SPIRITUAL DEVELOPMENT

SPIRITUAL DEVELOPMENT

An Interdisciplinary Study

Daniel A. Helminiak

LOYOLA UNIVERSITY PRESS
Chicago

Quotation from *The Nature of Sympathy* by Max Scheler reprinted with permission of
The Shoe String Press.

Six quotations from *Ego Development* by Jane Loevinger (with Augusto Blasi)
reprinted with permission of the publisher, Jossey-Bass, Inc.

Four quotations from *Method in Theology* by Bernard, J.F. Lonergan, S.J., reprinted with
permission of Winston Press, Inc., © Seabury and Harper & Row, Publishers, Inc.

Loyola University Press
3441 North Ashland Avenue
Chicago, Illinois 60657

Library of Congress Cataloging in Publication Data
Helminiak, Daniel A.
Spiritual development.
Bibliography: p. 215
Includes index.
1. Spirituality.   I. Title.
BV4501.2.H369554   1986   248'.01'9   86-11384
ISBN 0-8294-0530-5

Design by C. L. Tornatore

To my Mother,
Cecilia Ziołkowska Helminiak

Contents

Introduction

Traditional theology teaches that there are three stages in the spiritual life: the purgative, wherein one moves away from sin; the illuminative, wherein one grows in virtue; and the unitive, wherein one attains abiding union with God.[1] This conception was never meant to define discrete successive stages. At any time in one's spiritual journey, any of the three emphases—purgative, illuminative, or unitive—might take priority over the others, or in some way one may be at all the stages simultaneously.[2] Or again, if strict succession was suggested, it was only that of "beginning, middle, and end."[3]

The history of spirituality provides many accounts of the "scale" or "ladder" of perfection.[4] Scattered throughout the voluminous writings of Augustine of Hippo alone are at least eight accounts of the path of spiritual development, most with seven stages and some with three, but all different.[5] Clearly those accounts intended a suggestive and inspirational presentation and not a strictly systematic one. Nonetheless, inherent in these and all conceptions of spirituality is the notion of a path, a journey, a process, a developmental sequence.

Contemporary psychology also speaks of the human in terms of development. But with the rigor of a methodical science, psychology attempts systematically to delineate the stages of that development. *If spiritual development were conceived as human development viewed according to a particular set of concerns, the stage theories of psychology could significantly contribute to defining systematic stages of spiritual development.* Then spiritual development would stand with other psychologically defined conceptions of human development: Piaget's cognitive development, Kohlberg's moral development, Fowler's faith development, and Loevinger's ego development.

Psychology, Theism, and Christianity

That is the hypothesis pursued in this essay. Acceptance of that hypothesis necessitates separate treatment of the psychological and the theological questions. Accordingly, Part I of this essay begins by critically reviewing the scant literature that theoretically either treats spiritual development from a psychological point of view or attempts to integrate psychological developmental findings into theological concern for spiritual growth. Borrowing on the reviewed literature, the second chapter of Part I develops an initial definition of spiritual development and a list of the distinctive factors that determine it in contrast to other specific facets of human development. Next Chapter 3 presents an overview of current research on the stages of human development. Although all conclusions in this domain remain tentative, according to the purposes of this essay, focus will be on the integrative position in James Fowler's *Stages of Faith* and of the encyclopedic statement in Jane Loevinger's *Ego Development.* Insofar as developmental research hazards to suggest such a conclusion, the result is a sketch of the more or less currently determined lines and stages of human development within the populations studied. Finally, integrating this developmental material with the understanding developed in Chapter 2, Chapter 4 suggests a summary understanding of spiritual development and its stages.

Part I uses a critical, analytical, synthetic approach, sorting out the issues as they arise, consolidating issues where possible, introducing new material when necessary, all the time forging a progressively more coherent understanding of a very elusive subject. In the end the hope is to have justified as reasonable that psychology properly conceived can appropriately and adequately deal with many of the questions about spiritual development traditionally treated in theology. Indeed, within the contemporary context of extensive differentiation and specialization of disciplines, an adequate psychology and not theology is the discipline that properly treats questions of spirituality, at least insofar as practical issues are concerned.

Part II of this essay turns to the question of God and theist faith. Three chapters present a summary of theodicy, treatment of practical religious issues related to spiritual development, and the question of growth in holiness. The overall argument is this. Theism adds a further dimension of meaning to even an adequate psychological understanding of spiritual development. This is a contribution to a comprehensive theoretical account of the matter. But granted that God exists and is active whether acknowledged or not, theism as such offers no answer to practical questions about spiritual development. An adequate psychological account already provides this. Finally, growth in holiness, understood as a profound relationship with God, is not the same as spiritual development. The different possible coincidences of the two are multiple.

Part III treats the still further question about Christian faith and its contribution to a comprehensive understanding of spiritual development. In the present context, the distinctive contribution of Christianity is the conception of human life as a process of divinization. Because of the redemptive work of Christ and the sanctifying mission of the Holy Spirit, the human life created by God and studied by the human sciences is actually a growing participation in divine life. Granted the incarnation and resurrection of the Eternal Son, Jesus Christ, an understanding of the Holy Spirit as God's own Love poured into the human heart[6] is the key to this specifically Christian contribution. But once again, since divinizing grace is available to all whether they recognize it or not, Christianity's contribution is a further theoretical understanding of this matter rather than a distinctive prescription for living it.

Throughout, when practical issues of spiritual development are at stake, adequate psychological treatment retains the priority. It explains the process of development, and it defines the stages. Yet a comprehensive theoretical understanding of spiritual development is incomplete without the theist and Christian components.

Interrelationship of Different Disciplines

The working hypothesis is that spiritual development is nothing other than human development viewed from a particular perspective. This hypothesis necessitates that the contributions of various pertinent disciplines, constituted by different sets of presuppositions, be distinguished and treated separately. But there is an additional consideration. If the end product is to be a coherent and adequate account of spiritual development, this hypothesis also necessitates that these same disciplines be related within a comprehensive theoretical system. To meet this latter necessity, the present account employs an interdisciplinary position developed and explicated in detail elsewhere.[7] The basic outline of this conceptual schema is already obvious in the immediately preceding paragraphs.

This interdisciplinary approach presumes to pinpoint the specific and unique contribution of a cumulative series of different theoretical positions: positivist psychology, "humanistic" psychology, theism, and Christianity. Part I of this essay accepts the findings of developmental theorists, actually an unwitting mixture of positivist and "humanistic" psychology, and transposes the matter into an adequate psychological statement. "Humanistic psychology"[8] is an ambiguous title for the result. More accurately, Part I develops a "psychology within the philosophic viewpoint." "Philosophic" may be understood in contrast to "positivist." Whereas the positivist is content to determine the facts of the matter without concern for the values involved or the truth claims inherent in those facts, the philosopher—the lover of wisdom—is also concerned precisely about truth and real value. The contention here is that psychology is inadequate to the human unless the discipline explicitly allows for questions of truth and value, for an intrinsic dynamism toward those transcendent realities is constitutive of the human.[9] So Part I defines *spiritual* development by adding explicit concern for this human dynamism to the available psychological developmental research. By the same token, Part I delineates a psychology adequate to the present topic, a psychology within the philosophic viewpoint. The distinctive concern of such human science is human authenticity, defined in a technical sense by Bernard Lonergan.

But human authenticity does not necessarily entail belief in God, so introduction of the question of God broadens the theoretical presuppositions and calls for another specialized discipline and treatment. Part II provides this treatment in the present essay. But then again, belief in God is not the same as belief in the Trinity or in a divine-human one, Jesus Christ, or in the possibility of universal human participation in divinity through the mission of the Holy Spirit and the consequent indwelling of the Trinity. Yet Christianity envisages all this. So treatment of these still further issues requires still another discipline, specifically Christian theology, whose presuppositions transcend even theism.

While the movement within this interdisciplinary system is toward an ever broader perspective, the presupposition is that nothing is lost in that outward movement. So Christianity presupposes theism, and theism presupposes the human sciences within the philosophic viewpoint, and these in turn presuppose positivist sciences. The higher viewpoints sublate the lower.[10] Within this cumulative perspective it becomes obvious that theism and Christianity as such make no practical contributions to an understanding of spiritual development. Whatever practical contributions these two as lived religions have to make is already included within the theoretical purview of the philosophic viewpoint. The human issues are addressed within the philosophic viewpoint, and there explanations about the "what" and the "how to" of spiritual development are properly treated. Nonetheless, this conceptual schema also makes it obvious that theism and then again Christianity make important theoretical contributions to an adequate understanding of spiritual development.

Such is the interdisciplinary position that unites the various parts of this study. As the essay unfolds, these methodological issues will be treated further and will be clarified through application to concrete questions.

The Nature of this Essay

The paragraph before last introduced the distinction between Christianity as a lived religion and Christianity as a theoretical position, a set of peculiar presuppositions. This distinction requires explanation.

Religions are actually complexes of many related but conceptually different realities. Especially insofar as they structure cultures, religions contain customs, practices, taboos, and other social norms for living. These aspects of religions are what they are simply because that is how they happened to develop; they have no inherent claim to universal and absolute validity. Over and above these, all authentic religions also contain ethical prescriptions, authentic indications about how humans qua human ought to behave, some vision of life that would be valid universally. Over and above these, if the religions in question are theist, they also contain and foster belief in the one God of the Universe. Such belief about God is clearly a different reality in comparison with a valid understanding of life and ethical prescriptions about humankind. Theology and authentic humanism are distinct and even separable realities. Finally, if the religions in question are also Christian, they will contain some notion of God as Trinity, of Jesus Christ as a divine-human one, and of the possible divinization of human beings because of the mission of the Holy Spirit. These different realities, all possibly part of one lived religion, exemplify the four viewpoints introduced above: positivist, philo-sophic, theist, and Christian.

Each of these four sets of realities is different, though they may all be packaged up in one bundle in lived religions. Within such a differential analysis of religion, the term "Christian" takes on a dis-tinctive meaning. It indicates that and only that which distinguishes authentic Christianity from other aspects of religion found within the particular religion in question as well as from other religions that are not Christian. The term "Christian" takes on a theoretical meaning. It no longer refers to some concrete religion but only to one specific aspect of concrete Christian religions. It now specifies the essence of Christianity.[11]

A similar account could be given for the term "theism," for it is an exact parallel. Yet because the term "theism" does not generally sug-gest a particular, concrete, lived religion, this term is more self-ex-planatory than the term "Christian" used in a parallel sense. We readily understand the term "theism" to apply to many different religions. Moreover, we are comfortable asking whether a particular supposedly theist religion is authentically theist or not, whether it actually reverences the true God of the Universe or not. On the other hand, we are not accustomed to applying the term "Christian" in the same way. We generally predicate this term on the basis of externals: customs, practices, historical connections. Only speculative—and

now generally distasteful—concerns about orthodoxy and hetero-
doxy have highlighted the possibility that some who call themselves
"Christian" may not be Christian at all. And until now, history has
tolerated this state of affairs. When Christianity was the only religion
in its sphere, there was no real need to determine clearly what is
Christian and what is not. But the situation on a shrinking planet has
changed. Now further precision is necessary. Just as interdisciplinary
concerns raise methodological issues that were previously unsuspect-
ed, so do comparative-religions concerns. The present peculiar understanding of the term "Christian" is one result.

This essay is a theoretical study. It is an attempt to situate in one
comprehensive account a variety of issues that all impinge on spiritual
development. As with every theoretical study, the present one is not
without far-reaching practical implications. It is vitally relevant to
anyone's interest in spirituality. Yet the practical is not the explicit
concern here. This is not a study in piety, its various expressions, and
its effects on personal growth. For like religion, any piety might em-
body a number of significantly different realities: positivist, philosophic, theist, and Christian. To sort these out and to interrelate them
responsibly in a comprehensive theoretical account is the task of the
present essay.

For example, correctly understood, the above-stated fact is obvious: "theism and Christianity as such make no practical contributions
to an understanding of spiritual development." Misunderstood, tak-
en out of its theoretical context, this statement is atrocious. For as
lived religions, both theism and Christianity include prescriptions for
living, required practices, and support systems that do, indeed, affect
one's spiritual development. But within a theoretical analysis, these
practical helps are recognized as proper to the positivist and/or philosophic viewpoints; so in the present essay, they fall within the purview of an adequate psychology. Then, not theism or Christianity but
psychology properly determines the structures, mechanisms, and
processes of spiritual development.

It is to be hoped that these considerations make the exact nature
of this essay clear at the outset. Of course, the matter will arise again,
and it will be noted when it does.

There is need to note yet one other aspect of this essay. Theoretical concern in a field not yet well charted requires the review, some-

times in extensive detail, of other works related to the topic. In the present essay especially Chapters 1 and 3 satisfy this exigency. Some readers, interested primarily in practical things or wanting to get immediately to the heart of the matter, may prefer to skim over parts of these chapters, especially on first reading. But in the end complete understanding of the argument will be impossible on that basis. Integration of aspects of others' works results in the position developed here, comparison with other positions clarifies it, and appeal to elements found in other positions legitimates it.

As an interdisciplinary project, this essay begins with a psychological study but treats a topic that is of interest primarily to religious believers and theologians. A systematic treatment of spirituality—a comprehensive explanatory account—much needed today, requires that various disciplines be distinguished and interrelated clearly and that questions be answered by the discipline proper to each question. The present essay is a contribution to such a systematic spirituality.[12] Within a broad interdisciplinary context, this essay will argue that spiritual development is human development, conceived within a particular viewpoint.

Acknowledgments

I owe thanks to several people for various kinds of input into this book. Once again supporting interdisciplinary scholarship, at Boston University Philip E. Kubzansky directed my psychology studies, which culminated in what was the basis for Part I of this essay. Almost daily during the summer of 1982, conversations with Jacob Czapiewski allowed me to resolve the intricate issues in that same Part I. In a similar way Paula Rieder helped me to organize Part III. With insightful questions and gentle persistence, my students, Sylvia Maddox, Nancy Schweers, and Nedra Voorhies, motivated me to complete the theist and Christian sections of this study and then generously offered the thoughtful criticism that helped me to revise this work. Patrick Guidon, President, Oblate School of Theology in San Antonio, and Kirby Garner, Pastor, Cristo Rey Parish in Austin, accorded me the hospitality that allowed me to complete this writing. And Sylvia Chávez-García, faithful friend, supported me throughout the difficult process.

Notes

Introduction

1. Tanquerey, *Spiritual Life;* Groeschel, *Spiritual Passages.* The Bibliography provides complete documentation on works cited in the text and in the notes.

2. Groeschel, *Spiritual Passages,* 119, 160.

3. Aquinas, *Summa Theologica,* IIa IIae, q. 24, a. 9, ad 1; Squire, *Asking the Fathers,* 205-207.

4. Holmes, *History of Christian Spirituality,* 30-31.

5. Bourke, "Augustine of Hippo."

6. Rom. 5:5.

7. Helminiak, "One in Christ," "Four Viewpoints," "Where Do We Stand?"

8. Cf. Misiak and Sexton, *Phenomenological Psychologies;* Maddi, *Personality Theories,* 88-155.

9. Cf. Doran, *Psychic Conversion.*

10. Lonergan, *Method,* 241.

11. Rahner, "Christianity," *Sacramentum Mundi,* I, 299-313.

12. Helminiak, "Lonergan and Spiritual Theology."

PART I

The Contribution of Psychology

Authentic Human Processes and Stages

Psychological Accounts of Spiritual Development

Despite the recent mushrooming of interest in spirituality, surprisingly little has been written that specifically treats spiritual development from a psychological point of view. What has been written is tentative, difficult to interpret, and for the most part merely suggestive. Especially studies written from the perspective of religious faith tend to be inspirational and practical, pastoral contributions. Theoretical studies of spiritual development, attempts at some scientific account, are few.

Some General and Mostly Pastoral Studies

James Gwaltney's article, "Spiritual Development through Designed Exercises in a Small Group Setting," has practical concerns. He suggests group exercises that might further the "spiritual development" of divinity students. The spiritual development in question here is limited to the integrative task of young adulthood that results in "a greater sense of religious maturity and a motivation leading to responsible Christian behavior."[1] This conception sheds little light on the present study.

Similarly, Janice Brewi and Anne Brennan's *Mid-Life: Psychological and Spiritual Perspectives* is wholly lacking in any explicit theoretical interdisciplinary position. This book treats only one developmental transition, a most important and probably the most surely documented transition of adult development: mid-life. The book is loosely written, at points almost a collection of aphorisms and anecdotes, very popular in nature, and so perhaps ideally suited from a practical point of view for people undergoing a disorienting "mid-life crisis." The psychological undergirding of the book is completely and uncritically Jungian. As other contemporary spiritual writings in the Jungian mode, this book avoids the pitfalls of Jung's system[2] through its unselfconscious presupposition of the Judeo-Christian tradition. Indeed, the assumption throughout is that human life lived well and healthily *is* one's spiritual and Christian life.

W. Harold Grant, Magdala Thompson, and Thomas E. Clarke's *From Image to Likeness: A Jungian Path in the Gospel Journey* presents a superbly consistent and coherent application of Jungian psychology to Christian concern for spiritual growth. Focus is on the process of individuation, conceived here in terms of the integration of the four Jungian functions as measured on the Myers-Briggs Type Indicator: sensing (S), thinking (T), feeling (F), and intuiting (N). As is well known, these four are divided generically into two groups: sensing and intuiting are treated as expressions of the generic function, perceiving (P); and thinking and feeling are treated as expressions of the generic function, judging (J). The explicit position is that psychological growth is spiritual growth, that spiritual perfection entails psychological wholeness or individuation, integration of all four functions, and that God—and, indeed, the divinizing grace of the Trinity—is at work in the integrative process of individuation.

This book summarizes the authors' experiences in retreat/workshops (R/W) on spiritual growth and so is predominantly a pastoral statement. Four long chapters spell out aspects of the Roman Catholic tradition that tend to facilitate integration of each of the four Jungian functions. Yet Chapter 1 provides a brief account of the theory behind this team's work. Most provocative here is Harold Grant's projection of four stages of human development—actually six, when infancy and later adulthood are added on either end—inspired by, but not strictly derived from, the Jungian tradition. These stages are complexly deter-

2

mined by three factors: 1) alternations between the two contrasting attitudes, extroversion (E) and introversion (I); 2) alternations between the two generic functions: judging (J) and perceiving (P); and 3) the step-wise integration of the the four functions—S, T, F, and N—in a sequence peculiar to each of sixteen different possible personality types. The suggested stages are Infancy, where the two attitudes and all four functions operate in a random and tentative fashion; Childhood from age 7 to 12, where either the extroversion or the introversion attitude and either the judging or the perceiving generic function prevail, and one function—S, T, F, or N—emerges as dominant; Puberty from ages 13 to 20, where both the attitude, I and E, and the generic function, J and P, reverse and a second function—S, T, F, or N—is developed as an auxiliary; Young Adulthood from ages 21 to 35, where the E/I switch occurs again but not a switch in J/P, and a third function is developed; Midlife from ages 35 to 50, where again both the E/I attitude and the J/P generic function change, and the last of the four functions, the "shadow" or inferior function, is finally integrated; and the Golden Years, a kind of second childhood, where once again the two attitudes and all four functions operate but now as integrated and under the deliberate control of a person.

Although it has some support from the authors' "dealing with several hundred people in the context of the R/W, and from experience with several thousand students in two universities,"[3] this model of development remains tentative. A critical treatment of its contribution must be left for a later occasion. The particular significance of this model is that, based on a Jungian perspective, it arrives at stages of development that generally parallel the stages proposed by theorists working with very different presuppositions. As the present survey indicates, spiritual writers at the present time have a predilection for Jungian psychology. Grant's theory of "Jungian" stages offers the possibility of integrating the Jungian perspective into the mainstream of developmental research. Moreover, grounded in depth psychology, this model suggests an account of the psychodynamic mechanisms at work within the process of human development. Although this matter is relevant to the discussion in Chapter 4, this tenuous account remains but a provocative suggestion.

Raymond Studzinski's fine work on *Spiritual Direction and Midlife Development* focuses on counseling for spiritual growth—spiritual direction—and, again, on only one life transition, that of midlife. Obviously, the concern here, too, is practical. This work briefly states a methodological position for relating spirituality and psychology: complementarity of perspectives and vocabularies. "Each of these perspectives has illuminated different aspects of the transition. At times both have pointed to the same experiences of the midlife transition but have labeled them with names drawn from their respective vocabularies."[4] This theoretical position does not make it clear whether the different vocabularies actually highlight different aspects of the same reality or merely offer alternative ways of speaking about something. Specifically theist and Christian contributions may get lost in so unspecified a correlation. Certainly, Studzinski retains some form of the theist contribution when he considers life process "in terms of God's actions within people."[5] His narrative shifts easily between a psychological/developmental and a theist presentation. The clear assumption is that one and the same human experience is the arena for two different movements, or better, can be conceived according to two complementary perspectives. Human life is spiritual life. But a promised treatment of specifically Christian terms like "grace" never materializes.[6] Yet, in so pastorally oriented an account, such treatment may really never be missed—which fact is revealing in itself.

Helen Thompson's *Journey Toward Wholeness: A Jungian Model of Adult Growth* accounts for spiritual growth as a process of integration of opposites. The intended contribution is clearly theoretical. This book is treated here because of its association with other works on Jungian psychology and because of its relatively minor importance.

Thompson's little 108-page book is an overly ambitious attempt to integrate the work of several major theorists: Pierre Teilhard de Chardin, Carl G. Jung, Evelyn Underhill, William Johnston, Erich Neumann, and Robert Ornstein. Focus is on only one adult transition, and treatment of it is reduced to one process: integration of a basic polarity in the human. This polarity is styled in many ways: material vs. spiritual, unconscious vs. conscious, rational-analytical vs. intuitive-holistic, mind vs. body, reason vs. passion, "masculine" vs. "feminine." Overall, the presentation is too brief, too sketchy, and too uncritical of its sources. Use of image, metaphor, and suggestive terminology allows an all too easy correlation of those many theorists' positions. The most blatant example is the supposed parallel of a simplistically conceived physiological right-brain vs. left-brain duality with those other polarities. The Grant, Thompson, and Clarke model presented above shows that the Jungian approach is more complex.

Thompson suggests that every life transition has a three-part structure: "(1) a period of disintegration, a separation from the former ways, (2) a period of painful transition and awkward behavior, and (3) a period of integration around a new way of organizing one's life."[7] Although Thompson nowhere makes the connection, these three are strikingly similar to the traditional three stages of the spiritual life: purgative, illuminative, and unitive. This similarity suggests that the traditional "three ways" retain some validity, not in indicating the stages of spiritual development across a person's life span but in highlighting experiences that are integral to every respective transition through those stages, integral to every "conversion." Others make this point explicitly. Evelyn and James Whitehead point to anthropological theory that discerns a three-part structure in every life passage.[8] A careful reading of Groeschel's *Spiritual Passages*, discussed below, supports this interpretation. Finally, according to Adrian van Kaam, "all spiritual passages are marked by the three fundamental ones of purgation, illumination and union."[9]

Thompson certainly assumes that psychological integration *is* spiritual growth and that its goal is wholeness. This is so, perhaps, even to a fault. *Journey Toward Wholeness* is an almost clean specimen of psychology within the positivist viewpoint. Emphasis is on integration of opposites, but no explicit concern is given to the wholesomeness and ethical appropriateness of this integration process or, conversely, to the possibility of aberrant development. Need one, should one, unquestioningly follow one's inner drive without assessing the ethical implications? What exactly is meant by this inner drive, and so what is it that one should or should not be following?[10] Is a human being, as Ira Progoff's notion of the dynatype suggests, really like an acorn whose fullness is already somehow contained and predetermined in it from the beginning, or like a robin whose genetic endowment will lead it always to build a particular kind of nest in a particular way just by following its "instinct"?[11] The explicit assumption, borrowed from Jung, is that the integration process is good and ought to be fostered.[12] In Thompson's case, as in those others cited above, the faith presupposition that God—and so, the good—is, indeed, at work in the human[13] validates the Jungian assumption; but in all these works precisely this faith presupposition is so taken for granted that there is no awareness of the need to raise the ethical question. Still, those others sprinkle their pages with references to God and belief, the saints and the Scriptures, resurrection and church, and similar religious symbols. There religious intent, theoretically explicated or not, is in the forefront. Thompson, on the other hand, attempting to develop a fully psychological model of spiritual growth, leaves room for the critical ethical question only rarely, always in passing, and under the guise of anemic appeal to Christian symbol. For example, she speaks of the possibility that the integration process will unfold "graciously" when touched by the Holy Spirit:[14] The word "Holy Spirit" is mentioned, but there is no awareness of the specifically Christian work usually attributed to the Holy Spirit: human divinization. So as it stands, the usage is not substantively Christian but only nominally so. Moreover, it is not even clear if the symbol "Holy Spirit" is being used in a sense that makes its referent different from the transcendent urges of the created human spirit. There is no clear distinction made between the Creator and the created. Given the confusion within contemporary theological and especially sprirtual circles, this distinction may no longer simply be presumed. So as it stands, the usage may not even be theist. Finally, whether or not the word "graciously" has ethical connotations must depend on the mind of the reader. So the usage might mean nothing more than "comfortably," and all concerns that determine the philosophic viewpoint may also be absent. Thompson's presentation may be wholly positivist. This example is important. It highlights the difference between psychology within the positivist viewpoint, on the one hand, and psychology within the philosophic viewpoint and the other higher viewpoints on the other. When the issue is spirituality, that difference is crucial, and it may not be taken for granted.

Benedict Groeschel's *Spiritual Passages: The Psychology of Spiritual Development* is a disappointment. The title is an obvious reference to Gail Sheehy's best-seller and holds a promise of an up-to-date treatment of spiritual development. The book offers no such thing. Its two parts actually take two different stands vis-à-vis the psychology of human development. Part I, following especially Erikson and Levinson, presents some account of the spiritual implications of the developmental process and its stages as delineated by developmental theorists. Here, at least until Chapter 5's harsh criticism of contemporary psychology, developmental psychology is granted some credibility. In contrast, however, Part II presents the traditional three ways of the spiritual life as the definitive account of stages in spiritual growth. A highly questionable appendix even notes psychologists and other spiritual writers who allegedly also endorse this opinion. In this part psychological notions—especially, and ironically, isolated elements of Freudian psychoanalytic theory—are used to illustrate and explain issues traditionally associated with each of the three ways: moral rationalization and intellectualization are defense mechanisms;[15] pathology explains some habitual sins;[16] decrease in anxiety and fear is a major explanatory principle of the dynamics of the spiritual life (Groeschel's own theory);[17] pride, sensuality, and spiritual avarice in the illuminative stage are expressions of denial, repression, and reaction formation;[18] the Dark Night of the Senses results from the collapse of the last of the defense mechanisms, sublation;[19] the sense of rejection and persecution associated with the unitive way may simply reflect the saints' experiences of a midlife crisis;[20] the Dark Night of the Soul may represent the final disintegration of the ego in the face of union with God.[21] The division between the first and second parts of this work symbolizes a theme that seems to underlie the whole of Groeschel's thought: the psychological and the spiritual are like separate parts of a two-layered universe. At points the two touch, but in general they have their independent existence.[22] On this issue Groeschel differs with the basic presupposition of all the other opinions presented here. The difference is intentional, as the dogmatic, moralizing, romanticized, and defensive tone of the book indicates. Claiming to integrate the insights of contemporary psychology into theology and spirituality, this regressive presentation deepens the gap between them.

In fact, Groeschel's use of psychology is highly selective and generally superficial, and his theology is inadequate. Introduction of psychological terms often becomes the occasion merely to expound personal opinion.[23] Or again, ignoring the bulk of recent research and professional opinion on sexuality, this book represents homosexuality as a sexual fixation, pathological and deviant, an instance of arrested sexual development.[24] Without negative criticism or even a word of caution, Groeschel approvingly relates the case of Leon, homosexual for many years, who through a charismatic experience "has changed sufficiently so that he hopes he may one day marry and have a family."[25] The ethics in this book disregards recent and generally accepted positions among the best contemporary theologians.[26] The use of the Bible continues the subjective inspirational approach of the classical spiritual writers and ignores historical-critical method, accepted within all mainline Christian churches today.[27] Overall, this book is oblivious to the central issues in contemporary theological circles: history and hermeneutics. Indeed, because of its outdated and uncritical position and despite its solid wisdom at many points, this book may even be unintentionally harmful to the spiritually inexperienced, "those who seek," to whom it is addressed. It certainly makes little contribution to the present discussion.

An Empirical Study on Spiritual Growth

Edwards, Mead, Palmer, and Simmons's study, *Spiritual Growth: An Empirical Exploration of its Meaning, Sources, and Implications*, acknowledges widespread confusion about the term "spiritual growth." To bring some clarity to this and other issues, these authors contacted twenty-nine clergy from representative congregations—Episcopal, L.C.A. Lutheran, Roman Catholic, Presbyterian, U.C.C., Baptist (Black), and Conservative Jewish. The clergy were to identify "spiritually mature" lay people in their congregations. The clergy were to presume their own understanding of "spiritually mature." One lay person from each congregation was given a one- to two-hour interview about their "life-line" and its critical points and their spiritual growth.

The researchers were disappointed with the results and themselves sufficiently criticize the adequacy of this study.[28] They thought they were directed toward lay people who were socially mature and institutionally loyal rather than toward people with a sense for the spiritual. Furthermore, the interviewer did not obtain sufficient data to allow the researchers even to suggest what the subjects considered spiritual maturity to be. Supposed representative data on this topic gathered among some of the clergy present so broad a range of characteristics that no synthetic statement is possible. Some of these suggested characteristics of spiritual maturity are integration of religion with life, knowledge of God and the religion, inner strength, trust in providence and awareness of the mystery that pervades experience, regular corporate worship and private prayer, and attractiveness to others who are in need of help.

In an appendix the researchers present their own individual statements about spiritual maturity, written prior to the study. The researchers never discussed these statements sufficiently to arrive at a consensus understanding of spiritual maturity. Their statements stand as individual testimonies. The common elements in those statements include 1) openness of the person to 2) some transcendent principle beyond the empirically experienced self, whether within the person (one's essence, the "inner man") or beyond the person ("God," the "Spirit"); and 3) insistence that the *whole* person is involved in spiritual maturity and growth and not just some aspect of the person; this wholeness entails both the harmony of all aspects of the person considered in him- or herself and the harmonious relationship of the person vis-à-vis other people and, indeed, the whole cosmos.

The Center for Human Development

The Center for Human Development (CHD), originally at the University of Notre Dame and now located in Washington, D.C., has described spiritual growth by nine empirically measurable criteria. The staff of CHD arrived at these nine criteria "through an intuitive reflection upon certain themes in the Catholic tradition of spirituality and certain trends in philosophy and the behavioral sciences" and has available no theoretical statement of their position.[29] However, they indicate that a research project by P.J. Henry treats some related material. Using the Personal Orientation Inventory, the Tennessee Self-Concept Scale, the Loevinger Ego Development Scale, and the Survey of Ministerial Effectiveness developed for his research project, Henry showed that there is a significant correlation between clergy effectiveness and degree of self-actualization, self-concept, and ego development in his subjects.

A report on the Ministry of Priests Program in the Diocese of Pittsburgh, executed by the Center for Human Development,[30] does explain the general lines of the CHD conception of spiritual growth and reveals similarities with Henry's procedure. CHD adopts a "holistic approach to spirituality. According to this viewpoint, a healthy spirituality informs all of one's life: intellectual, emotional, physical, relational."[31] That this list of aspects of human life does not include "spiritual" emphasizes the conviction that the spiritual is not one aspect among others but rather names a particular way of viewing human life as a whole.[32]

Given this presupposition, CHD uses standard personality inventories which can isolate "some of the manifestations of wholeness" and provide "ways to measure them":[33] the Personal Orientation Inventory (POI), which assesses how closely a person approximates Maslow's concept of a self-actualizing person; the Tennessee Self-Concept Scale (TSCS), which measures self-esteem; the Loevinger Ego Development Scale (LEDS), which can measure ego strength and indicate how deeply principles are being internalized; the Defining Issues Test of Moral Judgment (DIT), based on Lawrence Kohlberg's stage theory of moral development; and the Spiritual Orientation Inventory (SOI), constructed by CHD to reflect its holistic conception of spirituality, which measures and correlates attitudes, behaviors, and satisfactions and concerns in one's religious life. The results obtained with these instruments are combined as appropriate and used to measure spiritual growth.

As already noted, CHD presumes that nine criteria can adequately describe spiritual growth for their purposes. These nine criteria and the instruments used to measure them are as follows:

> 1. A Developing Self-Concept . . . which includes an accurate self-perception and loving self-acceptance. Without this, paradoxically, surrender of the self to radical conversion is probably impossible.[34] (TSCS)
>
> 2. A Responsible Self-Awareness . . . an ability to be present to one's needs, feelings, and emotions which may signal the movements of the Holy Spirit within.[35] (SOI, POI, LEDS)
>
> 3. A Sense of Autonomy or Inner-Directedness . . . a basic trust in the validity of one's own experience and values which can allow one to leave behind a conventional viewpoint and move toward a personally integrated faith.[36] (POI, LEDS, SOI)
>
> 4. An Appreciation of Genuine Authority . . . which mediates social interactions and balances individual experience with traditional norms.[37] (POI, DIT)

5. A Principled Morality . . . based on self-chosen but universally valid principles ultimately reducible to one: in the Christian tradition, Love. From this vantage point laws derive their validity or are judged wanting.[38] (LEDS, DIT)

6. A Person Orientation . . . in which one places highest priority on relating to another person as a "Thou," rather than an "It."[39] (SOI, TSCS, POI)

7. A Holistic View of Development . . . in which physical, emotional and intellectual development are seen as intrinsically related to spiritual development.[40] (POI, SOI, LEDS)

8. A Present Centeredness . . . which allows one to live and encounter the richness and depth of reality as revealed in the sacrament of the present moment.[41] (POI)

9. An Openness to the Transcendent . . . a readiness to find mystical experience in the reality of self, others, and the world.[42] (SOI)

The CHD Report also contains a general notion of spiritual development:

Growth toward a deeper spirituality involves a movement, sometimes hesitant, painful and intermittent, from a conventional viewpoint to an integrated viewpoint. A conventional viewpoint focuses on externals and is characterized by adherence to the rules and regulations of organized religion and a piecemeal appropriation of reality. An integrated viewpoint moves away from concern for externals toward a personal faith. It is characterized by an internalization of the principles which rules and expectations only imperfectly express. The integrated viewpoint grasps and appreciates the unity of meaning in all of reality. The movement away from a conventional to an integrated viewpoint involves much more than an intellectual shift in thinking. It corresponds closely to the biblical concept of "metanoia," or conversion, which involves a radical reorientation of one's whole being.[43]

According to this statement, CHD views spiritual development as the result of an ongoing process of self-transformation (metanoia or conversion). There is no mention of discrete stages of spiritual development. However, use of the terms "conventional" and "integrated" and the description given to those terms clearly reflect the usage in Kohlberg's and Loevinger's developmental stage theories.

11

Evidently the CHD conception of spiritual growth is fully compatible with an assumption that stages of spiritual development would parallel the general stages of human development delineated by psychological developmental theorists. CHD's holistic approach to spirituality supports the hypothesis that spiritual development is human development conceived from a particular view. Indeed, of CHD's nine empirically measured criteria of spiritual growth, only the ninth, openness to the Transcendent, has a specifically theist reference. And even it is open to non-theist interpretation if, besides "God," another referent for "the Transcendent" could be provided. Even as the eight other, more psychologically defined criteria are open to theist religious applications and so are indicated in the CHD Report also by religious symbols—"radical conversion," "movements of the Holy Spirit," "the sacrament of the present moment"—so this ninth criterion might also be indicative of a fully human reality which is itself open to theist interpretation and application. If this is so, there arises the possibility of dealing, at least initially, with the whole reality of spiritual development in a strictly psychological context. The CHD understanding of spiritual growth is not adverse to such a conception; indeed, it presupposes it.

CHD conceives spiritual growth as movement beyond "a conventional viewpoint."[44] As will be clear in the summary of Fowler and Loevinger in Chapter 3 below, such movement is proper only to adults. Implicit, then, in the CHD conception is the assumption that spiritual development is a properly adult phenomenon.

Assagioli's Psychosynthesis

Roberto Assagioli's *Psychosynthesis* provides the richest study of spiritual development in a psychological context that I have found. As its subtitle indicates, *Psychosynthesis* is *A Manual of Principles and Techniques*. Yet it contains important theoretical sections. Assagioli's topic is clearly spiritual growth. He distinguishes two major phases in the process of psychosynthesis: personal psychosynthesis and spiritual psychosynthesis. The first treats the very issues considered to be spiritual development in the works already cited. Furthermore, personal psychosynthesis is the presupposition of spiritual psychosynthesis, and so the two are part of one process. Thus, despite

Assagioli's particular use of the term "spiritual," his entire work can be considered a study of spiritual development.

An understanding of Assagioli's specific definition of "spiritual" presupposes his "pluridimensional conception of the human person."[45] First, the field of consciousness and the conscious self or "I" represent the contents of ordinary awareness of the conscious subject. Then, as Freud was significantly instrumental in showing, there is also the "lower unconscious," which contains drives and primitive urges and all dreams and imaginations of an inferior kind and lower, uncontrolled parapsychological processes. Beyond this there is the "higher unconscious or the superconscious." The superconscious is the source of all higher intuitions, inspirations, and feelings—artistic, philosophical and scientific, ethical, and altruistic; it is the source of genius, the source of states of contemplation, illumination, and ecstasy, and the realm of the higher psychic functions and, presumably, of the higher parapsychological processes.[46] For Assagioli, the term "spiritual" is a correlative of the superconscious and refers to any experiences that would be rooted there. But "spiritual" also refers to experiences of the "higher Self." Thus, "spiritual" is defined by experience both of the superconscious and of the higher Self, but clearly the greater emphasis is given to experience of the superconscious. The exact relationship between the superconscious and the higher Self is not made clear. Here is a basic ambiguity in Assagioli's understanding of "spiritual."

Nor is it clear what Assagioli means by the "higher Self." The term is one of those undefined metaphors, so common in "spiritual writings." Assagioli's attempted definition[47] mixes psychological, metaphysical, and mystical considerations. He further confuses the issue by insisting that the duality between the conscious self and the higher Self is not real. "There are not really two selves, two independent and separate entities. The Self is one."[48] Assagioli relates the Self to the "Supreme Spirit" and to the "universal Self" of Vedanta philosophy: "'*Tat Twam Asi*' (Thou art That)"; but he is unconcerned whether one conceives the individual Self and the universal Self "as identical or similar, distinct or united."[49] It appears, then, that for Assagioli the term "higher Self" is supposed to indicate some transcendent principle internal to the human.

An analysis of Assagioli's understanding of spiritual growth and its goal confirms the above interpretation of the "higher Self" and highlights again the ambiguity in Assagioli's understanding of "spiritual." The goal of psychosynthesis is "organic unity,"[50] the integration in "a harmoniously functioning organism" of the "different drives and the various psychological functions within the individual."[51] Talk of integration presupposes that all the "drives" in question are internal to the human. This integration occurs in two phases. The first, called personal psychosynthesis, entails "the development and perfection of the personality"; the second, called spiritual psychosynthesis, entails the personality's "harmonious co-ordination and increasing unification with the Self."[52] In other words,

> The basic purpose of psychosynthesis is to release or, let us say, help to release, the energies of the Self. Prior to this the purpose is to help integrate, to synthesize, the individual around the personal self, and then later to effect the synthesis between the personal ego and the Self.[53]

Note that here Assagioli defines *spiritual* psychosynthesis by reference to the higher Self. But he fills out the meaning of spiritual psychosynthesis by reference to experiences of the superconscious. Incorporating into his understanding Abraham Maslow's conception, Assagioli refers to this second phase of psychosynthesis also as "self-actualization" and means "psychological growth and maturation, . . . the awakening and manifestation of latent potentialities of the human being—for instance, ethical, esthetic, and religious experiences and activities."[54] Assagioli specifically intends Maslow's[55] meaning of the term "self-actualization" indicating a development of personality that frees one from preoccupation with deficiency problems of growth and the unreal, neurotic problems of life and directs one to the real, existential problems of life. Insisting with Maslow that the phase of self-actualization is not a static state of already perfect integration, Assagioli speaks of "the successive stages of self-actualization."[56] This is spiritual growth.

Introducing a further clarification, Assagioli contrasts self-actualization with Self-realization (upper case "S," referring to the higher Self), "the realization of the Self."[57] Self-realization is also a goal of psychosynthesis. It is the subject's momentary experience of the

14

higher Self. It is what is generally referred to as a "religious" experience or a mystical experience. Assagioli describes it in detail.

> Self-realization, in this specific well-defined sense, means the momentary or more or less temporary identification or blending of the I-consciousness with the spiritual Self, in which the former, which is the reflection of the latter, becomes reunited, blended with the spiritual Self. In these cases there is a forgetfulness of all contents of consciousness, of all which forms the personality both on normal levels and those of the synthesized personality which include superconscious or spiritual levels of life and experience; there is only the pure intense experience of the Self.[58]

Now, in what may stand here as a summary of Assagioli's understanding of the "spiritual" and of "spiritual development," he writes,

> We are using the word "spiritual" in its broader connotation which includes, therefore, not only the specific religious experience [Self-realization], but all the states of awareness, all the functions and activities which have as common denominator the possessing of *values* higher than the average, values such as the ethical, the esthetic, the heroic, the humanitarian, and the altruistic. We include under the general heading of "spiritual development" then, all experiences connected with awareness of the contents of the superconscious, which may or may not include the experience of the Self.[59]

With that background, the ambiguity in Assagioli's understanding of "spiritual" and so of "spiritual development" can now be pinpointed. For Assagioli the second phase of psychosynthesis, spiritual psychosynthesis, is specifically spiritual development. It is defined by reference both to the superconscious and to the Self. It entails both self-actualization and Self-realization. But self-actualization means integration of the superconscious into the permanent personality, while Self-realization means the blending of the Self with the personality. Self-actualization is an ongoing process; Self-realization is a momentary experience. The two are significantly different, yet Assagioli confuses them. Are they related? Assagioli evidently thinks they are. In fact, he as much as identifies the two when he defines spiritual psychosynthesis as the personality's "harmonious and increasing unification with the Self";[60] for in this statement the distinction between superconscious and Self and the distinction between self-actualization and Self-realization collapse. Yet if here spiritual psycho-synthesis means "increasing unification with the Self," elsewhere spiritual development "may or may not include the experience of the Self."[61]

In summary, Assagioli has two understandings of "spiritual" and of "spiritual development." One relates to the superconscious and the other, to the higher Self. Assagioli never clearly distinguishes, relates, or reconciles these two.

Assagioli notes four stages in the attainment of the goal of organic unity.[62] First, Thorough Knowledge of One's Personality. One comes to know both the empirical, conscious elements in oneself but also especially the hidden dark forces of the unconscious. Second, Control of the Various Elements of the Personality. One generally appropriates all of what one is but does not identify with it all; one allows that there is a self beyond what is happening to it. Third, Realization of One's True Self—The Discovery or Creation of a Unifying Center. In a series of intermediate stages or plateaus, one strives to become one's Self by identifying with external models or ideals. And fourth, Psychosynthesis: The Formation or Reconstruction of the Personality Around the New Center. One builds a new, coherent, organized, and unified personality either by projecting an ideal self-image and trying to live up to it or by more spontaneously following a call from within.

What Assagioli calls "stages"[63] are not intended as discrete achievements along the way to spiritual integration: ". . . all the various stages and methods mentioned above are closely interrelated and need not be followed in a strict succession of distinct periods or phases."[64] These "stages" rather represent general aspects of a growth process and could conceivably be relevant to the transition between any real stages of spiritual development that might be discerned.

That same applies to the second and different account of "four critical stages" that Assagioli relates to disturbances that can arise during the process of spiritual growth.[65] First, an upheaval of normal living, often occurring with no apparent cause, results in despondency, lack of meaning and purpose in life, and serious questioning. What Assagioli describes here sounds like the classic "mid-life crisis," popularized by Gail Sheehy. Second, a breakthrough, "the spiritual awakening," brings an emotional high.[66] Third, cessation of the initial high causes doubt, confusion, and discouragement. Assagioli sees reference to this effect in Plato's account of the pain of the prisoners in the cave when they first see the light and in John of the Cross's account of the Dark Night of the Soul. And fourth, acceptance of the necessarily transitory nature of the initial experience allows one to begin the long process of restructuring the personality in light of the already experienced goal.

As noted above, these two different accounts of four stages offer no help in delineating really discrete stages of spiritual development. Rather, as suggested above regarding the traditional "three ways," they seem to describe the experience of passage through the transition of any stage whatever. However, Assagioli's distinction between personal psychosynthesis and spiritual psychosynthesis does provide some help. Despite the generality of definition given these two "phases" of psychosynthesis and despite the far-reaching ambiguity inherent in the description of spiritual psychosynthesis, the delineation of these two phases stands firm. These phases find some correlation with the stages of development proposed by the developmental psychologists to be considered in Chapter 3 of this essay.

Furthermore, Assagioli's notion of increasing unification of the personality with the Self and his notion of the reconstruction of the personality in view of that unification suggest development of the intrinsic structures of the personality—an understanding highly compatible, if not identical, with Loevinger's conception of ego development. Assagioli's conception also suggests heuristically the ultimate goal of that development, namely, that the personality become a perfect expression or reflection of the Self. At that ultimate point in development one would have attained not a momentary but an abiding state of Self-realization. These notions, though not consistently presented by Assagioli, are a part of his thought. They are valuable contributions for an understanding of spiritual development.

Four other aspects of Assagioli's position are relevant to the goal of this essay. First, Assagioli presupposes that psychosynthesis is an adult affair. That the first stage in the process is thorough knowledge of one's personality confirms this. Likewise, the conception of intentional integration of all aspects of the person, that is, eventual reconstruction of the personality, also confirms this. Assagioli's overall

17

presentation and his recommendation of specific techniques are obviously geared toward adults. He notes that there are two periods of particularly intense upheaval during life: "first, the tumultuous awakening of new tendencies at the time of adolescence, and second, the awakening of religious aspirations and new spiritual interests, particularly at middle age."[67] The latter is Assagioli's concern. Note that Grant, Thompson, and Clarke indicate these same two periods as critical and explain the crises in terms of alternations in the generic Jungian functions, perceiving and judging.

Second, Assagioli adopts an explicit, neutral stance toward religion. Of course, Assagioli is concerned about religious or spiritual experiences, but not about the religious formulations of those experiences nor about institutionalized religion.[68] Assagioli's indifference about how the higher Self is related to the universal Self, as noted above, is evidence here. Psychosynthesis is a "scientific conception" and does not "appropriate to itself the fields of religion and of philosophy. . . . Psychosynthesis does not aim nor attempt to give a metaphysical nor a theological explanation of the great Mystery—it leads to the door, but stops there."[69] Assagioli's position represents a clear and nuanced insistence that certain aspects of spiritual development can be adequately treated apart from theological presuppositions.

Third, Assagioli insists that there are "higher urges within man which tend to make him grow towards greater realizations of his spiritual essence."[70] He relates these "urges" to the Self and the superconscious, namely, to what he describes as the spiritual. Assagioli holds that "spiritual drives or spiritual urges are as real, basic and fundamental as sexual aggressive drives."[71] Although Assagioli's account of these spiritual urges in terms of the Self and superconscious is basically ambiguous, as noted above, his insistence on them provides a valuable clue about the nature of spiritual development.

Finally, given his insistence on the reality of the spiritual, Assagioli argues for a conception of psychology broad enough to deal with spiritual development. He explains, "We are not attempting to force upon psychology a philosophical, theological or metaphysical position, but essentially we include within the study of psychological facts all those which may be related to the higher urges. . . ."[72] Assagioli's presupposition squares with that of this essay, that certain aspects of spiritual development can be treated within a psychological perspective when adequately conceived. However, I am less optimistic than he that this can be achieved apart from acceptance of a particular philosophical position. This is not naively to suggest that psychology as presently conceived does operate apart from philosophical presuppositions.[73] It is simply to suggest that to deal adequately with spiritual—that is, with human!—issues psychology needs a different philosophical foundation.[74] Moreover, unlike Assagioli, I would not lump together philosophical and theological concerns.

Relevant Theological Papers

Articles by three other authors are particularly relevant to the concerns of the present essay. These approach the topic of spiritual development primarily from a theological perspective but relate seriously to the theories of developmental psychologists. None speaks explicitly of "spiritual development," yet it is clear that that is their concern, veiled under topics of very broadly conceived faith development, conscience development, religious maturity, full personal development, and the like.

Henry C. Simmons explicitly acknowledges that maturational crises intrinsically affect one's spiritual development. He considers those developmental issues that are pertinent to religious growth at or around age thirty[75] and between the ages thirty and sixty.[76] Simmons follows the developmental sketches of Jung[77] and Erikson,[78] arguing generally that maturational crises are to be expected, that they do affect one's religious growth, and that concern should be taken to help people negotiate them. Simmons notes that "affective autonomy" and "social responsibility" are conditions for adult faith at age thirty. Affective autonomy implies "a sense of self which is so integrated that one's own needs, wants, desires, fears, loves and hates no longer distort the perception of the other person with whom we are in relation."[79] One is ready "to assume and maintain personally chosen values" and "is really able to be oneself, and allow the same to the other person, in a close and therefore emotionally charged relationship.[80] Social responsibility entails "a commitment to the social order as it is in process of becoming whole, a commitment which is neither a simple 'selling out' to prevailing cultural values nor an overenthusiastic idealism which cannot commit itself within a real social context."[81] Social responsibility allows one to accept the reality that "Everything human is messy."[82]

Simmons does not speak of any explicit stages of spiritual development, yet in an undifferentiated manner his descriptions correlate with Fowler's and Loevinger's various upper stages of development. Simmons asserts that merely living through maturational crises does not insure development; people must be aided to grow spiritually as a result of maturation. That is to say, although Simmons uses a maturational outline to speak of spiritual development, his very presentation suggests that a theoretical account of that development requires other criteria.

Paul Philibert[83] criticizes Kohlberg's[84] notion of conscience as a Stage-6, postconventional development. This notion is too merely rational. It considers only the issue of knowing or deciding what ought to be done but ignores the question of actually doing the good. Philibert appeals to Rogers's[85] account of the stages of psychotherapy for a more adequate treatment of the affective aspects of moral development and for some understanding of the agent who not only comes to know the good but also does it. Rogers points to an energizer in the subject—the need to achieve congruence between ideas and experiences, the need to correlate ideas with feelings. In this energizer Philibert sees an explanation for "the *energy* in the agent's pursuit of the good, the *impulse* to pursue the object of duty"[86] and so speaks of "an intrinsic orientation of the moral agent to the good."[87] "The person is fundamentally obliged not just to do certain expected things, but to *be* and to *become* fully in accordance with 'reasons which the heart alone knows.'"[88] Philibert insists, "The issue here is self-transcendence. Another way of putting it is that the person has a vocation to become more than that which describes him statistically."[89] One has an "openness to transcendent value."[90] Thus, Philibert argues for a broader notion of conscience: conscience is operative in all the stages of moral development—in different ways at different stages, to be sure. Expressing itself through an urge toward self-congruence, it moves one not only to know the good but also to do it. It is thus a factor in one's being and becoming and leads one in growth toward transcendent value.

Philibert's account of conscience is closely linked to his theological presuppositions. He admits, "What I am looking for is something akin to the dynamic present in Augustine's 'Our hearts are made for Thee, and they shall not rest until they rest in Thee.'"[91] Or again, he speaks of "alert listening for the voice of the Creator whose world is not finished."[92] And again, conscience according to Philibert entails "originary consciousness," an inchoate form of religious experience, the awareness that "our being, our freedom, and our consciousness are limited and originated. We have not created ourselves; we have been created in love."[93]

Philibert's primary contribution to an understanding of spiritual development is his insistence that only some intrinsic principle of self-transcendence will account for one's actually doing the good, over and above one's deciding what is the good to be done. His appeal to affective consonance in Rogers's theory of psychotherapy as an explanation at least of the operation of that intrinsic principle of self-transcendence offers an entryway to some psychological understanding of that principle. Significant, too, is Philibert's insistence that that intrinsic principle affects not only one's doing but also one's being and one's becoming. This, along with the notion of self-congruence borrowed from Rogers, presents a picture of the whole human being— not just any one aspect—changing and developing in self-transcendence toward transcendent value. Only that Philibert links these notions so closely to belief in the Creator, the theist viewpoint, prevents his conception from being a wholly non-theological account of these important aspects of spiritual development, an account wholly within the philosophic viewpoint.

Walter Conn's "Moral Development As Self-Transcendence" argues that every stage in cognitive,[94] psychosocial (Erikson), and moral (Kohlberg) development evinces an advance over the previous stage and as such represents an instance of "self-transcendence." Conn concludes that "the theories of Erikson, Piaget, and Kohlberg, by defining personal maturity in terms of self-transcendence, point to a 'natural law' of the human spirit grounded in a radical drive of the human spirit for self-transcendence."[95] He explicates the meaning of self-transcendence by reference to Bernard Lonergan's analysis of intentional consciousness. Following Lonergan, Conn speaks of the "dynamism of the human spirit"[96] and of the human's "radical drive for self-transcending authenticity."[97]

21

Lonergan's Analysis of Dynamic Human Consciousness

In his major works, *Insight* and *Method in Theology*, Bernard Lonergan explains that the dynamism of the human spirit expresses itself initially in questioning. "Questioning" does not refer to the articulated expression of curiosity about something, the formulated question, but rather to that primordial curiosity or wonder that expresses itself in formulated questions. On the most fundamental level of human consciousness, one becomes aware that one is experiencing. Then questioning may spontaneously arise. One wants to know what it is that one is experiencing. The question here is, What is it? As soon as an answer arises, the further question spontaneously demands whether or not it really is what one thinks it is. The question now is, Is it so? If one pursues this further question, if one allows "the pure desire to know,"[98] one is led not only beyond what one had experienced, mere data to be understood, but also beyond what one thinks about the data and to the reality as it is in itself. One concludes, "Yes, it is so," or "No, it is not so." Now one knows something. Already inherent in this pursuit of questioning is a process of self-transcendence. But more important, if one does indeed attain to what is "so" in itself, one is engaged in a process of *authentic* self-transcendence. But questioning continues, and the dynamism of the human spirit leads one spontaneously to the further question, "What am I going to do about it?" If one responds appropriately, one achieves still another step in self-transcendence. One moves from knowledge to decision and action that are in accord with what one knows. But more importantly, again, one transcends oneself along the line of *authenticity*.

Lonergan conceptualizes the basic dynamism of the human spirit, which expresses itself in questioning, by speaking of "levels of consciousness."

> There is the *empirical* level on which we sense, perceive, imagine, feel, speak, move. There is an *intellectual* level on which we inquire, come to understand, express what we have understood, work out the presuppositions and implications of our expression. There is the *rational* level on which we reflect, marshal the evidence, pass judgment on the truth or falsity, certainty or probability, of a statement. There is the *responsible* level on which we are concerned with ourselves, our own operations, our goals, and so

deliberate about possible courses of action, evaluate them, decide, and carry out our decisions.[99]

According to Lonergan's analysis, human spirit has that inherent four-level structure, and it unfolds according to inherent principles. These principles are normative for all human activity. Objectified and articulated as parallels to the "levels of consciousness," they are "transcendental precepts" for humankind: "Be attentive, Be intelligent, Be reasonable, Be responsible."[100] *To the extent that one follows these precepts, one is authentic.* The ultimate goal of the dynamism of the human spirit is reality and value or, said otherwise, truth and goodness. For, by definition, the authentic person rests satisfied only with what is actually true and what is really worthwhile.

With such an analysis, Lonergan defines an intrinsically constitutive principle of the human, whose ultimate goal is absolute self-transcendence unto all that is true and good. Lonergan understands this principle to be completely human; it represents the dynamism of the human spirit. Of course, the ultimate goal of this dynamism, all that is true and good, is open to a theist interpretation. The believer names full Truth and Goodness "God," the concern in Part II of this essay. But Lonergan's analysis does not necessitate a theist interpretation: one does not deduce the existence of God.[101] Thus, Lonergan's detailed analysis of intentional consciousness provides an account of an intrinsic human principle of ultimate, authentic self-transcendence.

Walter Conn makes a valuable contribution to the understanding of spiritual development by linking Lonergan's notion of dynamic human spirit to growth through the stages of human development. He introduces a pervasive motive force that can account for post-conventional development and ultimate self-transcendence apart from theist presuppositions. This contribution is central to any possible non-theological account of spiritual development.

However, there is one oversight in Conn's presentation. While growth across any of the developmental stages could be called self-transcendence, not all such growth is automatically an instance of *authentic* self-transcendence. A development from pre-conventional to conventional morality in Kohlberg's scheme would be an instance of authentic self-transcendence only if the conventions which one

internalized were themselves authentic. Otherwise such development would indeed represent self-transcendence in the sense of a
move from a more to a less self-centered stance; but the development
would not be toward further authenticity. Lonergan writes that sometimes

> the unauthenticity of individuals becomes the unauthenticity of a
> tradition. Then, in the measure a subject takes the tradition, as it
> exists, for his [or her] standard, in that measure he [or she] can do
> no more than authentically realize unauthenticity.[102]

Growth toward authenticity entails self-transcendence; the reverse is not always true. This consideration does not disqualify
Conn's important contribution. Rather, it merely calls for further nu-
ance. It suggests that authenticity—and not simply self-transcendence—is the condition for development beyond a conventional
stage, howsoever conceived. Then it follows that if an intrinsic principle of *authentic* self-transcendence is to be one factor in a non-theological account of spiritual development, the post-conventional or adult
nature of this development must be another factor. The following
chapter will explicate this issue as it presents a definition of spiritual
development.

Notes

Chapter One

Psychological Accounts of Spiritual Development

1. Gwaltney, "Spiritual Development," 1.
2. Doran, "Jungian Psychology and Christian Spirituality."
3. Grant, Thompson, and Clarke, *Image to Likeness*, 3.
4. Studzinski, *Spiritual Direction*, 50.
5. *Ibid.*, 51.
6. *Ibid.*, 52, 135-136.
7. Thompson, *Journey Toward Wholeness*, 26.
8. Whitehead and Whitehead, *Christian Life Patterns*, 62-64.
9. Dust jacket of Groeschel, *Spiritual Passages*.
10. Brewi and Brennan, *Midlife*, 102.
11. Progoff, *Symbolic and Real*.
12. Doran, "Jungian Psychology and Christian Spirituality."
13. Thompson, *Journey Toward Wholeness*, 96, 97.
14. *Ibid.*, 42, 44, 78, 94.
15. Groeschel, *Spiritual Passages*, 104.
16. *Ibid.*, 106.
17. *Ibid.*, 117-119.
18. *Ibid.*, 153.
19. *Ibid.*, 174.
20. *Ibid.*, 175.
21. *Ibid.*, 185.
22. *Ibid.*, 35, 42, 49, 50, 66, 71-72, 94, 99, 122, 145, 189.
23. *Ibid.*, 59-61, 84.
24. *Ibid.*, 46, 52-53.
25. *Ibid.*, 76.

26. *Ibid.*, 106-111.

27. *Ibid.*, 21, 56, 67, 84, 107, 120, 130, 156.

28. Edwards, Mead, Palmer, and Simmons, *Spiritual Growth*, 13-1

29. Personal communication.

30. *CHD Report.*

31. *Ibid.*, 31.

32. Personal communication.

33. *Ibid.*, 50.

34. *Ibid.*, 51.

35. *Ibid.*

36. *Ibid.*, 52.

37. *Ibid.*

38. *Ibid.*, 53.

39. *Ibid.*, 54.

40. *Ibid.*, 55.

41. *Ibid.*

42. *Ibid.*, 56.

43. *Ibid.*, 50.

44. *Ibid.*

45. Assagioli, *Psychosynthesis*, 16.

46. *Ibid.*, 17-18.

47. *Ibid.*, 18-19.

48. *Ibid.*, 20.

49. *Ibid.*, 44-45.

50. *Ibid.*, 37.

51. *Ibid.*, 36.

52. *Ibid.*, 30.

53. *Ibid.*, 65.

54. *Ibid.*, 37.

55. Maslow, "Critique of Self-Actualization."

56. Assagioli, *Psychosynthesis*, 39.

57. *Ibid.*, 37.

58. *Ibid.*, 202.

59. *Ibid.*, 38.

60. *Ibid.*, 30.

61. *Ibid.,* 38.
62. *Ibid.,* 21-28.
63. *Ibid.,* 21.
64. *Ibid.,* 29.
65. *Ibid.,* 40-53.
66. Cf. also Groeschel, *Spiritual Passages,* 73-75.
67. Assagioli, *Psychosynthesis,* 37.
68. *Ibid.,* 194-195.
69. *Ibid.,* 6-7.
70. *Ibid.,* 193.
71. *Ibid.,* 194.
72. *Ibid.,* 193.
73. Woolfolk and Richardson, "Behavior Therapy."
74. Doran, *Subject and Psyche, Psychic Conversion.*
75. Simmons, "Human Development."
76. Simmons, "Quiet Journey."
77. Jung, "Stages of Life."
78. Erikson, "Eight Ages of Man."
79. Simmons, "Human Development," 565.
80. *Ibid.,* 566.
81. *Ibid.,* 567.
82. *Ibid.,* 568.
83. Philibert, "Conscience."
84. Kohlberg, "Implications of Moral Stages."
85. Rogers, *Becoming a Person.*
86. Philibert, "Conscience," 15.
87. *Ibid.,* 22.
88. *Ibid.,* 18.
89. *Ibid.*
90. *Ibid.,* 16.
91. *Ibid.,* 15.
92. *Ibid.,* 19.
93. *Ibid.,* 23.
94. Piaget, *Moral Judgment, Origins of Intelligence.*
95. Conn, "Moral Development," 205.

96. *Ibid.*, 190.
97. *Ibid.*, 192.
98. Lonergan, *Insight*, 348.
99. Lonergan, *Method*, 9.
100. *Ibid.*, 20, 302.
101. Lonergan, *Philosophy of God.*
102. Lonergan, *Method*, 80.

A Definition of
Spiritual Development

The above review of literature about a possible psychological account of spiritual development confirms at least this: there is no consistent and generally accepted understanding of the term "spiritual development" or "spiritual growth." With Tilden Edwards and his associates, all may legitimately wonder "what in the world someone is talking about when 'spiritual growth' comes into his [or her] conversation."[1]

Nor does consultation of standard texts on the "spiritual life" shed significantly more light. Given definitions are multiple and often enigmatic. Jordan Aumann offers no explicit definition for "spiritual life" but explains it with reference to "mystical" and "ascetical" theology and trusts that the exposition of his text itself makes clear what he is writing about.[2] Adrian Van Kaam states that spirituality pertains to what is beyond "mere ego identification in a functional society." It pertains to the "deepest self in God" or again, to "our true self in Christ."[3] Carl Vladimir Truhlar writes that "spiritual" designates "a life according to the 'spirit', understood in a Christian sense, in the sense of the New Testament, especially in Paul, and in contrast to life according to the 'flesh', again taken in the New Testament sense."[4] The biblical duality "spirit/flesh" has varied and complex meanings. It contrasts the "Holy Spirit" with sinful humanity. But most basically it implies the tension between good and evil—and not a dichotomy between body and soul, as the Hellenic mind would have it. For Louis Bouyer the "spiritual life" involves the development of an interior life "not in isolation but in the awareness of a spiritual reality, however this be understood, a reality that goes beyond the consciousness of the individual. Yet this 'spiritual reality' is not necessarily apprehended as divine; this character may even be expressly denied it."[5] Significantly, Bouyer insists that the "spiritual life" is not simply the "interior life," that rich realm of imagination, thought, and emotion generally associated with poets and artists. Finally, Adolphe Tanquerey does define "spiritual life" technically within the system of scholastic theology: its proper concern is "the perfection, of the Christian life . . . not only of the natural life of the soul but also of the *supernatural life,*—the life of *grace.*"[6]

No easily recognizable, generally accepted understanding of spiritual development is available. Still, common elements in the various understandings are discernible. Accordingly, assembling these common elements where possible and filling in the gaps and making reasonable choices where necessary, I shall proceed as any explorer must in areas not yet well charted and myself propose a systematic understanding of spiritual development.

An Intrinsic Principle of Authentic Self-Transcendence

In one way or another, most of the authors cited above note that a transcendent principle is a key factor for any understanding of spiritual development: "one's essence, " the "inner man," "God," "Christ," or the "Spirit";[7] the "Transcendent," the "Holy Spirit," "God";[8] the "superconscious" and the "higher Self";[9] "conscience" and "the voice of the Creator";[10] "the dynamism of the human spirit" and "the radical drive for self-transcending authenticity";[11] "what is beyond mere ego identification," the "deepest self," or the "true self";[12] the "spirit";[13] and a "spiritual reality that goes beyond the consciousness of the individual."[14] Diverse terminology points to a common factor.

That transcendent principle central to spiritual development is conceived freely both in theist and non-theist terms. A purely psychological understanding of spiritual development must be able to account for that transcendent principle in non-theological terms. Assagioli's "higher Self" and Lonergan's "dynamism of the human spirit" meet this requirement. The overall arguments of both Assagioli and Lonergan explicitly prescind from theological presupppositions. Both speak merely of human realities.

Lonergan provides a technical and fully coherent account of the dynamism of the human spirit. He grounds his statements in the subject's own experience of him- or herself as subject. He moves beyond metaphor and suggestive rhetoric and expresses the matter systematically, by means of a nest of interlocking, mutually defining terms.[15] Lonergan's analysis of the dynamic human spirit is an account of an intrinsic, human principle of authentic self-transcendence that can ground a non-theological exposition of spiritual development. Furthermore, it appears that this dynamic human spirit is what others intend by suggestive phrases like "higher Self," "inner man," "deepest self," "true self," "the spirit," and the like. This inner principle of authentic self-transcendence is also apparently behind what Philibert means by "conscience." That one notion includes and accounts for all the others. Therefore, this essay accepts the dynamism of the human spirit toward authentic self-transcendence, as explained by Lonergan, as the intrinsic principle of transcendence needed to explain spiritual development in a non-theological context.

Granted that understanding of the matter, it is clear that all metaphorical talk of "inner" selves and "higher" selves and "deeper" selves is inherently inaccurate and misleading. Such talk is the source of much of the "paradox" and, indeed, confusion in spiritual literature. Assagioli is right when he fumbles to explain, "There are not really two selves."[16] There is only one; but it is neither the "Self" nor the "self." There is really no "inner" self—and no "outer" self; no "higher" self and no "lower" self. Each individual, every person, is simply one human reality, one self. If there is within the human an intrinsic principle of self-transcendence, this is not to say there is another "self" within. It is simply to posit one factor among others as also necessary to explain the complex human reality and complex human experiences. Eschew all talk of a multiplicity of "inner" and "outer" and "deeper" and "truer" and "higher" and "lower" selves. Lonergan's notion of an intrinsic principle of self-transcendence and his definition of "authentic" render all those others obsolete. The "true self" or the "higher self" is merely oneself when one is acting authentically, for authenticity entails fidelity to the self-transcending dynamism of the human spirit.

Some Methodological Considerations

This acceptance of a completely human factor to explain spiritual development may cause uneasiness among some theologians. Still, most would acknowledge the validity of spiritual development in non-theist religions, and that acknowledgment presupposes the possibility of some non-theological account of spiritual development. Bouyer allows as much: "Yet this 'spiritual reality' is not necessarily apprehended as divine; this character may even be expressly denied it."[17] On the other hand, in both Lonergan's and Assagioli's accounts, insistence on an intrinsic transcendent principle does not deny the theological. While, indeed, pointing to it, it merely prescinds from it. Psychosynthesis does not explain "the great Mystery—it leads to the door, but stops there."[18]

Nor does the present approach deny the further questions that may arise in a theological context: creation, sin and forgiveness, divine revelation, grace, indwelling of the Trinity, participation in divinity, eternal life. These are legitimate issues, but they entail a set of presuppositions different from what is presupposed at this point. They belong to different disciplines. Indeed, they do add to what is said here; but they do not invalidate it. Rather, they presuppose and expand on it.[19] These other issues will be treated later in this essay. The very position of that treatment in a separate part of this study highlights the fact that, while different disciplines must be brought to bear on this complex topic, the scope of validity of each distinct discipline must be clearly defined, and the application of the different disciplines must not be confused. This approach does not belittle the contribution of any of the disciplines. While applying them separately, this approach nonetheless gives each its due and relates all coherently to one another. It provides a comprehensive, systematic treatment.

If this procedure may be offensive to some theologians, it may likewise, but for opposite reasons, be offensive to some psychologists. Can one allow within psychology notions like the "dynamism of the human spirit" or a "principle of authentic self-transcendence"? It seems so. If, on the one hand, these notions are not theological and yet, on the other hand, they are necessary for a complete explanation of the human, then they fall to psychology, the science of the human—if only by default. But more positively: understanding "spirit" to mean intentional consciousness as in Lonergan's analysis, it can be argued that some notion of "spirit" is necessary if psychology is to account for those phenomena that are distinctively human: understanding, self-determination, creativity.[20] Sigmund Koch,[21] Robert MacLeod,[22] and others[23] argue for such a broadened view of psychology.

Nor does this insistence on an intrinsic principle of authentic self-transcendence import into psychology preconceived beliefs and values—except commitment to accurate understanding and wholesome living, a commitment constitutive of modern science in its formative years. For that principle is a completely formal one; it is a wholly heuristic principle. The true, toward which it tends, is that which *will be known* when all questions on a particular issue are correctly answered. The good is that which the authentic person *will choose* in any particular case. But what the true and the good are in the concrete in any given case remains to be seen. Acceptance of an intrinsic human principle of authentic self-transcendence introduces only this into psychology: the presupposition that the concern for what is really so and for what is really worthwhile is a necessary factor for a complete explanation of the human.

Acceptance of this presupposition distinguishes irreducibly different realms within psychological studies, for that presupposition is the very one that distinguishes the positivist from the philosophic viewpoint.

Psychology within the positivist viewpoint, rigorously following the model of the natural sciences, limits its concern to human realities available to public observation and as they in fact are. It determines the publicly observable structures, mechanisms, and processes that explain the human. It correlates with a sociology or an anthropology that determines what are the actual structures or mores of a given

33

society. But it prescinds from the further questions, whether or not things ought to be as they are, whether or not the determined structures, mechanisms, and processes are being used correctly. In brief, it prescinds from the question of authenticity. As a practical discipline such psychology is adjustive; it helps clients to live comfortably within the expectations of a given society. But it does not ask whether or not such adjustment is really good, whether or not the expectations of the society in question are wholesome. Freudian analysis, behaviorism, and biological psychology are examples of psychology within the positivist viewpoint.

In contrast, the presupposition accepted here determines psychology within the philosophic viewpoint. Acceptance of human spirit as an intrinsic, human self-transcending principle directed toward the true and the good opens psychology to those further questions of meaning and value. Indeed, the suggestion is that without such openness one has missed the distinctively human factor, one is not really dealing with humans, one does not have an adequate human psychology.

Obviously, this presupposition is major. Yet it is not without parallel within the broad field of psychological studies as currently known. Humanistic psychology—as perhaps in Gordon Allport, Roberto Assagioli, Erich Fromm, Abraham Maslow, Ira Progoff, or Carl Rogers—has presuppositions similar if not identical to the presupposition accepted here. So, if this approach is offensive to some psychologists, it may well be congenial to others. Granted, the line between disciplines that this presuppposition draws, cutting right through the broad field of psychological studies, is decisive. It even implies a normative redefinition of human psychology. Still, its legitimacy can be argued within psychological studies themselves.

Finally and more immediately: it will be evident in Chapters 3 and 4 below that developmental theory cannot avoid consideration of some intrinsic principle of self-transcendence. For ultimately, something is needed to account for the undeniable human drive toward development, especially in its post-conventional achievements. Thus, whether commonly welcome or not, the issue of an intrinsic human principle of authentic self-transcendence—human spirit—has clearly entered the realm of psychological concern; and at least in the present study, it is posited as a basic presupposition.

The Definition of "Spiritual"

This essay defines *spiritual* development by reference to an intrinsic principle of authentic self-transcendence, the dynamic human *spirit*. This understanding, presupposing Bernard Lonergan's analysis of intentional consciousness or spirit, has been explicated in some detail, especially by insistence on authenticity as the prime criterion of spiritual development. In all this, this account remains in substantial agreement with the other authors cited in Chapter 1.

Note that this position clarifies—and, in comparison with most other usage, redefines—the meaning of "spiritual." Here the term refers to a strictly human reality. The term has no necessary theist or Christian connotations; there is no inherent reference to "religious" faith or practice, as generally understood in the Judeo-Christian world. Within a comprehensive and systematic account of the matter, other terms must be provided to account for those other connotations. Parts II and III of this essay address that issue. Finally, this position assumes that, in the contemporary world of increasing specialization of fields, psychology—within the philosophic viewpoint—is the discipline that properly treats the spiritual. Though theologians and religious believers, probably more than any others, will be concerned about spiritual development, theology and theist or Christian religion as such are not the appropriate arenas for the study of spiritual development as defined technically in this essay.

The Subject's Openness to the Spiritual

A first key factor in the definition of spiritual development has already been noted—an intrinsic principle of authentic self-transcendence. A second factor is the subject's openness to that principle. An increased sensitivity to the urge of that drive is an indication of increased spiritual maturity and a determinative of possible further spiritual development. Assagioli, the CHD Report, Tilden Edwards and his associates, and Henry Simmons support this understanding. In their pastoral presentation, mixing psychological and theological terms, Grant, Thompson, and Clarke speak of this same factor in terms of human freedom, choice: "While there is an element of givenness and grace in every coming to wholeness, it is also contingent on choice—we must *desire* wholeness, as a pearl of great price, and be willing to let go of everything else in order that we may gain it."[24]

Personal Integrity or Wholeness

A third characteristic of spiritual development is that it involves the whole person; it entails personal integrity or wholeness. Not any one or some few aspects of the person, but the development of the whole human is at stake in spiritual development. "Wholeness" is one of the common factors in the descriptions of spiritual development in *Spiritual Growth* by Edwards and his associates. In its holistic view of spirituality, the *CHD Report* assumes the same major starting point. Philibert's appeal to Rogers's consonance of experience or feelings with ideas insists again on integration of the whole person as an essential characteristic of spiritual development.[25] Likewise, all the other authors reviewed in Chapter 1 share this presupposition, except perhaps Benedict Groeschel.

The specific intent of this insistence on wholeness or integrity is that the intrinsic dynamism toward authentic self-transcendence must not be forgotten when one speaks of human development. It, too, is a part of the whole person. Thus, wholeness implies a growing self-consistency, a consistency within the whole. It implies a mutual influence between the concrete structures of human being and acting, on the one hand, and the intrinsic dynamism of the human spirit, on the other, resulting in an increasingly self-consistent being.

Wholeness also implies self-constitution. It suggests that human being is becoming, that in the process of daily activity humans gradually make themselves to be what they are. As humans follow the drive toward authentic self-transcendence and not only come to acknowledge what is really "so" but also then decide and act appropriately on what they know, they effect changes not only in the external world on which they act but more importantly on themselves who are acting. Their decisions affect what they themselves are as well as what other things will be. They become as they do. They constitute themselves in an ongoing dialectic between themselves as agents in an outer world and their own dynamism toward authenticity in the realm of interiority.[26] Spiritual development concerns this ongoing process whose result is the whole human being as he or she is.

This conception further explicates what Philibert indicates when he argues for an understanding of conscience broad enough to account not only for one's knowledge of what is to be done but also for the doing and so the very becoming of the agent. The review of Jane Loevinger's conception of ego development below—concerned with an all-pervasive yet, from the point of view of spiritual development, still partial aspect of the human—will shed more light on these issues.

An Adult Phenomenon

Those considerations lead to a fourth characteristic of spiritual development—its adult nature. All human development is a process of self-constitution. This is true not only of adults who think and weigh evidence and judge and decide for themselves what they will do and so become. It is also true, but in a different way, for children who unthinkingly and unknowingly and so without responsibility, uncritically caught up in the world of intimates, "go along with" whatever is offered. They, too, make themselves be what they will be, but in the process they really have little choice. Max Scheler makes this point clearly.

> The ideas, feelings and tendencies which govern the life of a child, apart from general ones such as hunger and thirst, are initially confined entirely to those of his immediate environment, his parents and relatives, his elder brothers and sisters, his teachers, his home, his people, and so on. Imbued as he is with "family feeling," his own life is at first almost completely hidden from him. Rapt, as it were, and hypnotized by the ideas and feelings of this concrete environment of his, the only experiences which succeed in crossing the threshold of his inner awareness are those which fit a kind of channel for the stream of his mental environment. Only very slowly does he raise his mental head, as it were, above this stream flooding over it, and find himself as a being who also, at times, has feelings, ideas and tendencies of his own. And this, moreover, only occurs to the extent that the child *objectifies* the experience of his environment in which he lives and partakes, and thereby gains *detachment* from them. The mental content of experience that is virtually absorbed "with one's mother's milk" is not the result of a transference of ideas, experienced as something "communicated." For communication entails that we understand the "communicated content" as proceeding from our informant, and that while understanding it we also appreciate

its origin in the other person. But this factor is just what is absent in that mode of transference which operates between the individual and his environment. For in this case we do not primarily "understand" the passing of a judgment or the expression of an emotion, or regard it as the utterance of another self. We fall in with it, without being consciously aware of the element of co-operation involved.[27]

In an unthinking, uncritical, undifferentiated way, children do have a part to play in what they become as they are reared. With adults, however, the case is significantly different. Still the agent of their self-constitution, they can be so reflectively, critically, analytically. To some extent, at least, they can reflect on what they are because of earlier experience, can evaluate that, and can decide what they will retain and what they will work to change. When they can begin the process of self-constitution from a reflective, critical stance, they have come to a critical turning point in life: "One has to have found out for oneself that one has to decide for oneself what one is to make of oneself."[28]

Spiritual development properly speaking begins only at that critical turning point. Spiritual development entails self-critical and self-responsible growth. All that comes before that critical turning point does, in fact, concern one's growth in authenticity. Children grow in authentic virtue as well as adults do. Indeed, one's childhood significantly sets the condition for the possibility of one's subsequent self-responsible self-constitution. Yet different phenomena are at stake in child and in adult self-constitution. The former is adequately named "learning," "upbringing," "education," or "formation." These terms imply the influence predominantly of an extrinsic force on the individual. But self-responsible self-constitution alone is properly the stuff of spiritual development. And when it moves along the line of authentic self-transcendence, it is spiritual development.

In one way or another, all the sources cited above presume that spiritual development is an adult phenomenon. More specifically, Assagioli's overall program for *Psychosynthesis*, George Simmons's concern that at about thirty years of age and beyond people receive special help for growth in their religious life, and the *CHD Report's* understanding of spiritual growth as movement from a conventional to a post-conventional viewpoint, all explicitly acknowledge the adult nature of spiritual development. Subsequent consideration of theories of adult development will further explicate this issue, for it is clearly a developmental one.

Departures from Assagioli's Position

I have defined spiritual development according to four distinctive characteristics and have emphasized authentic self-transcendence as a key factor. Precisely here, this position represents a significant departure from Assagioli's richly developed one.[29] Insofar as the dynamic human spirit accurately represents also the intent of Assagioli's metaphor "the higher Self," both positions are in accord. Moreover, in this case it appears that his "Self-realization" represents the subject's possible extraordinary experience of the dynamism of his or her own spirit, which in principle is open to transcending all space and time.[30] Yet for Assagioli reference to "the higher Self" as definitive of the spiritual is secondary in comparison with reference to the superconscious. This issue is significant and deserves treatment.

There are at least two separate sets of contents in Assagioli's "superconscious": first, the ethical, humanitarian, and altruistic; second, the esthetic, artistic, philosophical and scientific, mentally superior (genius), ecstatic, and "higher" psychic and parapsychological. Insofar as the first intends movements toward authentic self-transcendence, they are already adequately accounted for by the above-mentioned intrinsic principle of authentic self-transcendence; they pertain to the essence of spiritual development, as defined here. But the second do not.

There is no reason for naming "spiritual" what is unusually intelligent or giftedly creative, what pertains to artists, poets, and geniuses. No doubt, these phenomena are expressions of the human spirit—and not merely expressions of the "imagination," according to the now popular but ambiguous usage of the term.[31] But these phenomena participate in human spirit in a way significantly different from what is categorized here as definitive of spiritual development. Artistic and intellectural genius is a function of the first and second levels of consciousness in Lonergan's analysis, whereas spiritual development is a function of the fourth level of consciousness, which sublates all the other levels in an integrative process of self-constitution. Other categories indicate these phenomena sufficiently well:

intelligence, creativity, genius, giftedness. They are but unusually intense instances of the intelligence and creativity that all humans share in a more prosaic degree. So these phenomena are no more "spiritual"—and so no more to be named as such—than those similar occurrences in all human beings.

As for the rest—the ecstatic, psychic, and parapsychological: common usage does speak of these as "spiritual." The reference is to "spiritualism," the belief in communication with the dead by means of a medium. The reference is to the "supernatural," the eerie, ghostly, and inexplicable. And the reference is to psychic and parapsychological phenomena like psychokinesis, "out-of-the-body experiences," automatic writing, levitation, and extra-sensory perception: telepathy, clairvoyance or distant viewing, and precognition. There is reason to believe that these extraordinary phenomena are easily possible for people who have significantly integrated within themselves the full capacities of the human spirit.[32] That is to say, these phenomena may accompany high levels of spiritual development as understood in this essay. Yet these phenomena are not essential to spiritual development. Traditional Christian theology calls these phenomena "extraordinary" or "charismatic"—distinguishing them from what is "essential," "concomitant," or "constitutive"—and insists that they are not determinative of intense spiritual development.[33] Tibetan Buddhist teaching likewise minimizes the importance of these phenomena.[34] Moreover, all religious traditions warn against the possibility of using psychic and parapsychological powers for evil.[35] That is to say, one could have such powers and still be operating at a petty self-serving level of moral development comparable to a child's in Kohlberg's pre-conventional level.

Psychic giftedness, possible in a child, and levels of even ordinary adult human development are separable realities. All the more so is psychic giftedness not a necessary concomitant of authentic self-transcendence.[36] If possibly related, the two realities are significantly different. Accordingly, the term "spiritual development" is reserved here for growth along the line of authentic self-transcendence. The terms "psychic" and "parapsychological" adequately name the other reality.

The insistence here is parallel to Bouyer's[37] concern in distinguishing the "interior life" of poets, artists, and other gifted people from the "spiritual life." On this point I emphatically depart from Assagioli's conception and usage. Indeed, I veiw them not only as confusing but also as dangerously misleading. This is not foolishly to deny the reality of "psychic phenomena" nor to discourage the study of them. It is merely to insist that psychic and parapsychological phenomena and other examples of extraordinary human giftedness are not essential factors in spiritual development.

A Definition of Spiritual Development

I have proposed four distinctive characteristics of spiritual development: 1) an intrinsic principle of authentic self-transcendence, 2) openness in the subject to this principle, 3) the integrity or wholeness of the subject in question, and 4) the self-critical self-responsibility of an adult. Thus, *spiritual development is the ongoing integration that results in the self-responsible subject from openness to an intrinsic principle of authentic self-transcendence.*

That represents an initial statement. Subsequent discussion will further explicate and expand it. Yet this initial statement is sufficiently detailed to clarify the basic hypothesis of this essay: spiritual development is human development conceived according to a particular set of concerns. The four elements in the definition specify the concerns according to which human development is spiritual development. So conceived, spiritual development is not to be considered primarily a religious or theological phenomenon. It is a human phenomenon. As such, it is essentially the proper object of study not for theology but for the human sciences and particularly for psychology within the philosophic viewpoint.

All the sources quoted in Chapter 1 acknowledge the relevance of psychology to an understanding of spiritual development. In *Holiness Is Wholeness* Goldbrunner argued convincingly that holiness is not antagonistic to psychological wholeness but, on the contrary, precisely entails such wholeness, despite the sometimes bizarre spiritual ideals prevalent in former times. The *CHD Report* deals with spiritual growth according to empirically measurable criteria; and Assagioli argues explicitly for a non-theological account of spiritual development. Thus far, this essay has taken these positions and integrated them into a theoretically coherent one. An initial definition of spiritual development is the result. The following chapter will review the research of developmental psychologists in order to determine the discernible stages of adult human development. Then, again assuming its fundamental hypothesis, this essay will accept those conclusions to propose the stages of spiritual development.

Notes

Chapter Two

A Definition of Spiritual Development

1. Edwards, Mead, Palmer, and Simmons, *Spiritual Growth*, 1.

2. Aumann, *Spiritual Theology*.

3. Van Kaam, *In Search of Spiritual Identity*, 5.

4. Truhlar, *Structura Theologica*, 1.

5. Bouyer, *Introduction to Spirituality*, 4.

6. Tanquerey, *The Spiritual Life*, 1

7. Brewi and Brennan, *Mid-Life*; Edwards, Mead, Palmer, and Simmons, *Spiritual Growth*; Grant, Thompson, and Clarke, *From Image to Likeness*; Groeschel, *Spiritual Passages*; Studzinski, *Spiritual Direction*; Thompson, *Journey Toward Wholeness*.

8. *CHD Report*.

9. Assagioli, *Psychosynthesis*.

10. Philibert, "Conscience."

11. Conn, "Moral Development"; Lonergan, *Method*.

12. Van Kaam, *In Search of Spiritual Identity*.

13. Truhlar, *Structura Theologica*.

14. Bouyer, *Introduction to Spirituality*.

15. Cf. Lonergan, *Insight*, 10-13; Helminiak, *The Same Jesus*, Chapter Four, n. 9.

16. Assagioli, *Psychosynthesis*, 20.

17. Bouyer, *Introduction to Spirituality*, 4.

18. Assagioli, *Psychosynthesis*, 6-7.

19. Helminiak, "Four Viewpoints," "How Is Meditation Prayer?" "Meditation," "One in Christ," and "Where Do We Stand?"

20. Helminiak, "Consciousness."

21. Koch, "Reflections on Psychology," "Nature and Limits of Psychological Knowledge."

22. MacLeod, "Newtonian and Darwinian Conceptions," "Phenomenological Approach."

23. Woodfolk and Richardson, "Behavior Therapy."

24. Grant, Thompson, and Clarke, *Image to Likeness*, 184-185.

25. Philibert, "Conscience."

26. Lonergan, *Second Collection*, 79-84; *Collection*, 254; *Method*, 74-81; Helminiak, "One in Christ," 311-331.

27. Scheler, *Nature of Sympathy*, 247.

28. Lonergan, *Method*, 121.

29. Assagioli, *Psychosynthesis*.

30. Helminiak, "How Is Meditation Prayer?"

31. Helminiak, *The Same Jesus*, Chapter Three, n. 9.

32. Tart, *Transpersonal Psychologies*, 150-151.

33. Johnston, *Inner Eye*, 30; Tanquerey, *Spiritual Life*, 700; Bouyer, *Introduction to Spirituality*, 298-303.

34. Trungpa, *Cutting Through, Myth of Freedom*.

35. Johnston, *Inner Eye*, 97-98

36. Helminiak, "Where Do We Stand?"

37. Bouyer, *Introduction to Spirituality*.

CHAPTER THREE

Stages of Human Development

Theories of human development may be categorized according to two general approaches. There is the maturational or psychosocial approach, and there is the constructivist developmental approach.[1] See Table I for an overview of this material.

Maturational Theories of Human Development

The maturational—or psychosocial—approach presumes that changes that occur are the result of ordinary growth. New life situations bring forth new development. Stages in development are age-related.

Erikson's "Eight Ages of Man" is an example of a psychosocial scheme of development. According to Erikson's theory, eight successive maturational tasks entail eight successive psychological "crises." For Erikson the term "crisis" does not necessarily mean a difficult and threatening experience; rather, it means simply an important, a critical, transition. The possible result of each crisis is expressed as an antinomy with a possible positive or negative outcome. Thus, basic trust vs. basic mistrust is at stake in the infant oral stage; autonomy vs. shame and doubt, in the anal stage; initiative vs. guilt, in the phallic stage; industry vs. inferiority, as the child enters the new world of school; identity vs. role confusion, at puberty; intimacy vs. isolation, at the young adult marrying age; generativity vs. stagnation, at the middle adult time of responsibility for the succeeding generations; and integrity vs. despair, as one faces the decline of life in old age.

Erikson's theory of development has been popular with people writing from a religious perspective. Since the theory notes major issues to be faced along life's way, it provides an easy outline within which one can discuss various questions of meaning and value generally considered to be religious. In fact, Erikson's presentation provokes such religious consideration. The three adult crises in his account clearly entail values: intimacy, generativity, and integrity, and he even relates the positive competency to be developed at each crisis to traditional virtues: love, care, and wisdom.[2]

Daniel Levinson's *Seasons of a Man's Life* provides another example of a maturational theory of development. Levinson proposes four major eras of male life, with transition periods between each. In Childhood and Adolescence boys have the task of learning the rubrics of living and social skills and knowledge about various types of adult activity. In Early Adulthood a man must learn to choose, create, and maintain his own life structure. In Middle Adulthood a man must bear the major responsibility for family and profession; growingly aware of his mortality, he may also review and revise his life structure. Late Adulthood allows a man, as a wise and experienced senior, to assert significant influence but mostly from the sidelines of life's activity.

Roger Gould's *Transformations: Growth and Change in Adult Life* is another example of a psychosocial theory of human development. Gould developed his account of adult development working with numerous clients as a psychoanalyst. Gould's and Levinson's initial research is the material Gail Sheehy borrowed to write her best-seller, *Passages*. Gould understands development primarily as an internal shift in a person's "consciousness." In the face of the passing years one gradually may give up false assumptions about life. One moves from "childhood consciousness" to "adult consciousness." Maturity means the ability to allow one's deepest needs without fear of being overwhelmed and so sabotaged by them. It entails slowly disengaging the defense mechanisms that shield one from oneself, from deep intimacy with others, and from energetic engagement with the world. Insofar as this account focuses on inner changes in a person's way of experiencing life, it really does treat the development of the human individual and not just changes in patterns of external behavior. To this extent, Gould's theory also has characteristics of constructivist developmental theories, to be discussed presently.

According to Gould's explicit acknowledgment, two factors account for adult development, an external factor: age-related social expectations, and an internal one: the individual's prior developmental achievement.[3] As one ages and the new situations dictated by one's culture bring new challenges, one brings one's resources to bear and so achieves some growth. Here is obviously one of those cases in which "to him who has will more be given."[4] Those who have successfully negotiated prior transitions are more likely to do well in later ones. But underlying these explicit factors is another, an unacknowledged but pervasive presupposition in Gould's theory. This further factor could be described as a drive toward transparency or as a basic need to be one's full self. Such a thing would explain why one works to eliminate childhood misconceptions and their concomitant defense mechanisms. Gould comes closest to acknowledging this critical factor when he notes that the rate of one's growth "is determined by how capable and efficient an individual is at processing psychological material—in particular, how willing that individual is to abandon the irrational protective devices and reexperience childhood anger and hurt in order to reach inner freedom."[5]

Gould projects five stages of adult development. From about 16 to 22 years old, young men and women begin to launch out and leave their parents' world, both emotionally and geographically. They develop their own opinions, assert their independence, and become romantically involved, but they still remain considerably ambivalent about their independence. From 22 to 28, as they set up their own lives, especially through marriage and career, they begin to realize the fact that no one can live their lives for them; they are on their own. They develop independence and competence in their external life, but their intimate relationships still often represent attempts to recover or rework parental relationships. Ages 28 to 34 bring a shift to awareness of inner reality. Young adults realize the complexity in themselves and others and learn that life is not as simple as it once seemed, that it is not fair, and that it is not what it is "supposed" to be. Ages 35 to 45, the mid-life decade, bring a sense that time is running out. Action is called for. Now adults come to grips with the passions in their core, accept themselves realistically for what they are, and learn to tap the power of their inner resources. Finally, in the Beyond-Mid-life period, inner-directedness finally prevails. Adults give up the standards of childhood and society—competition through power and size—and in the face of death become their own persons. They live with a sense of acceptance, saying, "That's the way it is, world. Here I am! This is me!"[6]

The maturational approach assumes that personal development corresponds automatically to age-related changes. Yet this presumption raises significant questions. Can this approach determine universally valid stages of human development or are its results significantly culture-bound (as seems clear in Levinson's account of the American male or in Gould's account of middle- to upper-class heterosexual couples)? Do all who pass through the maturational crises by sheer dint of age actually experience the appropriate personal development as a result of that passage? Or, as seems more likely, are these crises only likely occasions for possible growth? Then, are the same age-related crises actually significantly different experiences for people of different degrees of personal integration? And would not these "degrees of personal integration" be more valid indicators of actual stages of development?

Constructivist Theories of Human Development

An alternative, the constructivist developmental approach, attempts to avoid the possible shortcomings of the maturational approach. What is here called "constructivist" is most widely known in the form of *structural* theories of development. These conceive development by analogy to the growth of an organism. The specialization of cells, the combination of like cells into different tissues, and the combination of like tissues into separate systems in the growing organism: digestive, circulatory, reproductive, nervous systems—these suggest a process wherein the subsequent result at each stage is actually different from the antecedents and yet proceeds from them.[7] James Baldwin, Heinz Werner, and Jean Piaget pioneered this organismic notion of development. In its theoretically refined form,[8] this approach describes the various stages of development according to the different structures that characterize them.

A structure is the ordered set of relations among all the elements internal to the organism. A structure exhibits an equilibrium, a balance, a certain harmony among all its elements; a structure is recognizable as an integrated whole, a unity. A structure tends toward such a stage of equilibrium. It maintains this equilibrium by assimilation of new experiences (selectivity) and by accommodation to new experiences (flexibility), within the limits possible to its present organization. Yet, because of its structural properties, when faced with internal need or environmental demand, the organism is able to change its structure to meet the new situation and so arrive at a new state of equilibrium.

Development is precisely such a structural change. Development can be expected to continue until the organism reaches a stage of structural equilibrium adequate to all its experiences.[9] The alternative is for it to die.

Lawrence Kohlberg summarizes Piaget's conception of structural developmental theory in four principles.[10] Each stage represents a structural whole. Each is qualitatively—not just quantitatively—different from the others. The stages of development follow an invariant sequence: the stages always follow in the same order, and no stage can be skipped. Finally, the stages are hierarchical integrations: higher stages displace and reintegrate lower structures at a level of increased differentiation and adequacy to need.

That is the theory. Of course, empirical research provides results that are less clean-cut.[11] Above all, the first principle, "structures of the whole," suggests an emergence of stages as finished and integrated units, as if one moves from one plateau to another, having either wholly arrived at the next level or not. In actuality, as a result of individual differences and of the complexity of human development in general, elements constitutive of the successive stages as theoretically defined may emerge separately and on different schedules. At any one time but with respect to various domains of learning or behavior, a subject will provide evidence of being in several of the stages simultaneously. This empirical fact poses a serious challenge to the notion of structually conceived stages. Current practice determines one's stage of development by noting where the preponderance of one's responses to a measuring instrument, in an interview, or on a skills test fall.

Piaget himself rejected the notion of "structures of the whole" in his later writings, yet he still retained a modified notion of internal structures to characterize different stages—even as many developmental theorists continue to do. However, Robert Campbell and Mark Bickhard's *Knowing Levels and Developmental Stages* provides a recent, profound, and devastating criticism of any structuralist explanation of development. In contrast to the structuralist approach, Campbell and Bickhard elaborate other aspects of Piaget's theory: the subject's interactive engagement with the environment that results in the emergence of new stages and the determination of stages according to levels of reflective abstraction. On this view, determination of developmental stages by appeal to supposed internal "structures" is misguided. The notion of structure appears to be but a metaphor, internalized and reified, for one aspect of a complex human phenomenon that still needs to be explained.

Nonetheless, on that same view and although its theoretical underpinnings are significantly different from the structuralist approach, the delineation of stages that results retains a substantive relationship with Piaget's model. Moreover, there still emerges a logically necessary sequence of stages that are invariant and hierarchical. Finally, these stages do not emerge automatically. In clear contrast to a maturational model of development, the age markers in the constructivist developmental model, howsoever conceived, merely indicate the earliest likely emergence of a new stage. Beyond childhood, age in no way guarantees that one will achieve the stage whose emergence may be theoretically associated with a particular age. Thus, it appears that, despite the lack of consensus among psychologists regarding important theoretical issues inherent in the constructivist developmental approach, the delineation of stages of human development, such as are summarized in the present chapter, retains a qualified validity.

Stages of Cognitive Development

Jean Piaget's own stages of cognitive development represent the prototypical example of a structural developmental theory. Intelligence first expresses itself in a sensori-motor period, lasting from birth till the emergence of language. During this period the infant achieves control over the body and learns to use the senses in their multiple possible combinations. By the end of this period the infant also has some working understanding of space, time, and causality, develops some sense of the permanence of objects apart from personal visual or tactile experience of them, and acquires the ability to reproduce various behaviors at will, apart from a physically present model. Then, to some extent the infant is at home in his or her body and in the physical world. Such sensori-motor achievement is the adequate expression of human intelligence at this stage of development. Next, in the pre-operational stage, lasting till about seven years of age, the use of language allows for representational thinking. Yet thinking remains dominated by immediate perceptions and does not allow for the mental reversibility of a process. Thus, a child at this stage is unable to solve problems of conservation and will opine that there is more liquid in a tall, slender cylinder than in a short but fat one. Or again, a child at this stage cannot follow a map. In the concrete operational period, lasting from about seven years to adolescence, the child can mentally conceive classes and series and so perform logical operations on concrete problems, that is, when the materials are there before her or him. But only in the formal operational stage, beginning at puberty, is the adolescent capable of complex and abstract hypothetico-deductive thinking, conceiving an array of possibilities about any particular issue and spinning out coherent theories in an abstract world.

Research confirms that human intelligence does develop in some such way as this; yet, depending on the measure one uses, research also shows that only about seventeen to sixty-seven percent of college students ever develops formal operations.[12] An invariant sequence is given, but there is no promise of universal achievement.

Recent research in post-formal operational thinking extends Piaget's own theory and proposes further stages of cognitive develop-

51

ment. Researchers vary widely in their suggested accounts of these further stages.[13] One approach, consistent with Piaget's own later thinking, proposes that the emergence of each cognitive stage results from successive reflexive appropriation of the distinctive factor only implicit in the functioning of the next lower stage.[14] Pre-operational thinking deals with objects. Concrete operational thinking deals with the relations—groupings and classes—among objects. Formal operational thinking deals with theories, or systems of relations. Post-formal operational thinking deals with consciousness as the source of all systems. The final attainment is some kind of unitive experience. Thus, Bernard Lonergan can write, "Thoroughly understand what it is to understand, and not only will you understand the broad lines of all there is to be understood but also you will possess a fixed base, an invariant pattern, opening upon all further developments of understanding."[15] On some such basis, Philip Powell and Herb Koplowitz, for example, each in his own way, derive two stages beyond formal operations. These stages seem to parallel the upper two in the theories of Fowler and Loevinger treated below (see Table I) and so suggest an inner logic in these highest stages of human development, a logic coherent with that of all the lower stages. Though still tentative and highly debated, such research and theorizing in cognitive development may provide a systematic and explanatory account of all stages of human development on the basis of the human cognitive—that is, spiritual—capacity.

Stages of Moral Development

Kohlberg's analysis of moral development is another example of structural-stage theory.[16] Kohlberg proposes three main stages of moral development—pre-conventional, conventional, and post-conventional—and subdivides each into two. The result is a six-stage theory of moral development.

But more accurately, Kohlberg's is a theory of moral reasoning or moral judgment. For based on a Kantian conception of ethics, this theory presumes—and quite questionably so[17]—that the heart of morality lies in knowing what is required of one. So the final stage in Kohlberg's theory conceives conscience in terms of comprehensive, universal, and timeless principles, "objectively" distant from particular concrete situations. Entering the discussion from the point of view of her research on women, Carol Gilligan has argued that women are not morally underdeveloped, as application of Kohlberg's theory to data on women would suggest.[18] Rather, insofar as women tend to make moral decisions more on the basis of community concerns, personal commitments, and human relationships, they are simply responding to other values, equally as lofty as those highlighted by Kohlberg's theory. "Gilligan has called the approach that she finds more typical of women 'the ethic of responsibility'. We might characterize the approach that Kohlberg represents as 'the ethic of duty or obligation'."[19] These two ethics represent long-standing traditions in Western civilization. Then the telling issue here may well not be male-female differences at all but rather the effect of Kantianism on Kohlberg's theory.

The stages of Kohlberg's theory unfold as follows. In Stage 1 fear of punishment and deference to superior power are the dominant orientation; the physical consequences of an action determine its goodness or badness. In Stage 2 right action is what satisfies one's own needs or occasionally the needs of others; fairness and reciprocity interpreted as "tit for tat"—and not loyalty, gratitude, or justice—is the rule. In the conventional Stage 3, the good-girl/good-boy orientation holds sway; good behavior is what pleases or helps others and gains approval from them. In Stage 4 law and order is the dominant concern; right behavior consists in doing one's duty, specified by fixed rules for the maintenance of the social order. The post-conventional morality of Stage 5 adopts a social-contract orientation; right action is defined by standards known to be agreed upon by, and for the good of, the whole society. At this stage there arises the notion of possibly changing the law in favor of what is more equitable. Finally, the morality of Stage 6 is determined by conscience and self-chosen ethical principles; such morality appeals to logical comprehensiveness, universality, and consistency.

Kohlberg has proposed variations on that basic outline of his theory. For example, he suggests the addition of a metaphorical "Stage 7."[20] It entails a perspective on life's ultimate meaning that allows one to ask the ultimate moral question, Why be moral at all? and to act ethically in the face of this question. "Stage 7" represents the epitome of moral maturity. In the present context it is useful to note that, since concern for the ultimate meaning of life is taken to be a religious issue, Kohlberg allows that "Stage 7" is religious. However, this fact does not suggest that "Stage 7," any more than the rest of Kohlberg's theory, might be particularly relevant to the topic of spiritual development. Rather, the emergence of a religious "Stage 7" in Kohlberg's ongoing theorizing highlights the narrowness of his initial conception of moral development in terms of moral reasoning. Philibert's criticism of this issue has already been noted in Chapter 1, and Fowler's criticism of it is noted below.

Clear in both Piaget's and Kohlberg's theories is the delineation of discrete stages, each internally coherent and consistent, each transcending the ones before it, and all arranged in a hierarchical order. Both Piaget and Kohlberg claim universal validity for their theories. That is to say, these theories supposedly spell out an invariant pattern of human development. They prescind from the cultural context and the particular content pertinent to the thinking or moral reasoning in question in any instance. They are strictly formal theories. As such, they indicate the intrinsic development of the relevant structures of the human, as such. Of course, this is an optimistic assessment of the matter; but to attain such universal validity and theoretical sophistication is the intended strength of the constructivist developmental approach. It is this approach that both James Fowler and Jane Loevinger follow.

Fowler's Notion of Faith

James Fowler first became interested in faith development when, in 1968-69, as associate director of a house for the continuing education of clergy and for lay retreats, he listened to over two hundred stories, the stories of people's pilgrimages of faith. Erik Erikson's model of human development helped him to sort out and organize what he was hearing at that time. Later, teaching at Harvard Divinity School, he became familiar with Lawrence Kohlberg and his work. Then Fowler began to systematically work out stages of faith development.[21] Since that time he has published a number of preliminary statements about his research.[22] *Stages of Faith* is the comprehensive statement of his position. His later book, *Becoming Adult, Becoming Christian*, makes no further significant contribution on this matter.[23]

For Fowler, faith is an exceedingly broad and complex reality. Basically, it is "an orientation of the total person, giving purpose and goal to one's hopes and strivings, thoughts and actions."[24] Spelled out in more detail,

> Faith is a person's or group's way of moving into the force field of life. It is our way of finding coherence in and giving meaning to the multiple forces and relations that make up our lives. Faith is a person's way of seeing him- or herself in relation to others against a background of shared meaning and purpose.[25]

Thus, the central issue of faith is the meaning and purpose which structure a person's world. Elsewhere Fowler speaks of the same issue in terms of *"center(s) of value and power"*[26] or "transcendent centers of value and power"[27] or "the human quest for relation to transcendence."[28] Fowler also provides a formal and comprehensive definition of faith.[29] However, that long and convoluted formula would be more confusing than helpful here. Fowler's mention of transcendence introduces a provocative ambiguity into his presentation, which will be treated below. Here it suffices to indicate his general understanding of faith.

Faith so conceived is not necessarily a religious phenomenon. Following Wilfred Cantwell Smith, Fowler sees religion as "cumulative tradition."[30] Religion entails sacred texts, laws, teachings, doctrines, creeds, rites, formulas, etc. All these are the expressions of faith of people in the past. Neither is faith to be confused with belief, "the holding of certain ideas."[31] Faith is a subjective activity, the process of "setting one's heart on" something and so construing the meaning and purpose of one's world. Far from being proper to any one religion or even to religion in general, it is a wholly *"human phenomenon, an apparently generic* consequence of the universal human burden of finding or making meaning."[32]

Faith is a relational reality. It relates (1) one to (2) others against (3) a background of shared meaning and value. Faith has a "triadic shape."[33] The background of shared centers of value and power can be "polytheistic," that is, a constellation of multiple centers of interest and concern; or "henotheistic," that is, a single ultimate center of commitment acknowledged as one among many possible others; or "monotheistic," that is, *the* "transcendent center of value and power, that is neither a conscious or unconscious extension of personal or group ego nor a finite cause or institution."[34] The latter may be construed in a theist or nontheist way.

Faith acts as a kind of imagination—in German, *Einbildungskraft*: "literally, the 'power (*Kraft*)' of 'forming (*Bildung*)' into one (*Ein*)'."[35] "Faith forms a way of seeing our everyday life in relation to holistic images of what we may call the *ultimate environment*."[36] Presupposing the commonly held understanding that images are the primordial currency of the human mind, Fowler insists on the essential role of imaging in the construction of one's worldview. Evidently, "imaging" is the specific activity through which one "constructs a world," "finds coherence," "gives meaning," "gives purpose and goal" to life.

Stages of faith can then be construed as various, successive ways that one "images" one's world. Fowler explains, "The images of faith are not static. By virtue of our research and observation I believe that we can identify reasonably predictable developmental turning points in the *ways* faith imagines and in the way faith's images interplay with communal modes of expression."[37] These stages of faith are purely formal in nature; they are defined by the manner of one's "faithing" apart from consideration of any particular content of one's belief.

Piaget and Kohlberg highly influenced Fowler's work, and he incorporates their thought into his own. But he criticizes them on two important points reminiscent of Philibert's[38] criticism of Kohlberg: they separate cognition from affection and emotion; and they ignore the symbolic process, the role of imagination in knowing. Fowler insists that faith development is not reducible to cognitive or to moral development nor to a combination of the two. He tries to take into account those factors neglected by Piaget and Kohlberg. His necessarily complex understanding of faith is the result.

Faithing as Self-Constituting

Faithful to his broader concerns, Fowler points out the further implication. In some way faith development is concerned not only with some activity or function of the human subject but also with the very constitution of the subject. Of course, the same is true of Piaget's cognitive and Kohlberg's moral development, but it can be easily overlooked in their restricted intellectual contexts. Where there is emphasis on the affective, however, this implication may not be neglected.

In both faith knowing and the kind of moral-knowing which gives rise to choice and action, the constitution or modification of the self is always an issue. In these kinds of constitutive-knowing not only is the "known" being constructed, but there is also a simultaneous extension, modification, or reconstitution of the *knower in relation to the known.*[39]

". . . our previous decisions and actions shape our character, as do the stories and images by which we live."[40] Thus, the stages of faith development are stages of development of the human subject him- or herself. Faithing is a self-constitutive activity: it makes one be what one will be. And the same is also true of the more restricted cognitive and moral functions of the human being.

That emphasis is important. It suggests developmental stages for the human personality, and so it provides an obvious link with Loevinger's conception of ego development. Moreover, it envisages the development of the individual him- or herself as a whole, and so relates to the central concern here, spiritual development.

Stages of Faith

Fowler discerns six stages in faith development. A pre-stage called Undifferentiated Faith is proper to the infant up to about one and a half years of age. This pre-stage is unavailable to empirical research. It is parallel to the period when, according to Erikson's scheme, the crisis of trust vs. mistrust is being worked through. The faith of early infancy is characterized by the mutuality between infant and nurturers. The infant lives in an unthinking world, held together by the presence of significant others. The importance of this pre-stage is the possibility it holds for the affective development of trust, autonomy, hope, and courage—or their opposites—which will condition all further development of faith.

Stage-1 Faith, called Intuitive-Projective Faith, is typical of the child of three to seven. The emergence of language, that marvelous tool for concretizing thought, effects the transition from the pre-stage to Stage 1. At Stage 1 the child constructs an ever-shifting world by means of imitation, fantasy, and rich imagination. Thinking is fluid and episodic. Associations are formed according to subjective experience and are not governed by any logic. Unable to make comparisons or shifts of perspective, the child unquestioningly assumes that things simply are as he or she experiences or perceives them. The child's world is circumscribed by the orbit of the family. The example, moods, actions, and language of primal others are powerfully influential for good and for possible irreparable harm. Relationships of attachment and dependence and the authority of those who are bigger and more powerful provide anchorage in the Stage-1 child's world.

Stage-2 Faith, called Mythic-Literal Faith, is normative for children from about seven to twelve; but as all the subsequent stages of faith, it can remain the effective mode throughout life. The emergence of concrete operational thinking precipitates the transition of Stage 2, and resolution of the Oedipal issues is a significant affective factor. Now the child wants to know how things really are and to clarify this for him- or herself. A newly acquired ability not only to appreciate but also to tell stories gives to narrative, drama, and myth the power to hold one's world together. But unable to step back from the flow of the stories or critically to formulate their meaning, children at this stage accept the stories and symbols of their community's beliefs in a one-dimensional, literal way. A strict sense of reciprocal, impersonal justice contributes further to the coherence of the school child's relatively simple, orderly, temporally linear, and dependable world. The authority of "those who know" provides the anchorage for this world. With Mythic-Literal Faith one holds one's sheltered world together by recounting the party line, which tells the way things really are.

Stage-3 Faith, called Synthetic-Conventional Faith, can begin to evolve at adolescence. The emergence of formal operational thinking allows critical reflection on the myths that are so central to Stage-2 Faith. Literalism breaks down; implicit contradictions demand explanation; disillusionment with previous teachers and teachings may result; and the emergence of the mutual interpersonal perspective calls for a world in which interpersonal relationships carry more weight. All this leads to Stage-3 Faith. The adolescent's world broadens to include a number of spheres: family, school, work, peers, friends. Faith must hold all these spheres together meaningfully, providing a basis for identity and outlook. The adolescent accepts a world-synthesis globally and non-analytically. The synthesis is an "ideology," a coherent set of beliefs and values, which the adolescent feels deeply but has not actually objectified. In a sense, then, he or she is not aware of having it. The authority for this worldview is the consensus of the valued groups or the word of personally worthy leaders. Stage-3 Faith is a conformist faith: it is acutely tuned to the expectations of significant others; it rests on an authority external to oneself. Yet, it allows one to approach a complex world with a coherent and satisfactorily reasonable stance.

Stage-4 Faith, called Individuative-Reflective Faith, begins to emerge when geographically or emotionally one "leaves home" and from outside takes a look at one's own self and outlook. Then one may not only see one's own identity as formed by one's upbringing but may also see those formative influences as a *system* and come to recognize other such systems with conflicting values. Awareness of social systems and their formative influence on individuals is characteristic of Stage-4 Faith. Because of this awareness, Stage 4 works to see people in terms of personal qualities, while at the same time taking into account the formative influence of ideologies. But "no longer constructing social relations as merely the extension of interpersonal relations, Stage 4 thinks in terms of the impersonal imperatives of law, rules and the standards that govern social roles."[41] A genuine move to Stage-4 Faith requires both the interruption of reliance on an external authority and the relocation of authority within the self. Fowler calls this internal authority *"the executive ego."*[42] The essential determinant of Stage 4 is the personal construction of one's own worldview on the basis of one's own self. Stage-4 Faith realizes that meaning is separable from the symbols and rituals which convey it. Stage 4 is a demythologizing stage. As a result, it tends toward reductionism and the flattening of meaning. Its dangers are "an excessive confidence in the conscious mind and in critical thought and a kind of second narcissism in which the now clearly bounded, reflective self overassimilates 'reality' and the perspectives of others into its own world view."[43] In Stage 4 a person finds meaning and purpose by personally making rational sense of his or her world.

The transition to Stage-4 Faith is normative for young adulthood. Yet for many it does not occur until the thirties or forties, if at all. Others experience only a partial emergence of Stage-4 Faith. Becoming aware of the relativity of their inherited identity and outlook, they fail, nonetheless, to relocate authority within themselves. Either they continue to rely on external authority or they do develop a personal position, which is, however, only a variant of the inherited ethos. Thus, they do not really take responsibility for themselves. They do not find out for themselves that it is up to themselves to decide for themselves what they will make of themselves.[44] In one way or another, they attain a potentially longlasting equilibrium in transition between Stages 3 and 4, and spiritual development, an adult phenomenon, becomes a moot issue for them.

Stage-5 Faith, Conjunctive Faith—formerly called Paradoxical-Consolidative Faith[45]—is rare before middle age. It emerges with the awareness that reality is more complex than what one's Stage-4, highly rationalized view can contain. Externally, Conjunctive Faith realizes the validity of systems other than one's own and so goes beyond the dichotomizing logic of Stage 4's either-or thinking. One's world stretches to embrace even what is outside one's own realm. If one is not able to reconcile with full coherence the truth one recognizes in divergent opinions, one affirms that truth, nonetheless, and rests content with "paradox." Internally, Conjunctive Faith begins to come to grips with unconscious forces—the Jungian emphasis[46]—and realizes that the conscious ego is not always master in its own house. One begins to reclaim and rework one's past. A mellowing sets in. Symbols regain their value—"second naivete"[47]—as one realizes that their richness cannot be fully expressed in logical propositions. Grasped by the depth of reality to which they refer, one again appreciates symbols, myths, and rituals, one's own and others'. Conjunctive Faith constructs a world by realizing that reality is bigger than logic and by accepting a humble place in the affirmation of that reality, wherever it is experienced.

Stage-6 Faith, Universalizing Faith, represents the "normative endpoint"[48] of faith development. In describing it, Fowler struggles to be true both to his pervasively motivating teleological conception and to empirical data on a few actual examples of Universalizing Faith.

Basically, Stage-6 Faith is the lived perfection of Stage-5 Faith. Universalizing Faith represents the "disciplined, activist *incarnation*— a making real and tangible—of the imperatives of absolute love and justice of which Stage 5 has partial apprehensions."[49] People of Stage-6 Faith often are experienced by others as subversive, die a martyr's death, and are more revered in death than in life. Stage-6 Faith super-sedes the conflicting loyalties—to a vision and to the present order, institutions, groups, and compromise procedures—that are part of Stage-5 Faith. Stage-6 Faith constructs an ultimate environment that includes all being. It cherishes particularities as "vessels of the univer-sal" and so "as valuable apart from any utilitarian considerations." Universalizers live out of a "felt participation in a power that unifies and transforms the world."[50] Fowler proposes Gandhi, Martin Luther King, Mother Teresa of Calcutta, Dag Hammarskjold, Dietrich Bon-hoeffer, Abraham Heschel, and Thomas Merton as examples of Uni-versalizing Faith.

Note some significant issues about Fowler's presentation of Stage-6 Faith. First, more than in the other stages, in Stage-6 Faith Fowler emphasizes the subject's actual being and doing rather than the subject's way of construing a world of meaning and purpose. The self-constitutive dimension of faithing comes to the fore here so much as to suggest a sharp contrast with the presentation of previous stages. Second, Fowler implies that people of Universalizing Faith might appropriately be called "saints."[51] Third, Fowler notes that to say someone embodies Stage-6 Faith is not to say that he or she is perfect, neither in a moral nor psychological nor leadership sense. He recalls Erikson's letter of reprimand to Gandhi for his unfair and mutedly violent treatment of his wife, Kasturba, and his sons. And Fowler explains that Universalizing Faith does not necessarily imply that one is "a 'self-actualizing' or a 'fully functioning human being'—though it seems that most of them are or were, if in somewhat differ-ent senses than Abraham Maslow or Carl Rogers intended their terms."[52] Fourth and finally, Fowler admits that the Jewish-Christian image of the Kingdom of God and H. Richard Niebuhr's notion of radical monotheism[53] are the dominant influences in his conception of Stage-6 Faith. He correctly insists that one may gain insight and inspiration from a particular, even a religious, perspective and apply them in a universally valid presentation. Yet his procedure raises a question about the introduction of crucial content into a supposedly purely formal account.

These four issues are pertinent to understanding spiritual devel-opment. Final discussion of them will come after a presentation of Jane Loevinger's conception and theory of ego development.

Loevinger's Notion of Ego

In her *Ego Development* Jane Loevinger assembles a remarkable array of data from numerous researchers. More remarkable still, however, is the general consistency she discerns in that mass of data. A compelling convergence from widespread sources supports her central claim, "that many diverse aspects of thought, interpersonal relations, impulse control, and character grow at once, in some more or less coherent way."[54] "Ego" is what accounts for that coherence.

Loevinger is reluctant to state an outright definition of ego. Rather, she points toward the reality and expects the accumulative effect of her writing to clarify the issue. Ego is "the 'master trait' in the personality";[55] it is "a central core of personality."[56] It is that which organizes into a coherent whole the "functions" and "structures" of the personality. So Loevinger's ego development subsumes Piaget's and Kohlberg's cognitive and moral development; and it easily correlates with, and in many ways duplicates, Fowler's faith development. Loevinger's appears to be *the* synthetic theoretical statement on human development, if such a thing is possible.

Loevinger notes the "Attributes of the Ego."[57] First, "The ego is above all a process, not a thing."[58] "The striving to master, to integrate, to make sense of experience is not one ego function among many but the essence of the ego."[59] Second, the ego is also a structure. It is the organization of the personality. It represents a person's self-consistency and ordered pattern of meaning. Third, the ego has a social origin: "the ego would never come into being for a person raised in isolation. . . ."[60] Loevinger's reference is to George H. Mead's account of the emergence of the "self."[61] The self arises from the internalization of the "generalized other," the societally provided system of roles and rules. When appropriated by the individual, it becomes the organizing principle of the individual personality, making the individual a reflection of the culture which formed him or her.[62] The ego, the key structuring factor of the personality, arises in social interaction. Fourth, a holistic conception of personality insists that the ego functions as a whole. Inner conflicts are explained not by positing a variety of entities alongside the ego—like id and superego and collective unconscious—but by acknowledging that the person may hold some memories and experiences outside the frame of reference of the ego. While the function of ego is to provide overall organization, that organization is hardly perfect. Finally, ego is not merely reactive or mechanistic. Rather, it is the ongoing structural effect of a basic human striving for meaning and purpose. Loevinger summarizes, "The fundamental characteristics of the ego are that it is a *process*, a *structure, social* in origin, functioning as a *whole*, and guided by *purpose* and *meaning*."[63]

Loevinger is not completely consistent in her account of ego. While the brunt of her presentation shows ego to be the key organizational factor in the personality, she also writes as if ego is rather the tendency itself toward organization. For example, she says, seemingly with approval, "The striving to make experience meaningful is for Fingarette not something that a thing called *ego* does; the striving for meaning is what ego is."[64] And so, "the ego is seen as striving (or as *the striving*) for self-consistency and meaning."[65] But though the two are certainly closely related, ego cannot be both the ongoing human drive for meaning and purpose, the striving itself, and the successive patterns of organization, the products of the striving. The burden of Loevinger's presentation indicates that ego is the latter, not the former. So, except for the reference to ego as process, that is how I have presented the issue above.

In Loevinger's overall presentation this discrepancy is minor. Yet in the present context it is crucial. I consider "the striving itself" to be but another way of speaking of the dynamism of the human spirit, central to the definition of spiritual development. The dynamic human spirit—intentional consciousness—is an intrinsic principle of human self-transcendence, constitutive of the human. But it is a completely formal factor in human development. Though it does have a determined structure and inherent norms of operation, it necessitates no particular content but is open to all contents. Ego, on the other hand, is the product of this dynamism operating in a particular place and time. Ego is the concrete result of the formal principle. Ego is the actual central organization of the personality, the ordering constellation of biographical and cultural factors that allows meaningful, purposeful, viable living in a real world.

Loevinger's presentation is not adverse to that understanding. The ambiguity just highlighted provides evidence here. Moreover, she acknowledges that at some level she is "also making a case for a view of human nature."[66] Augusto Blasi, who contributed the third chapter to Loevinger's book, is more explicit. He notes that developmental psychology "must look those ghosts in the face": "natural order" and "nature,"[67] something of "necessity and order . . . which transcends cultures and individuals and to which cultures and individuals have to submit."[68] Blasi goes on to discuss consciousness and freedom, and he argues their relevance: "If subjectivity and freedom are not simply the achievement of a few individuals but are also the universal orientation and goal, then a theory of personality development must be able at least to approach an explanation of them."[69]

Moreover, whereas in a more fundamental conception I speak of dynamic human spirit, Blasi speaks of cognitive structures—which are not the same thing. Yet his problem and argument are the same as mine. He clearly recognizes that a formal principle entails "an ensemble of possibilities" whereas "personality is factual and determined." That is, apart from terminological differences resulting from different theoretical traditions, Blasi's arguments and my own coincide. So Blasi concludes,

> Personalities are structures—*forms* of life, as Spranger and Wittgenstein called them—but structures of a different nature from cognitive structures. That human beings, developing, go through an ordered sequence of such structures is the premise of this book. In this context, cognitive structures are important as providing the individual with a more or less wide range of alternatives. Where within that range personality in fact develops is determined by different factors and different rules.[70]

Ego is one thing, and the dynamic human spirit is another. But the latter is also pertinent to ego development. Only acknowledgment of a principle of self-transcendence, intrinsic to the human as such, allows complete explanation of the dynamism manifested by ego development. Perhaps that is why Loevinger feels the need to include within the conception of ego, untidy though the result be, also some notion of process, of the striving itself. Then ego is not only manifested as a sequence of structures that organize the personality but can also appear to be its own principle of development. Then one could explain the development by saying, "It is the nature of ego to develop." I would prefer to say, "It is the nature of the human to develop," and to locate the dynamism of that nature in one of the factors constitutive of the human, namely, spirit, Lonergan's intentional consciousness, and to treat personality and its structures as aspects of another really distinct factor, psyche.[71] Perhaps in her own way and with different terminology, Loevinger is even trying to say the same thing. Whatever the case, Blasi devotes the final two-thirds of his chapter to the discussion of these issues, which resurface periodically throughout Loevinger's book.

In the present context and in light of previous discussion, only brief mention need be made here of the fact that ego development entails development of the human individual. Not just some function of the individual but the very organizing master structure of the individual him- or herself is explicitly at stake in ego development. This self-constitutive implication of all developmental theory is more obvious in Loevinger's than in any other of the theories presented here. For ego is, indeed, a central factor in the very constitution of the concrete individual.

Stages of Ego Development

The above discussion has already introduced the notion of *development* of the ego. As Loevinger's is a constructivist-developmental account, she proposes discrete stages in ego development. Each stage represents an intelligibility recognizable more or less as a unified whole. Each stage represents a discernibly different way in which ego structures the personality. As such, each stage also represents a particular type of personality, so Loevinger's stages of ego development are also a typology.[72] Unlike the other theorists noted above, Loevinger refuses to suggest what level of ego development is appropriate to what age. The stage theory of ego development arose from comparing different kinds of personalities, not from studying different ages. Yet parallels with other theorists' research make at least general correlations of ego level and age possible.

Loevinger presents a scheme of ten stages of ego development; but two of these are transition stages—which she calls "levels" rather than stages—and may not represent discrete stages. She names each with common-speech terms and also includes an arbitrary code symbol for each stage.

In the Presocial Stage (I-1) the infant has not yet clearly differentiated the self from the outer world and so is in the initial stage of forming an ego. The term "Autistic" is also used to refer to this stage.

The Symbiotic Stage (I-1) is still that of the infant. Even after the infant has achieved some sense of stability in the world of objects, he or she retains a symbiotic relation with the nurturer(s). Relationships are extremely dependent. The beginning use of language is significant in helping to consolidate the infant's sense of self as distinct from non-self.

The Impulsive Stage (I-2) is characterized by the child's inability to control impulses. The child is preoccupied with bodily impulses. In one way, these help him or her to affirm a separate identity. To the impulsive child good and bad mean "nice to me" and "mean to me."

In the Self-Protective Stage (Delta-Δ) the child can control impulses, but control is fragile and so there is a corresponding vulnerability and guardedness. People at this stage are much identified with their own immediate and self-centered desires. They are often highly manipulative, are characterized by caution, and act as if from behind a protective shell. At this stage there is an awareness that there are rules, but the main rule is "Don't get caught." The self-protective person is highly competitive and tends to believe that one's gain is always another's loss.

Fowler's Intuitive-Projective and Mythic-Literal Faith correspond somehow to Loevinger's Impulsive and Self-Protective Stages, but the parallels are far from perfect. More obvious is the correspondence between Fowler's Synthetic-Conventional Faith and the following, Loevinger's Conformist Stage. Still, because at this point Fowler ties his delineation of stages closely to Piaget's scheme and Loevinger does not, Loevinger's Conformist Stage appears proper at its onset to a younger age than could Fowler's Synthetic-Conventional faith. However, the correspondence between the two schemes from here on is striking, and all the more so in view of the fact that neither Fowler nor Loevinger seems to be aware of the other's work.

At the Conformist Stage (I-3) people are concerned primarily for approval of others. They not only conform and approve of conformity but also perceive themselves and others as conforming to approved norms. That is, they see others not as individuals but as members of generic groups. Externals—appearance, social acceptance and reputation, and material things—are more important than inner life and feelings.

Between the Conformist Stage and the next, the Conscientious Stage, Loevinger places a transition stage, which she calls the Self-Aware Level (I-3/4). It can be called the Conscientious-Conformist Level and appears to be a stable position in mature life, indeed, the modal level for adults in our society. Two salient qualities mark the move away from the Conformist and toward the Conscientious Stage: first, increased self-awareness resulting from greater sensitivity to one's inner life and from the realization that one does not oneself always live up to the expectations of social norms; and second, appreciation of multiple possibilities in situations. The latter allows for exceptions and contingencies, though not in terms of individual differences but still in terms of stereotypic categories like age, sex, marital status, and race. This transition level seems to coincide with the possible equilibration between Stage-3 and Stage-4 Faith in Fowler's presentation.

The Conscientious Stage (I-4) is characterized by complete internalization of rules. If various aspects of conscience are found in each of the preceding stages, adult conscience proper emerges only in the Conscientious Stage.[73] Now the person is governed by "long term, self-evaluated goals and ideals, differentiated self-criticism, and a sense of responsibility, . . . the major elements of an adult conscience."[74] There is room for conscientious objection. With a certain sense of moralism, the conscientious people feel responsible for others. They are concerned for privileges, rights, and fairness, the correlates of responsibility. They have a sense of choice in life and do not feel themselves the pawns of fate. No longer feeling that work is intrinsically onerous, they aspire to achievement. They tend to construe the world in terms of polar opposites: love vs. lust, trivial vs. important, dependent vs. independent, inner life vs. outward appearances. They have a rich and differentiated inner life, view behavior in terms of traits and motives, and are capable of real mutuality in interpersonal relations. Except for Loevinger's uncharacteristic aside that rarely people of age thirteen or fourteen attain this stage, the Conscientious Stage seems to parallel Fowler's Stage 4, Individuative-Reflective Faith.

The Individualistic Level (I-4/5) is a transition level from the Conscientious to the Autonomous Stage. Its characteristics are a heightened sense of individuality as evidenced in recognition of individual differences and increased tolerance for self and others; concern for emotional dependence, now recognized as different from physical or financial dependence; a sense that relations with others can be antagonistic to one's own striving for achievement or one's moralistically conceived responsibility for others; and the naturalness of thinking in terms of psychological causality or development.

The Autonomous Stage (I-5) is marked by the capacity to accept and cope with inner conflict as a normal part of living. Reality is seen as complex and multifaceted, and there is high tolerance for ambiguity, paradox, and contradiction. Autonomous people are somewhat freed from the oppressive demands of rigid conscience. They not only recognize but also cherish individuality and allow the autonomy of others. At the same time they recognize the limitations of autonomy and prize personal ties as a most precious value. They are aware of a rich inner life and express feelings vividly and convincingly. Self-fulfillment supplants personal achievement as a goal. The Autonomous Stage is a clear correlate of Fowler's Stage-5 Conjunctive faith.

The highest stage, the Integrated Stage (I-6), represents the perfection of the Autonomous Stage. It entails the transcending of the conflicts of that former stage and the consolidation of a sense of identity. Loevinger admits that as highest, this is the hardest stage to describe. The higher the stage, the rarer it is and the more surely it exceeds the development of the researchers. Loevinger points to Maslow's account of self-actualization as the best likely description of the Integrated Stage.

> The characteristics of self-actualization are, according to Maslow: not a fixed state but a changing process, thus, openness to development; more efficient perception of reality, that is, "lesser blindness"; availability of inner life; vivid perception of the outer world; capacity for both abstractness and concreteness; tolerance for ambiguity; capacity for guilt and sense of responsibility; capacity for spontaneity, as opposed to intensive striving; existential as opposed to hostile humor; gaiety, particularly in sexual and other love relations; transcending of contradictions and polarities; acceptance of reality; greater integration, autonomy, and

sense of identity; increased objectivity, detachment, and transcendence of self; democratic character structure.[75]

The formulation of this final stage remains tentative. Loevinger acknowledges this by concluding, "In some sense, moreover, there is no highest stage but only an opening to new possibilities."[76] There are similarities as well as differences between Loevinger's and Fowler's final stage. The two are not correlates, yet they both point in the same direction.

Polar Variables

As well as noting discrete stages of ego development—marked by "milestone sequences"[77]—Loevinger is also concerned about "polar variables, that is, aspects of ego that constantly increase during the period of development."[78] The distinction between polar variables and milestone sequences emphasizes that, on the one hand, development entails real discontinuities, qualitative and not merely quantitative differences. Yet on the other hand, development entails real continuity and augmentation of core human realities. The notion of polar variables also raises once again the question about the driving forces which move development along. These considerations clearly link Loevinger's ego development to spiritual development, which is specified by the unfolding influence of a spiritual, human constant: authenticity.

Loevinger lists the following as polar variables. *Internalization* or the turning of concern from the outer to the inner world increases with each stage of development. Higher capacity for *realistic thinking* corresponds with higher stages of ego development. *Moral progress,*[79] a complex variable defined by Flugel,[80] includes movement 1) from egocentricity to sociality, including ever widening classes within the community; 2) from unconscious to conscious, that is, toward bringing ever larger proportions of life to explicit awareness and control; 3) from autistic to realistic thinking; 4) from moral inhibition to spontaneous goodness; 5) from aggression to tolerance and love; 6) from fear to security; 7) from heteronomy to autonomy; and 8) from moral judgment to cognitive or psychological judgment, or said otherwise, from aggression to understanding.

It appears that many of those elements can be grouped together.

Movement from fear to security suggests self-confidence, integration, being at peace with oneself. So understood, it relates to internalization—or increasing self-consistency and harmony. Then, increased capacity for realistic thinking was mentioned twice. Thirdly, a growing self-responsibility—that is, responsibility both for one's self and on the basis of one's self (cf. Fowler's executive ego)—summarizes the movements from unconscious to conscious, from moral inhibition to spontaneous good, and from heteronomy to autonomy. Finally, increasing sociality includes also the movements from aggression to tolerance and love and from aggression to understanding.

Thus, in summary, the core polar variables in ego development appear to be four: self-consistency, realism, self-responsibility, and sociality. This supposition is very pertinent to an understanding of spiritual development, for those four variables are all expressions of increasing integration of the intrinsic principle of authentic self-transcendence, human spirit. How this is so in the case of the first three variables—self-consistency, realism, and self-responsibility—should already be clear from what was said in Chapter 2. The fourth variable, sociality, relates to spiritual development insofar as sociality is an expression of human wholeness or integrity. Chapter 4 will expand the notion of wholeness to apply not only within oneself but also to one's relation with the whole of humanity. The basic presupposition is that to be human is to be social. Thus the four polar variables in Loevinger's' theory of ego development are also expressions of the driving force of spiritual development, dynamic human spirit.

Chapter 4, the final chapter in the psychological part of this essay, will summarize and correlate all that has been said thus far. It will integrate and elucidate the suggestive correlations that have been noted in passing in the present chapter and will suggest the stages of spiritual development.

Notes

Chapter Three

Stages of Human Development

1. Lasker and Moore, "Current Studies"; Kohlberg and Armon, "Three Types of Stage Models." I am grateful to Mark Bickhard of the University of Texas at Austin for suggesting the term "constructivist." Cf. also Kuhn, "Cognitive Development."

2. Whitehead and Whitehead, *Christian Life Patterns*; Groeschel, *Spiritual Passages*.

3. Gould, *Transformations*, 41.

4. Mark 4:25.

5. Gould, *Transformations*, 41.

6. *Ibid.* 311.

7. Breger, *From Instinct to Identity*; Beard, *Outline of Piaget's Psychology*.

8. Piaget, *Structuralism*.

9. *Ibid.*

10. Kohlberg, "Stage and Sequence."

11. Case, Intellectual Development, 1-56; Kuhn, "Cognitive Development."

12. Santrok, Life-Span Development, 463-64.

13. Commons, Richards, and Armon, *Beyond Formal Operations*.

14. Bickhard, "Developmental and Psychological Processes," "Developmental Stages"; Campbell and Bickhard, *Knowing Levels*.

15. Lonergan, *Insight*, xxviii.

16. Kohlberg, "Child as Moral Philosopher," "Implications of Moral Stages," "Stage and Sequence."

17. Philibert, "Conscience."

18. Gilligan, *In a Different Voice*.

19. Fowler, *Becoming Adult*, 42.

TABLE I: *Putative Stages of Human Development*

Era and Ages	ERICKSON *Psycho-social Stages*	GRANT "Jungian" Stages	LEVISON *Seasons of Life*	GOULD *Transformations*
Infancy (0-1½)	Trust vs. Mistrust	INFANCY Attitudes E/I & Functions F,T,S,N, all operate randomly		Childhood Consciousness
Early Childhood (2-6)	Autonomy vs. Shame & Doubt Initiative vs. Guilt			
Childhood (7-12)	Industry vs. Inferiority	CHILDHOOD E or I and dominant function emerge	CHILDHOOD AND ADOLESCENCE Develop basic knowledge & skills	
ADOLESCENCE (13-21)	Identity vs. Role Confusion	ADOLESCENCE E/I & J/P alternate; auxiliary function emerges		
				Leaving Our Parents' World
			EARLY ADULTHOOD Choose, create, & maintain a life structure	I'm Nobody's Baby Now
Young Adulthood (21-35)	Intimacy vs. Isolation	YOUNG ADULTHOOD E/I alternates & third function develops		
				Opening Up to What's Inside
Adulthood (35-60)	Generativity vs. Stagnation	MID-LIFE E/I & J/P alternate; shadow function is integrated.		Mid-Life Decade
			MIDDLE ADULTHOOD Bear major responsibilities, revise life structure	Beyond Mid-Life
		GOLDEN YEARS Both attitudes & four functions operate deliberately		
Maturity (60+)	Integrity vs. Despair		LATE ADULTHOOD Influence as a wise senior from the side lines	

PIAGET *Cognitive Development*	KOHLBERG *Moral Development*	FOWLER *Faith Development*	LOEVINGER *Ego Development*	*Spiritual Development*
SENSORIMOTOR		Pre-Stage: Un-differentiated Faith	PRE-SOCIAL	
PRE-OPERATIONAL	PRECONVENTIONAL Punishment/reward & obedience orientation	INTUITIVE-PROJECTIVE Use of language, imitation, fantasy, rich imagination	SYMBIOTIC STAGE Use of language, great dependency	
			IMPULSIVE STAGE Concern to control (bodily) impulses	
CONCRETE OPERATIONAL	Hedonistic relativity; reciprocal relativity; tit for tat	MYTHICAL-LITERAL The family's story, drama, myth—taken literally—anchor one's world.	SELF-PROTECTIVE STAGE Vulnerable, guarded, self-centered	
FORMAL OPERATIONAL a.	CONVENTIONAL Approval/disapproval orientation—"nice girl/good boy"—mutual interpersonal relationships Law & order orientation. Social system & conscience	SYNTHETIC-CONVENTIONAL An ideology (coherent, rational, borrowed & supported by external authority) anchors a world of family, peers, school, work.	CONFORMIST STAGE Approval seeking; judges on externals	CONFORMIST STAGE
		3/4 TRANSITION Move from external authority and relocate authority in self	SELF-AWARE LEVEL (Conscientious Conformism) Sensitive to inner life & own failings. Allows stereotypical exceptions.	CONSCIENTIOUS CONFORMIST STAGE
b.	POST-CONVENTIONAL Social contract orientation, recognizes moral conflict	INDIVIDUATIVE-REFLECTIVE Leave home, recognize system, construct one's own rationalized worldview	CONSCIENTIOUS STAGE Self-determinative; driving moralism; rich inner life; real mutuality	CONSCIENTIOUS STAGE
			INDIVIDUALISTIC LEVEL Tolerance; emotional dependence; relationships vs. other responsibilities & goals; psychological & development outlook	
POST-FORMAL OPERATIONAL a.	Self-chosen ethical principles; comprehensive, universal, consistent	CONJUNCTIVE (Paradoxical-Consolidative) Validity of other systems; paradoxical resolution; confronts unconscious forces	AUTONOMOUS STAGE Accepts inner conflict & complexity of reality; freed from rigid conscience; cherishes individuality & relationships; prizes self-fulfillment over achievement.	COMPASSIONATE STAGE
b.	"Stage 7"	UNIVERSALIZING Lived perfection of prior stage; transcends conflicting loyalties, often prophetic	INTEGRATED STAGE Perfection of prior stage; transcends conflicts & consolidates sense of identity; open-ended; self-actualizing	COSMIC STAGE

20. Kohlberg and Power, "Moral Development."

21. Fowler and Keen, *Life Maps*.

22. *Ibid.*; Fowler, "Faith Development Theory," "Stages of Faith," "Toward a Developmental Perspective on Faith"; cf. Howe, "A Developmental Perspective on Conversion."

23. Helminiak, Review of Fowler's *Becoming Adult*.

24. Fowler, *Stages of Faith*, 14.

25. *Ibid.*, 4.

26. *Ibid.*, 17.

27. *Ibid.*, 33.

28. *Ibid.*, 14.

29. *Ibid.*, 92-93.

30. *Ibid.*, 9.

31. *Ibid.*, 11.

32. *Ibid.*, 33.

33. *Ibid.*, 17.

34. *Ibid.*, 23.

35. *Ibid.*, 24.

36. *Ibid.*

37. *Ibid.*, 31.

38. Philibert, "Conscience."

39. Fowler, *Stages of Faith*, 103.

40. *Ibid.*, 105.

41. *Ibid.*, 180.

42. *Ibid.*, 179.

43. *Ibid.*, 182-183.

44. Cf. Lonergan, *Method*, 121.

45. Fowler and Keen, *Life Maps*.

46. Brewi and Brennan, *Mid-Life*; Grant, Thompson, and Clarke, *Image to Likeness*; Thompson, *Journey Toward Wholeness*.

47. Ricoeur, *Symbolism of Evil*, 347-357.

48. Fowler, *Stages of Faith*, 199.

49. *Ibid.*, 200.

50. *Ibid.*, 201.

51. *Ibid.*, 202.

52. *Ibid.*, 201-202.

Spiritual Development and Its Stages

The presupposition was that spiritual development is human development conceived from a particular view. In an explication of that particular view, spiritual development was defined as the on-going integration that results in the self-responsible subject from openness to an intrinsic principle of authentic self-transcendence. Further elaboration is now possible.

An Adult Phenomenon

Spiritual development is a properly adult phenomenon. It is the growth in authentic self-transcendence that results from the individual's taking responsibility for her- or himself. The general line of human development, according to all theorists, moves from infant, impulse-dominated self-centeredness to conformist identity with one's social group and finally to post-conventional self-determination and integration of internal and external reality.

In some sense the end product is again a kind of self-centeredness, but it is of a very different kind from that of the child. Mature self-determination accords with reality; it is realistic and responsible.

Even if it appears to be—and is—spontaneous response, it is the result of long self-formation and explicit choice. It is the now "natural" activity of a self-formed individual. If the virtues of maturity can be called "childlike"—"Truly, I say to you, whoever does not receive the kingdom of God like a child shall not enter it"[1]—they are not the supposed virtue of childish "innocence," which is more accurately named ignorance, inexperience, and naivete. Mature virtue is not childish innocence, and only the former pertains to spiritual development as such.

The stages of human development sketched above allow more technical statement about the "adult" nature of spiritual development. If adult means "self-responsible," then spiritual development first becomes possible when one begins to move out of the Conformist Stage with its Synthetic-Conventional Faith. But that movement is difficult and precarious. Many people never completely transcend the Conformist Stage to achieve the Conscientious Stage. Rather, they remain in the half-way station, the Self-Aware Level or Fowler's transition stage 3/4, "the modal level for adults in our society."[2] They become, in Loevinger's all too accurate formulation, conscientiously conformist. So for most people spiritual development quickly becomes a moot issue.

Unfortunately, that comment often applies even to people committed professionally to religious pursuit and to others whose well-publicized avocation is interest in spirituality or whose recent "charismatic" conversion experience has brought new meaning and religious affiliation. Inspired by stories of the "saints," by models of "holiness" or "enlightenment," or by accounts of miraculous occurrences, they become but faithful imitators. Too intent on becoming "spiritual," they follow the master, keep the rules, affirm the teachings, all without question or responsible criticism. Good will is turned into slavery, often to the advantage of some sponsoring institution: almost no institution can afford to encourage people to grow and to think, to make decisions for themselves. So people "authentically realize unauthenticity."[3] They become skilled in the virtue of the child, obedience, and never experience the adult phenomenon, spiritual development.

In more ideal cases spiritual development begins in late adolescence or early adulthood, probably sometime during college years in our society. If the post-conformist transition is left until later years, it is more severe and protracted. Left until the thirties or forties, it is probably an exacerbating factor in a traumatic "mid-life crisis," which then can entail rapid growth through a number of successive stages, up to the Autonomous Stage and Conjunctive Faith. In such a case, which is not uncommon, spiritual development only begins at mid-life. This fact probably explains Simmons's concern for the religious life of people thirty and beyond[4] and explains the relevance of spiritual books and workshops focusing specifically on mid-life.[5] It is clear, then, that not chronological age but level of development defines what is meant by the "adult" nature of spiritual development. For spiritual development is proper to the self-responsible subject.

The Dynamism behind Human Development

As suggested above, an intrinsic principle of authentic self-transcendence can account for the dynamism manifested in human development. Blasi pointed out the need to posit such a principle if full explanation of development is to be achieved. Approaching the same need from a different perspective, Loevinger suggests that "conscience, or perhaps the ego ideal, is itself a moving principle of ego development."[6] For consideration of the process of ego development beyond the Conformist Stage highlights a perplexing problem. "We may desire to create or encourage maturity of conscience in our charges, but in the nature of things there is no direct way to lead them beyond the morality of obedience."[7] Whence comes the motivation toward post-conformist development?

To answer this question, Loevinger borrows Dember's notion of the "pacer,"[8] a motivating object of some novelty and complexity, neither too much nor too little, that leads a person to grow beyond his or her present ideal level. She suggests that conscience can act as an internalized pacer. She notes the

> sources that contribute to the evolution of the mature conscience. These sources are, in their developmental order, (1) the formation of a sense of self, (2) turning of aggression against the self, (3) the need for mastery, (4) adoption of parental precepts and standards, and (5) mutual love and respect.[9]

Those are indeed factors in the development of mature conscience. Yet, a factor which explains the movement through them and beyond is still missing. Only an explicit acknowledgment of an intrinsic principle of self-transcendence, which expresses itself through these factors, ultimately resolves the problem of post-conformist development. Only an intrinsic drive toward authenticity, which transcends the "is" with an "ought" and then urges self-consistency, finally accounts for self-principled authentic development. At points Loevinger's discussion of this issue approaches such a solution,[10] and her notion of conscience resembles, without its theist aspects, that of Philibert.[11]

It appears, then, that the intrinsic dynamism of the human spirit toward authentic self-transcendence is indispensable for explaining development beyond the Conformist Stage and Synthetic-Conventional Faith. Consideration of Fowler's presentation offers further verification. Recall the suggestion that Fowler introduces specific content into his supposedly merely formal account of stages of faith. Whereas in theory he defines faith with reference to an "ultimate environment," in practice that ultimate becomes *the* ultimate or the transcendent.

Fowler recounts how he would not fully accept a student's suggested definition of "ultimate environment" as "something we will enjoy when we're successful, rich, happily married, with children, about age forty. It's that environment we dream about and work for."[12] But suppose that that were indeed the ultimate environment structuring the life of that young man. Suppose that the content of that young man's faith could accurately be described as the much touted "American dream." Would that young man ever attain post-conformist Stage-4 Individuative-Reflective Faith? I think not. His "ultimate" vision could carry him at most to Stage 3/4, Conscientious Conformism. That is to say, the young man might arrive at a point where he really believes in the American dream with personal conviction and self-sacrificing dedication. But the very content of his faith would not allow him to become Conscientious nor, indeed, Autonomous, recognizing the truth in positions other than his own and allowing the validity for himself of others' systems of life. In order to grow further, he would have to change the content of his faith and introduce a self-critical, self-transcendent factor.

Now, Fowler admits that the image of the Kingdom of God is the motive force in his account of faith development. Indeed, without some such principle of ultimate self-transcendence, he would not be able to derive the upper two stages of faith development. Obviously, for this purpose an intrinsic human principle of authentic self-transcendence would work as effectively in Fowler's scheme as does the theist image "Kingdom of God." Such a substitution would actually strengthen Fowler's presentation as a formal theory of development. Still, the point here is not the theist nature of Fowler's transcendent principle; it is its transcendent nature. Fowler seems to be well aware that without some ultimately transcendent factor in his theory of development the final stages cannot be justified.

To that add Loevinger's presentation of the polar variables of ego development—summarized above as realism, self-responsibility, self-consistency, and sociality—and the argument is strengthened. The conclusion is not only that an intrinsic principle of authentic self-transcendence is definitive of spiritual development. Such a principle is also the presupposition of human development as such, at or beyond the Conscientious Stage. In one way or another, both Loevinger and Fowler acknowledge that presupposition in their presentations. One might, of course, imagine—or even know—individuals who appear to be Conscientious (They act according to their own dictates of what is right and wrong.) or even Autonomous (They are their own boss.) but who also appear in no way to be authentic, dedicated uncompromisingly to what is really true and good—Hitler, Nixon. One must conclude that they would not really be Conscientious or Autonomous people; they would rather be somehow successful Impulsive or Self-Protective or Conformist types. The inherent rationale of both Fowler's and Loevinger's stage theories necessitates this conclusion. An intrinsic principle of authentic self-transcendence is a driving force for post-conformist development.

Some suggest that the influence of a counter-culture community may explain post-conventional development, at least to some extent.[13] Granted, individual human development without a supporting community is difficult, if not impossible. Yet the introduction of the truly novel into society through the mediation of gifted individuals is a fact which remains to be explained.[14] Appeal to a counter-culture to explain post-conventional development may point merely to the trading of one conformity for another.[15] A truly theoretical account must explain precisely the post-conventionality which is the essence of adult development. The logic of the issue cannot be dodged.

Openness to the Dynamism of the Human Spirit

If an intrinsic principle of authentic self-transcendence is one factor necessary to explain post-conformist human development, openness to that drive toward full and authentic integration is a correlative and equally necessary factor. Authenticity is defined by reference to the transcendental precepts that parallel the four levels of intentional consciousness as analyzed by Bernard Lonergan: "Be attentive, Be intelligent, Be reasonable, Be responsible."[16] So wherever there is violation of these precepts, there is lack of openness to authenticity and so, according to the present argument, the impossibility of further post-conformist development.

Empirical testing of the role of openness to authenticity in human development is possible. Using an interviewing technique, the researcher need only determine whether or not there is openness or resistance in the subject. In fact, Perry[17] points to exactly this issue in his account of the developmental failure of some of his subjects: "Those whom we perceived as standing still, or stepping to one side, or reaching back, acknowledged that they were avoiding something or denying something or fighting something, and they regularly remarked on an uneasiness or dissatisfaction akin to shame."[18]

Furthermore, certain widely recognized psychoanalytic concepts point to the critical role of openness for human development. Noting them, Loevinger suggests that ego stability—and so, lack of development—results from what amounts to violation of the precept, "Be attentive."

> Thus the ego remains stable because the operations by which the person perceives his environment effectively admit only those data that can be comprehended already, hence are compatible with current ego structure. Incompatible situations are either distorted to conform to prior expectations, that is, assimilated, or else ignored. In Piaget's terms, the latter case implies that parts of the objective situation effectively do not exist for the person. Baldwin's *selective thinking*, Adler's *tendentious apperception*, and

Sullivan's *selective inattention* are similar ideas, and a subset of Piaget's assimilation.[19]

Schachtel's[20] study of perception again confirms the point.

> Much of perception in adult life is dominated by what Schachtel calls *secondary autocentricity*. . . . perception is limited to the way the object serves the person's needs and purposes; such perception helps the person to avoid encountering new aspects of reality. . . . The most usual form of secondary autocentricity is seeing everything in terms of labels and stereotypes. Corresponding to secondary autocentricity there is a secondary embeddedness in the person's own culture.[21]

Secondary autocentricity is a prime characteristic of the Conformist Stage of ego development. To move beyond that stage one must regain an openness to exterior reality, in some way characteristic of children.

> In what Schachtel calls the *allocentric attitude*, there is an interest in and turning toward the object; it involves the whole object and the whole being of the observer. Allocentric interest in an object leads to global perception of it, but it is a different kind of globality from that of infancy, which fuses subject and object, or of early childhood, in which the distinct features of the object are not perceived. Rather, it presupposes full objectification, that is, appreciation of the object as an object. Creativity is inhibited not so much by repression, as some psychoanalysts have maintained, as by encroachment of labels and stereotypes on our openness to the world. . . . What is decisive is the openness in the encounter with the object. . . .[22]

Finally, recall that from his narrow psychotherapeutic perspective Roger Gould also indicated a kind of openness as determinative of adult development: "how *willing* that individual is to abandon the irrational protective devices and reexperience childhood anger and hurt in order to reach inner freedom."[23]

Openness to the dynamism of the self-transcending human spirit is a condition for the possibility of adult development. Adult development is a process of self-determination, a process of deliberate self-constitution. Then spiritual development is, as well. Repetition of Grant, Thompson, and Clarke's religiously phrased statement will appropriately summarize the issue: "While there is an element of givenness and grace in every coming to wholeness, it is also contingent on *choice*—we must *desire* wholeness, as a pearl of great price, and be willing to let go of everything else in order that we may gain it."[24]

The Stages of Spiritual Development

Spiritual development is human development understood within a particular set of concerns. It must be clear, then, that the definable stages of adult human development are also the stages of spiritual development. Fowler's and Loevinger's developmental theories deal with very broad aspects of human development, and explicit introduction of the four defining characteristics of spiritual development does not alter or invalidate but, on the contrary, compliments and confirms their accounts. Accordingly—but leaving room for the possible and even likely reformulation of empirically verifiable stages of adult development—I propose their stages as the stages of spiritual development, at least within middle-class American and equivalent cultures.

Thus, the basic conception of the stages of spiritual development, expressed in the terms of Loevinger's and Fowler's theories, is as follows: the baseline of spiritual development is the Conformist Stage with its Synthetic-Conventional Faith. It is the *terminus a quo,* and spiritual development entails movement from that stage to subsequent ones. Some initial spiritual growth may be imputed to people in the transition level, Loevinger's Self-Aware Level or Fowler's Stage 3/4. Yet, if in any case this stage functions not as a transition stage but as a permanent resting place, then the possibility of spiritual growth has been stifled and one may well have settled for a lifetime of spiritual mediocrity. This point has already been made above.

The Conscientious Stage with its Individuative-Reflective Faith determines the next stage of spiritual development. But more accurately conceived, it is the first stage, the first achievement, of spiritual development.

The Autonomous Stage with its Conjunctive Faith determines the next stage of spiritual development. A transition stage, Loevinger's Individualistic Level, may serve as a bridge between the Conscientious and Autonomous Stages of spiritual development.

Beyond these lies the final stage of spiritual development. It remains relatively ill-defined but has qualities of Loevinger's Integrated Stage and Fowler's Universalizing Faith. More will be said about this stage presently.

Conceived specifically as stages of spiritual development, these stages could use the names of Loevinger's stages or even the less descriptive names of Fowler's. The reality in question, and not the terminology, is the important matter. And the theories summarized in Chapter 3 explicate the content of those stages, the reality in question. Still, in an attempt to focus those stages on issues that are more obviously spiritual, proposing a slight variation on Loevinger's terms, I will suggest another set of names here.

The baseline beginning point of spiritual development is the *Conformist Stage*. It is characterized by a deeply felt and extensively rationalized worldview, accepted on the basis of external authority and supported by approval of one's significant others. The *Conscientious Conformist Stage* is characterized by a person's beginning to take responsibility for him- or herself as awareness begins to dawn that because of unthinking adherence to an inherited worldview one has actually abdicated responsibility for one's life. One begins to learn for oneself that it is up to oneself to decide for oneself what one will make of oneself. The first true stage of spiritual development is the *Conscientious Stage*. It is characterized by the achievement of significantly structuring one's life according to one's own understanding of things, by optimism over one's newly accepted sense of responsibility for oneself and one's world, and by rather unbending commitment to one's principles. Next follows the *Compassionate Stage*, characterized by a certain mellowing. Here one learns to surrender some of the world one has so painstakingly constructed for oneself. One's commitments are no less intense, but they are more realistic, more nuanced, and more supported by deeply felt and complex emotion. One becomes more gentle with oneself and with others. Finally there is the *Cosmic Stage*. It will be detailed below.

Facilitating Spiritual Development

Fowler's and Loevinger's accounts and other developmental literature provide indications about what might facilitate growth at each particular stage. Those concerned about their own spiritual development or about directing others along the spiritual path could benefit from consultation of that literature. However, firm and generally accepted conclusions in the area of human development are rare. It still remains to be seen whether subsequent research will confirm the outline of stages presented here or, in the extreme, conclude that no stages can be delineated and that human growth slides along a continuum, varying significantly for every individual. Only after such confirmation or revision can research projects be designed to determine more accurately the concrete factors that facilitate human—and so, spiritual—development along its course. Nonetheless, this much is clear. The multiple contemporary techniques commonly called psychotherapy, especially those in the humanist and holistic traditions, are appropriate means for furthering spiritual development.[25] And traditional religious techniques—meditation, prayer, retreats, fasting, isolation, reading, spiritual direction, service, love, worship—need to be understood scientifically so that their valid mechanisms may be highlighted and their merely superstitious or actually deleterious aspects, eschewed.[26]

The Cosmic Stage

Both Fowler and Loevinger acknowledge the difficulties in describing the final stage of development. In one way or another both refer to Maslow's account of self-actualization as an appropriate description. To some extent this suggestion must be correct, especially if one presumes an understanding of psychology as within the philosophic viewpoint. For Maslow understands self-actualization as "ongoing actualization of potentials, capacities, talents, as fulfillment of a mission (or call, fate, destiny, or vocation), as a fuller knowledge of, and acceptance of, the person's own intrinsic nature, as an increasing trend toward unity, integration, or synergy within the person."[27] However, some determinants of self-actualization—like the turn from preoccupation with deficiency and unreal, neurotic problems to concern for the real, existential issues of life—can certainly occur in the Conscientious Stage. In seeming agreement, Assagioli understands self-actualization as a *first* achievement that opens one to a whole new possibility in development; indeed, according to his peculiar usage, he reserves the term "spiritual" to speak about that new possibility.

Nonetheless, Loevinger's account of the Integrated Stage, which appeals to Maslow's self-actualization, is sufficiently distinct from the Autonomous Stage and adequately described so as to represent some description of the Cosmic Stage of spiritual development.

Though some aspects of Fowler's Universalizing Faith correspond with Loevinger's Integrated Stage, not all do. Generally, lack of correspondence at this point occurs because of the fuzziness of that final stage of development for all researchers. Specifically, however, a difference arises because of the peculiarity of Fowler's derivation of Stage-6 Faith: he invokes the biblical image "Kingdom of God," he points to outstanding historical personages, and he emphasizes the lived implications of faith. All this makes it difficult to understand exactly what Stage-6 Faith is. As already noted, Fowler does allow that someone with Stage-6 Faith would likely be "a 'self-actualized person' or a 'fully functioning human being'"; but he suggests this must be understood "in somewhat different senses than Abraham Maslow or Carl Rogers intended their terms."[28] He does not explain that "somewhat different sense." Perhaps his later expressed concern about the supposed exaltation of self-seeking "destiny" and the depreciation of altruistic "vocation" in our society was already operative in his thinking.[29] Then his reservation may intimate what I have argued systematically, that apart from explicit acknowledgment of the philosophic viewpoint even the loftiest seeming humanistic psychology needs to be qualified. Or are there here echoes of the standard *caveat* from spiritual theology courses, that holiness, a gift of God, cannot be adequately measured by human standards? (More on this topic in Chapter 7.) Or might the implication here be that one could be a person of the most highly developed faith—in Fowler's sense—yet still not meet the contemporary qualifications of psychological wholeness?

Whatever the case, if spiritual development and human development are strict correlates, the "saints" in any particular historical period or culture would meet the standards of authentic human development current in their historical period or culture; and they would exhibit the same limitations characteristic of their time and place, as well. So the non-violent Gandhi's subtle violence against his wife and sons is understandable, as is St. Paul's blindness to the inherent evil in slavery. Understandable, too, is the recent discussion in Roman Catholic circles whether Mother Teresa of Calcutta's criticism of the "contemporary American nun" is fair or not.[30] In a society that accurately recognizes self-actualization as inherent to fully mature humanity and that is capable of fostering such maturity, the Cosmic Stage of spiritual development must be defined at least by self-actualization.

When Assagioli speaks of spiritual psychosynthesis as a form of development beyond self-actualization, there is no clarity about the ultimate development toward which he points. Loevinger also acknowledges that in some sense there is no highest stage but only openness to continuing growth. These comments envisage some development beyond the Cosmic Stage of spiritual development. But it is an open question whether that further development can be detailed as discrete subsequent stages or represents only a continuing perfection of the Cosmic Stage. Consultation of the classical spiritual masters might be helpful at this juncture. For example, traditional accounts of the unitive stage of spiritual growth suggest discernible discrete processes within the unitive experience.[31] Further research is needed here.

If adequate treatment of stages of spiritual development at or beyond the Cosmic Stage is not yet possible, one can at least project a theoretical account of the ideal perfection of the Cosmic Stage. Spiritual development is conceived here as an ongoing process of integration. Critical to this process is an intrinsic principle of authentic self-transcendence. Loevinger's account of ego development allows the conception of the ongoing transformation of the personality. Then, spiritual development is precisely the integration of the drive toward increasing authenticity into the master structure of the personality.[32]

The present account of spiritual development suggests that each of the subsequent stages of spiritual development represents a restructuring of the ego such that the overall personality and, indeed, the subject him- or herself become an ever more adequate concrete expression of the spiritual drive toward authenticity. As one approaches the ideal, one's habitual patterns of perception, cognition, interrelation, and all others would be those of an authentic person.[33] One would be fully open to all that is, ever willing to change and adjust as circumstances demand, alive always to the present moment, responding as one ought in every situation, in touch with the depths of one's own self, aware of the furthest implications of one's spiritual nature, in harmony with oneself and with all else—and all this, not as a momentary, passing experience but as a perduring way of being, now built into the very structure of one's concrete self. The concrete, space-time-bound structures of the personality would be the adequate historical embodiment of the trans-spatial and trans-temporal dynamic human spirit. There would be a coincidence, insofar as one is possible, between spirit and concrete self.

This account is similar to that suggested by Assagioli's notion of self-realization. Yet explicit definition of an intrinsic principle of authentic self-transcendence and a precise conception of ego development add theoretical clarity not found in Assagioli's account. This account is also similar to accounts of the highest state of spiritual development in both Eastern and Western traditions.[34] Yet there, again, there is no theoretical account of the intrinsic nature of that state. The final stage of spiritual development, conceived in a strictly heuristic fashion, is that state of full integration when the personality is the adequate instrument of the authentic person. This is nothing other than mysticism—*samadhi, satori, kensho, moksha,* cosmic consciousness, enlightenment—conceived not as a passing experience but as a way of life.

Personal Integrity in Spiritual Development

Unlike other accounts of human development, which remain partial, the present conception of spiritual development regards the development of the whole person, as such. Comparison with Loevinger's and Fowler's accounts of ego and faith development will explicate this aspect of spiritual development.

In the first place, Loevinger and Fowler both treat development from infancy on. Since spiritual development proper is a strictly postconformist reality, their concerns are not spiritual development and only part of their accounts is relevant to spiritual development. But there are other considerations.

Loevinger deals with ego development, the most comprehensive approach to human development hitherto available. Ego development does imply development of the human individual her- or him-self. And Loevinger's account of ego development does somehow acknowledge an intrinsic principle of self-transcendence as critical to the process of ego development.[35] Nonetheless, Loevinger's explicit concern is ego, the central organizing factor in the personality, but still only one aspect of the human being. Insofar as this is so, Loevinger's is not an account of spiritual development. But when those other factors—an intrinsic principle of self-transcendence, an implication of self-responsible self-constitution, and concern for the whole person as such—are explicitly allowed, then Loevinger's account does become an account of spiritual development, even as has been presumed all along.

In Fowler's case, because of the coincidence of spiritual development with the upper stages of human development, because of his explicit introduction of a principle of ultimate authentic self-transcendence into his account, and because of his explicit acknowledgment of the self-constitutive implication of "faithing," his account of faith development is actually also an account of spiritual development. This is clear in his presentation of "Mary's Pilgrimage." This case study in faith development is actually the story of Mary's comprehensive religious development in light of her Christian faith. A study in faith development, it is also a study in spiritual development—yet not a very good one: Mary is at the baseline of spiritual growth, the Conformist Stage; she is struggling to make the first advances toward self-responsibility.

Despite this essay's repeated insistence on the integral nature of spiritual development, there has yet been no mention of the body, which—in addition to spirit with its structured dynamism expressed in levels of consciousness and psyche with its images, feelings, and learned patterns of behavior (ego "structures")—is also a factor in the whole person. That one's psychological state affects one's somatic state is beyond dispute. Conversely, that diet, exercise, and environment affect one's psychological state is also beyond dispute. That consistent meditation affects the very contours of one's body is also well known.[36] Here I do no more than acknowledge one's physical bodiliness as also a factor to be considered in spiritual development. Further research needs to be done on this issue.

The Social Dimension of Spiritual Development

Spiritual writers often note that spiritual maturity entails not only integrity within the individual her- or himself but also integration, harmony, wholeness with others and, indeed, with the whole cosmos. Nothing about the "cosmic" implication of spiritual development will be said here apart from the above indication that physical bodiliness also plays a part in spiritual development. But some brief comment can be given about the social implications of spiritual development. As will be remembered, "sociality" is one of the polar variables in Loevinger's theory of ego development.

Elsewhere I have argued at length the intrinsic social nature of the human individual and have indicated the essential factors that structure human solidarity: physical embodiments, dynamic human spirit, and shared meanings and values.[37] The sharing—and so, self-constituting appropriation—of only *true* meanings and *real* values conditions the possibility of universal solidarity. In other words, increasing authenticity entails increasing solidarity; or, in the present context, spiritual development entails increasing solidarity. The individual and social dimensions of the human grow simultaneously. In Fowler's scheme, the very name "Universalizing Faith" and the characteristic of Universalizers to identify with, and give themselves for, others presupposes and expresses that fact. In Loevinger's scheme, the polar variable, increasing sociality, does the same.

This brief mention of the social dimension of spiritual development will have to suffice here. However, note especially that the present account of spiritual development—though it emphasizes self-responsibility and self-constitution in post-conventional experience—is not a narrowly individualistic conception. Built into it at its base, in the notion of authenticity, are concerns that point beyond the individual, concerns for reality and value, concerns for others, for social structures, and for the global environment.

Surrender of the "Ego" and Spiritual Development

R. Ravindra argues that surrender of the "ego" or "self" is the core of the spiritual life.[38] This is a common theme in spiritual literature.

Ravindra does not mean by "ego" what Loevinger means. For Ravindra "ego" means the image that one holds of oneself and that one tries to project to others. "Ego" is one's external self, defined by the prestigious credentials recognized in one's culture and social level; "ego" entails motivation by ambition, fear, or concern for self-protection. According to Ravindra, awareness of a broader sense of self is essential to the possibility of surrendering the "ego" and so growing spiritually. Ravindra describes this broader sense of self in religious and metaphysical terms: the bidding of a higher will; the Spirit, above and beyond any isolated, individualistic consciousness; the supra-individual, supra-personal, supra-cultural.

Considering Ravindra's position within the context developed here, one must immediately presuppose that the intrinsic principle of authentic self-transcendence adequately accounts for that broader sense of self. Next, it is obvious that the "ego" of which Ravindra speaks is proper to the Conformist Stage of ego development. To view oneself in terms of externals, credentials, social status, is precisely characteristic of people at that stage of development. Some of these personality traits may also be retained in the Conscientious Stage; Fowler's treatment of the possibly excessively rationalistic character of Individuative-Reflective faith and Loevinger's indication of the driving force of oppressive conscience at this stage bear witness here. Therefore, to say that spiritual growth entails surrendering that "ego" means simply that spiritual growth entails movement out of and beyond the Conformist Stage of ego development. Ravindra's comparative-religions account of the essence of the spiritual life squares with the presentation of spiritual development presented here.

Moreover, the present discussion clarifies the meaning of the term "ego," so much a part of spiritual literature. If spiritual development entails surrender of the ego in Ravindra's sense, it does not mean extinction of the ego in Loevinger's sense.[39] In Loevinger's sense it means merely development from one ego stage to a higher stage. Even in the highest conceivable stage one is not without ego. One maintains a personality and that personality retains some configuration, an ego. But the ego is such that it is perfectly harmonious with the intrinsic drive toward authenticity, the "higher bidding." At that point "ego" in Ravindra's sense is no longer there. But ego in

Loevinger's sense is and must be there—otherwise, one would be speaking of some non-worldly reality, not about a human being. A proper understanding of "surrender of the ego" is not lacking among the spiritual masters.[40] What is lacking is a theoretical account of it.

Summary of Part I

In his analysis of consciousness, Bernard Lonergan provides a non-theist account of an intrinsic human principle of authentic self-transcendence. When spiritual development is defined in terms of that principle, the locus of adequate treatment of spiritual development moves out of the realm of theology and falls to the field of psychology. However, most approaches to psychology prescind from concern for normative meanings and values, so psychology adequate to treatment of spiritual development—and to any really human issues!—must be transformed by addition of that essential human concern. There results psychology within the philosophic viewpoint in contrast to the more limited psychology within the positivist viewpoint. Once this distinction is made, purely psychological treatment of spiritual development may proceed without fear of reductionist over-simplification.

The presupposition is that spiritual development is not one more focus of study added to a list of other such foci—like physical, emotional, intellectual, and more technically conceived cognitive, moral, ego, and faith development. Rather, spiritual development embraces the whole. Spiritual development is human development when the latter is conceived according to a particular set of concerns: integrity or wholeness, openness, self-responsibility, and authentic self-transcendence. So spiritual development is the ongoing integration that results in the self-responsible subject from openness to an intrinsic principle of authentic self-transcendence. This conception envisages the ever fuller integration of the human spiritual principle into the very structures of the personality until, in the ideal, the personality becomes the adequate expression of the fully authentic subject.

Furthermore, if spiritual development is human development, the stages of both are one and the same, and the research of developmental psychologists can be used to determine the stages of spiritual development. Accepting the seemingly converging results of developmental theorists at least at this point in a far from complete research endeavor, one can sketch a number of stages of spiritual development: the baseline beginning point, The Conformist Stage; the initial but tentative start, The Conscientious Conformist Stage; the first true achievement, The Conscientious Stage; the period of mellowing, deepening, and broadening of spiritual commitment, The Compassionate Stage; and the culmination, The Cosmic Stage.

This account of spiritual development unfolds without explicit acknowledgment of God. But there is a further question, central to many religious accounts of spiritual development: What role do God and belief in God play in spiritual development? So that both theorists' needs for intellectual honesty and comprehensive explanation and believers' needs for devotional integrity may be respected, this further question must be addressed. The following parts of this essay turn to theological considerations about spiritual development.

Notes

Chapter Four

Spiritual Development and Its Stages

1. Mark 10:15.
2. Loevinger, *Ego Development*, 19.
3. Lonergan, *Method*, 80.
4. Simmons, "Spiritual Development," "Quiet Journey."
5. Brewi and Brennan, *Mid-life;* Studzinski, *Spiritual Direction.*
6. Loevinger, *Ego Development*, 410.
7. *Ibid.,* 408.
8. Dember, "The New Look in Motivation."
9. Loevinger, *Ego Development*, 408-409.
10. *Ibid.,* 410-411.
11. Philibert, "Conscience."
12. Fowler, *Stages of Faith*, 29.
13. E.g., Kegan, *The Evolving Person.*
14. Cf. Helminiak, "One in Christ," 303-308, 358-359.
15. Kohlberg and Gilligan, "The Adolescent as Philosopher."
16. Lonergan, *Method*, 20, 302.
17. Perry, *Forms of Intellectual and Ethical Development.*
18. *Ibid.,* 50, as cited in Loevinger, *Ego Development*, 131.
19. Loevinger, *Ego Development*, 310.
20. Schachtel, *Metamorphosis.*
21. Loevinger, *Ego Development*, 144.
22. *Ibid.,* 145.
23. Gould, *Transformations*, 41 (emphasis added).
24. Grant, Thompson, and Clarke, *Image to Likeness*, 184-185.
25. Matson, *P T Omnibook.*

26. Chávez-García and Helminiak, "Sexuality and Spirituality"; Dunn and Helminiak, "Spiritual Practices"; Helminiak, "How is Meditation Prayer?" "Meditation," "Neurology and Religious Experiences," "Modern Science on Pain."

27. Matson, *P T Omnibook*, 309.

28. Fowler, *Stages of Faith*, 202-203.

29. Fowler, *Becoming Adult*.

30. Cf. *National Catholic Reporter*, January 25, 1980, p. 2; May 28, 1982, p. 11; and November 18, 1983.

31. Groeschel, *Spiritual Passages*, 160-188.

32. Ibid., 185-187; Grant, Thompson, and Clarke, *Image to Likeness, 58-59.*

33. Helminiak, "Meditation."

34. White, *The Highest State of Consciousness*.

35. See Chapter 3.

36. Goleman, "Meditation as Meta-Therapy."

37. Helminiak, "One in Christ."

38. Ravindra, "Self-surrender."

39. Cp. Groeschel, *Spiritual Passages*, 185-186.

40. Cf. Trungpa, *Cutting Through, Myth of Freedom.*

PART II

The Contribution of Theism
The Human as Created by God

CHAPTER FIVE

The Theoretical Contribution of Theism

Thus far this essay has considered spiritual development as a concern proper to psychology within the philosophic viewpoint. That presentation treated the key questions and, especially from the practical point of view, appears to have exhausted the topic. Non-believers may even wonder why further discussion is needed. Yet belief in God raises other questions that also need to be addressed. Without a comprehensive presentation that includes also these further questions, the account of spiritual development given above may appear sufficient to the psychologist and reductionist to the theologian. Both assessments would be false. Only when the specifically theological issues are completely spelled out will the extensive but legitimate place of the psychological be secure in a field of concern, spirituality, that was long the exclusive domain of religion. On the other hand, only then will the proper and equally extensive place of theological studies be clear, as well. No short-cut approach or provocative suggestion is adequate to the important and delicate task at hand.

Accordingly, Part II treats the further question, What other considerations about spiritual development need to be made when one acknowledges God? To begin this treatment, the present chapter provides an extended explication of the understanding of God presumed in the notion of theism as used in this essay. The intent is to show that an accurate understanding of "God" and of God's relation to the universe in no way invalidates or changes the account of spiritual development already presented. Acknowledgment of God adds only a further dimension of meaning to that account. This account of "theodicy" or "philosophy of God" or "natural theology" is critical to the argument of this essay.

The Theist Viewpoint

Acceptance of concern for authenticity as essential to the human defines the philosophic viewpoint. Or again, the philosophic viewpoint is determined by the acknowledgment that a spontaneous dynamism toward accurate meaning and real value, toward the true and the good, specifies the human as such.

Yet even within the philosophic viewpoint further questions arise. Is there an ultimate truth and goodness toward which that human dynamism points? Can one speak of the true and the good if there is no ultimate truth and goodness? Can one really accept one's experienced dynamism toward accurate understanding and real value without in that very act trusting that there is in reality a term of that dynamism, full correct understanding and transcendent value? Does full acceptance of oneself entail also acceptance of an ultimate truth and goodness toward which one's spiritual dynamism points? These questions and the experience from which they arise are the stuff of belief in God. For the affirmative answer is acknowledgment of the existence of God: "Yes, there is an ultimate truth and goodness toward which my intrinsic self-transcending dynamism spontaneously moves." Such acknowledgment determines the theist viewpoint.[1]

Thus, the theist viewpoint arises out of the philosophic viewpoint—not, however, as a deduction but rather as a responsible choice. One chooses to believe in God since such belief appears to be a responsible choice in the face of one's own experience and the questions it raises.[2] One does not prove the existence of God: "proof is rigorous only within a systematically formulated horizon. . . ."[3] But acceptance of any particular horizon depends on choice. A shift in horizon entails some form of what may be called conversion. Kuhn's notion of "paradigm shift" is also apposite here.[4] So belief in God is ultimately a matter of choice, not a matter of deduction or proof, and not a matter of mere caprice, either. In this sense, what follows here, rigorous though it be, is not presented as proof for the existence of God. Much more humbly, what follows is merely a reasonable account of that belief which some—and quite reasonably so—may choose to hold.

That understanding entails a conception of God as the ultimate explanation of all things. For if God is the term of the intrinsic human dynamism toward complete correct understanding, i.e., explanation, then God is the explanation of all. But included in this "all" is also the existence of all things. For the fact that things exist also requires an explanation. The contingency of everything we know in this world points to the need for some necessary being; otherwise, contingent existence is not explained. Nor does appeal to some supposed eternal existence of the world or to an infinite series of contingent causes provide explanation; these approaches avoid the issue: contingent being, non-self-explanatory by definition, requires something else to explain it. So, if God really explains the existence of all things, God must explain that existence not only cognitively but also actually. When existence is in question, explanation is not only theoretical but also existential. In this unique case, that which explains not only makes sense of something; it also makes that something be—because its very being is precisely what is in question. So God is the explanation of things especially in this sense: God is the source of their existence.[5]

God as Creator

Within the theist viewpoint the primary conception of God is that of Creator. As Creator, necessary being, God stands over and against all else as creature, contingent being. The distinction between the two is inviolable. They are defined in contrast to one another.

This understanding of God is proper to Judaism and Islam. It also occurs in Christianity, although belief in the Trinity determines the specifically Christian, which will require special additional treatment. This understanding of God may also occur in Hinduism, though this is not likely. The Hindu tendency toward pantheism, or at least its gnostic- or neo-platonic-like identity between Brahman and Atman, precludes the distinction between Creator and creature. So Hinduism, like non-theist Buddhism, may be more accurately treated within the philosophic viewpoint. In any case, discussion about God here will rely on the Judeo-Christian tradition.

Acknowledgment of God as Creator implies that the structures, the mechanisms, the processes, and the very stages of human spiritual development are created by God. Then, if the above account of spiritual development is correct, it is a human account of a work of God. With no difficulty whatever the theist can accept the accurate conclusions of scientific research and affirm them as an explication of God's creation.

In referring creation to God, the theist does not usually expect to be adding any new content to that which has been explained scientifically. To acknowledge that God created something does not change the substance of that thing. Acknowledgment of God merely adds a further dimension of meaning to the understanding already available. Over and above what science explains, theist faith adds an explanation for the *givenness* of that which was explained. Faith holds that that thing is there to be understood in the first place because God created it. But given that the thing is already there, one may proceed to explain it without any reference to God, and one would not thereby necessarily be mistaken in one's explanation. Theism arises from a different kind of questioning than does science. Science questions the "what" and "why" and "how" of things, assuming all along that they are there to be understood. But theism is concerned about metaphysical issues; it questions the very existence of things. So, granted that things do exist, neither does prescinding from the question about the existence of things invalidate one's explanation of them, nor does acknowledgment of God as Creator add anything to scientific explanation.

This understanding allows the easy and accurate interrelation of human science and theology, for it specifies the different but related realms of concern of each. In particular, then, this understanding allows that, without any prejudice to theist faith, one can simply accept the above account of spiritual development as accurate and complete. Theism adds nothing except the acknowledgment that God is Creator of that human phenomenon.

Creation and Conservation

However, that last summary sentence presumes an adequate understanding of "creation." Such understanding entails three distinct considerations: creation, conservation, and concurrence (or concourse).[6]

In its restricted technical sense, *creation* refers to the beginning of all things. The term means that *out of nothing* God brought contingent reality into existence. Allowance of only this aspect of the total issue results in deism, the prevalent eighteenth-century position that compared the universe to a clock and God to the clock maker: God created the universe and set it in motion and then sat back to watch its ticking without any further involvement. Valid in the deist position is its acknowledgment that the universe does need some explanation for its beginning, God. Also valid is its insistence that God is not like a puppeteer, directing the course of natural and human events by routine miraculous and so manipulative intervention. There are discoverable natural laws that govern the universe. These, and not God's miraculous intervention, explain why things are as they are. Newton's remarkable synthesis, an important influence on the deist position, made this point stunningly. Any adequate account of God's relation to the universe must retain these valid insights. Yet there is more to the issue than God's creating the universe *ex nihilo*. Deism overlooked that "more."

In addition to the world's dependence on God in its beginning—creation—there is also its continued dependence for perduring existence. The term *conservation* indicates this aspect of the issue. God's creation of the universe is not like a builder's construction of, say, a house. When complete, the house will go on standing quite well without the builder. Creation is not construction. Construction presumes construction materials that already exist apart from the builder. But creation presumes the existence of nothing except the agent, God. Since the move from non-being to being is infinite and can never be presumed, a contingent being's perdurance in being continues to require explanation. To be contingent means precisely not to be self-explanatory as regards existence. Existence being what it is, what requires explanation in the beginning of its existence also requires explanation in the continuance of its existence. Only non-contingent

105

necessary being can provide the required explanation for the continued existence of contingent being. As in the case of creation, so here as well, any other explanation merely dodges the issue. So, if it is to be explained at all, continued contingent existence, like creation, must be referred to necessary being, "God." Conservation indicates that action of God that keeps things in existence once they are created.

God's Existence and the Meaning of "God"

Throughout the treatment on God at the beginning of his *Summa Theologica*, Thomas Aquinas states repeatedly, We do not know what God is, but we do know that God is. His meaning might come clear in the present context.

Granted that all things have an explanation, the existence of contingent beings and the continued existence of contingent beings must have some explanation. The critical presupposition here is that everything must have some explanation. If one is unwilling to grant this presupposition, one must give an account of one's position. Otherwise it is not a reasonable position but mere caprice, and no one need take it seriously. Such an account must state how one knows where to draw the line between what is explainable and what is not, why some questions are to be pursued and others disregarded. That one is not interested is not sufficient reason, for the issue is not one's personal propensities but a matter that lies beyond oneself. That pursuit of certain questions is difficult is likewise not sufficient reason, for the issue is not whether or not the matter is difficult but whether or not it needs to be addressed. Even that complete explanation is beyond human capacities is also not sufficient reason, for the issue is not one of consummate results but one of in-principle commitment to the on-going process of human understanding, however far one may legitimately follow this process. Not some reasons personal to the interlocutor but some explanation intrinsic to the subject matter must be given if questions about it are to be legitimately disqualified. But if one can give reasons intrinsic to the subject matter, how can one argue that that subject matter lies beyond the line of profitable questioning, beyond the line of all understanding, beyond the line of explanation? One cannot. If one can give reasons intrinsic to the subject matter, then some such explanation is possible, and one's case is lost. On the other hand, if in making one's point one cannot give reasons intrinsic to the subject matter, then one does not know what one is talking about, and the practical conclusion is the same.

To deny that everything has an explanation is to involve oneself in self-contradiction. This self-contradiction is not merely logical, as just explained. This self-contradiction is also existential. It is a contradiction within one's own self. Certainly human intelligence requires an explanation for everything. We spontaneously continue to ask questions; we want to understand. But if legitimate questions have no answers, then our spontaneous intellectual curiosity is inane, and the core tendencies of our humanity are misguided. We are miserable, deluded wretches seeking meaning in a meaningless world. Thus, to reject the possibility of explanation is to reject the validity of one's own questioning. It is to reject one's own intelligence, it is to reject one's own self. To reject the possibility of explanation is to reject the rejecter. It is to disqualify one's self from the discussion. This disqualification follows from one's self-contradiction. What one proclaims with one's actions, one denies with one's words. One's arguing the issue exhibits a firm commitment to the process of question and answer and the desire to achieve accurate understanding. Yet one's verbal argument denies the validity of that very process. One must with deeds contradict one's own argument with words or else one must admit the validity of questioning and so eventually admit that everything has an explanation. The only other consistent option is to affirm the inanity of one's own self and the meaninglessness of the universe, to cease asking questions, to despair of all answers, and to refrain from any discussion whatsoever. One must withdraw from this debate and from all human—that is, intellectual—intercourse. In sum, one may accept one's self, one's spontaneous questioning, the possibility of answers, and the possible explanation of everything about everything, and so be open to the existence of self-explanatory, necessary being. Or one may reject all that and descend into nihilism. The options are few, and they are clear. Acceptance of self-explanatory being is the only reasonable option—provided one grants the value of being reasonable, provided one grants the value of one's intellectual self.

Granted the presupposition that everything has an explanation, then, and to return to the main issue: contingent existence must have an explanation (creation), and continued contingent existence must have an explanation (conservation). That explanation must be self-explanatory, necessary being, and this "necessary being"—as Aquinas states at the end of each of his five arguments for the existence of God[7]—is what people call "God."

Note that the name "God" is a shorthand label put on the answer to a number of questions. How is it that things exist? How do things continue to exist? These are legitimate questions, and they must have answers. If they have no answers, then why should we expect that any questions at all have answers? The answer to these questions certainly lies beyond what is available to ordinary experience. Yet the questions themselves and their very pointing beyond are integral to the ordinary experience of questioning: to deny these is to deny one's own self. So the questions are legitimate, and the questions have an answer. But what that answer is, we do not yet know. When we will have correctly understood everything about everything, then we will know the explanation of everything. Then we will know that which we name with the label "God." For "God" is the name we put on the anticipated answer to our questions about the existence of things. We can indeed say something about what that answer will entail when we finally know it: it will be the explanation of everything about everything. And, insofar as we understand our own intrinsic dynamism toward complete explanation of everything, we do have some sense of what such explanation means. It is the ultimate, ideal fulfillment of that intellectual or spiritual dynamism within us. But until we actually attain that complete explanation, we do not know it. We conceive it analogously, on the basis of our own experience of the dynamism of human consciousness. And we speak of it heuristically; it is what will be known when everything about everything is understood.

Self-explanatory, necessary being is the known unknown that is the term of the human dynamism toward complete understanding of everything about everything. It is this self-explanatory, necessary being that is named "God." In this sense, "God" is a heuristic term. Like "x," the unknown, expressed in an algebraic equation in terms of other factors already known, "God" names an unknown about which we can speak in terms of things already known. In an algebraic equation we may be able to specify x in terms of, say, y and z. If on some basis we know that $x = y + 2z$ and that $y = 3$ and $z = 7$, we can determine that $x = 3 + 2(7)$, or $x = 17$. In a similar way, we might spell out the meaning of the heuristic concept, "God."

Our basic datum is that there is something that explains everything about everything. This we are calling "God." As already noted, this "God" must be necessary being. Otherwise it is contingent, something else must explain it, and it does not explain everything about everything.

Moreover, it must be eternal, that is, without beginning. Otherwise it had a beginning, something else must explain its beginning, and it itself does not explain everything about everything.

Moreover, it must be simple, that is, it must have no parts. Otherwise it is composite, something else must explain its composition, and it itself does not explain everything about everything.

Moreover, it must be unchanging. Otherwise it changes, something else must explain its change, and it itself does not explain everything about everything.

By the same token, it must be perfect, that is, it itself must determine the meaning of "perfection." Otherwise it is imperfect, there are perfections apart from it, something else must explain those other perfections, and it itself does not explain everything about everything.

Similarly, it must be good, that is, it itself defines what "good" means. For whatever is not attributable to it simply is not, and what is not is deficient in the most fundamental of qualities, existence. Apart from it is nothing, non-being. Of it is being, all that is. Since it itself is in no way deficient but is rather the source of all else that is, it is perfectly good.

Moreover, it must exist always in the present. Otherwise it is temporal, it experiences past, present, and future, it has within itself some basis for the determination of time, so it is not simple and it changes, and then, as already noted, it itself cannot be the explanation of everything about everything.

Moreover, it must be intelligent. Otherwise it cannot account for the intelligent order of the universe, and it does not explain everything about everything.

And it must be free and self-determining, that is, non-constrained in its creation of, and its relationship with, the universe. Otherwise it is dependent on the universe or on something else, and it itself does not explain everything about everything.

Moreover, it must be benevolent and well-wishing. The very fact of creation implies as much—granted that creation is free and unconstrained, entails sharing existence with others, and results in no possible benefit to the creator.

Then, in some sense it must be personal. Otherwise it is impersonal, it lacks what is generally meant by "personal," it is not intelligent and self-determining—as it must be, as has already been noted, if it is to explain everything about everything.

Moreover, it must be omnipotent, that is, able to account for everything that is possible, capable of whatever can be. Otherwise it would be limited, it would not be the explanation of everything about everything.

And the list could go on. In Chapter 19 of *Insight* Bernard Lonergan lists twenty-six charactristics that must logically be attributed to that which explains everything about everything.

Now, this whole exercise of listing qualities of self-explanatory being is but an explication of the notion, explanation of everything about everything. It is an intelligent expansion of the heruistic term, "God." So one could write the following:

$$\text{GOD, complete explanation} =$$
$$\text{necessary} + \text{eternal} + \ldots + \text{personal} + \text{omnipotent}.$$

The point is that "God" is a heuristic term, like "x" in the equation

$$x = y + 2z.$$

But now notice some significant differences. We can solve for x because we know that $y = 3$ and $z = 7$. Moreover, in some sense we know what 3 and 7 mean, so to some extent we also understand what $x = 17$ means. But in the case of the heuristic notion "God," we do not understand what "necessary" and "eternal" and "good" and all those other notions mean. For if in every case we conclude that those notions must be proper to "God," we also know that they are in "God" in a manner unknown to us. We do not understand absolute necessity

110

nor absolute eternity nor absolute intelligence nor absolute freedom any more than we understand absolute explanation of everything about everything. Perhaps those notions in our equation about "God" should be raised to the nth power, thus:

$$GOD = (necessary + eternal + \ldots + personal + ominpotent)^n.$$

But then, again, the series of pluses in this equation also calls for some qualification. If one of the qualities of "God" is simplicity, "God" cannot be accurately expressed as a list of qualities added together. There are no parts in "God," and there are no real distinctions in "God." So our heuristic expression about "God" needs to be revised again, thus:

$$GOD = (necessary\text{-}eternal\text{-}\ldots\text{-}personal\text{-}omnipotent)^n.$$

The upshot of this exercise in heuristics is this: though we can specify characteristics necessarily implied in the notion of complete explanation of everything about everything, if we are careful about our procedure, in the end we realize that we still do not really understand "God." Although the items on the right side of the heuristic expression about "God" help our finite minds to understand better what the notion "God" implies, in the end those items are no more intelligible to us than the x variable "God" on the left side of the heuristic expression.

Take omnipotence, for example. When predicated of "God," omnipotence simply means that whatever actually is and whatever could possibly be must be attributable to "God," for by definition "God" accounts for everything about everything. Then, does divine omnipotence mean that God can do anything? Can God create a square circle? Is God so great that God could create a rock God cannot lift? Note that "square circle" is a self-contradition; the two terms mutually cancel each other. A square circle is nothing. As such, it needs no explanation. The same is to be said about the rock too big for God to lift; and toward the end of this chapter, something similar will be said about sin.

To ask about what might explain a square circle is foolishness. So not even "God," that is, not even that which explains everything about everything, could account for a supposed square circle. A square circle has no explanation, no accounting for, because it needs no explanation: it is nothing to explain.

Omnipotence does not mean that "God" can do anything the imagination might suggest. Omnipotence simply means that whatever is or could be, must be attributable to "God." Since "God" is that which accounts for all, "God" must be capable of all that can be—by definition. Whatever is not self-contradictory can be, and whatever can be has some explanation. Since "God" is the ultimate explanation of all that is explainable, especially as regards existence, God can account for whatever is not self-contradictory, God is capable of it.

That is all divine omnipotence means. It, like the other characteristics attributed to "God," merely explicates the meaning already contained in the notion of complete explanation. In spelling out the implications of the heuristic notion, "God," we do not add to our understanding of "God." So we must not speak as if we are adding qualities to "God"—as if we knew "God" and so were able to detail the divine character. Calling "God" omnipotent does not imply some super power, capable even of the impossible, like a magic wonder-worker of childhood fantasy, animated cartoons, and science fiction. Calling "God" ominpotent or intelligent or personal or good adds nothing to what is already contained in the notion "God."

That which explains everything about everything we call "God." But what that actually is and what the qualities necessarily implied mean, we do not understand. We do not know what God is. Nonetheless, we do know that such a thing must exist. Affirming its existence is a most reasonable judgment. Suspending judgment about it may be a tolerable alternative: non-theism is not the same as atheism. But denying its existence can involve one in self-contradiction—not merely logically but also existentially. Echoing Thomas Aquinas, we must affirm that we do not know what God is even though we do know that God is.

The practical conclusion of this long digression on Aquinas's statement can be made quickly: we do not know what we are talking about when we talk about God! To pretend we do confuses the issue. "God" is the answer to a series of questions. We understand the questions. We also understand that there must be some answer to those questions. We can also project in broad outline—heuristically—

what that answer must be. But we do not understand what that answer is. To refer to that answer we say "God."

Unfortunately, once we have that name, we begin using it as the subject of sentences and go on making statements about the reality as if we really understood what we were saying. "God created the universe." "God is with you and me." "God loves each of us very dearly." "God guides our spiritual growth." Since our religious tradition has also spoken about "God" with similar declarative sentences, many of them in one way or another undoubtedly true, we are confirmed in our assumption that we know what we are talking about. We say, "God created the universe," and appear to understand the issue. What we really mean is this: Whatever explains the origin and continued existence of the universe, and there must be some explanation— that is "God."

The latter statement is more humble. It retains the question as well as the anticipated answer. It highlights the mystery, the inexhaustible surplus of meaning, that is at stake. It keeps things better in perspective. When this perspective is lost, theism appears immature. The pursuit of theological questions appears unscientific. Discussion of creation appears partisan. And the intelligent interrelationship of specialized fields of study becomes impossible.

Divine Concurrence

Some created beings not only exist but also act. They have certain capacities that allow them to do certain things. When a contingent being acts, it has some part in bringing into existence something new, namely, the very act in question and, by implication, its effect. But this something new is itself a contingent reality, so it also needs something to explain its existence. In this case, God must not only create the agent in question and sustain it in existence but also enable it in each case to act. *Divine concurrence* indicates this latter activity of God.

As should already be obvious, the question of concurrence is but another particular instance of the general understanding that was applied also in the question of conservation. Just as contingent beings cannot continue in existence apart from the sustaining act of the Creator, so they cannot act on their own without the concurrent act of

113

the Creator. Only appeal to necessary being provides explanation for contingent being of any kind whatsoever, including actions.

Insisting that creatures cannot act apart from an act of God raises the thorny question about human freedom.[11] How can humans be free if they are dependent on God in their very acts? If God's will is irresistible, how can there be freedom?

This issue is particularly important in light of the topic of this study, spiritual development. As noted above, a psychological account of spiritual development already seems to cover all the relevant practical issues. Theist belief changes nothing. Yet, once one affirms the existence of God and acknowledges God as Creator, as necessary explanation of all that is and happens, it may appear that the balance has shifted from the psychological to the theological. It may appear that spiritual development—and any other historical process—is determined by God and not by humans after all. So acknowledgment of God may seem to be not merely one more factor, broadening the psychological-scientific explanation to metaphysical limits; it may seem to be the only telling factor. The human may now appear to fall into insignificance. Psychological explanation may now appear to be a futile pastime. And these assumptions would certainly be accurate if God were indeed the only factor that really matters.

The resolution to this supposed problem is a correct understanding of the dependence of created reality on the Creator. It is, then, none other than that same understanding that is operative in the discussion of creation and conservation above.

Just as human construction is not an adequate analogy for God's activity in creation, so human assistance and support is not an adequate analogy for God's activity in concurrence. In fact, there is no adequate analogy. God is not like us. We do not really understand what God is. "God" is the answer to certain questions, the answer that intelligence demands. But we do not understand what that answer is; God is like nothing else we know.

Every other agent we know is contingent, this-worldly. Each can be adequately compared with others. The joint interaction of many such agents in any human undertaking is a kind of co-operation. One does this, and the other that. Differences of opinion are settled by negotiation or, if not in that way, by outright conflict. Agent vies against agent, and the strongest wins control. But God is not one more agent alongside the rest, not even if conceived as the most powerful of them all. So the notion of God as "Supreme Being"[12] may be misleading. God is not being like any other being we know.

Divine being transcends all other being and so exceeds any possible grasp by human understanding and belies any comparison with other beings. So it is mistaken to conceive God's concurrence with created agents as a kind of co-operation. And it is mistaken to imagine a conflict of wills between the divine and the human agents. Rather than conflict with the human agent, God constitutes and actualizes that agent. The contingent agent exists and acts precisely because God establishes and confirms that agent in its existence and activity. God makes everything be and be what it is. If the agent in question is a free agent, it is so precisely because God constitutes it as free. Its free acts are not in conflict with God's concurrent power but are precisely the result of God's power. Then, the more irresistible one understands God's action to be, the more surely one knows the created agent to act freely. God infallibly ordains the free acts of the creature. And because God's action is precisely that of Creator, incommensurable with any other agent, God's action is infallible and the creature's action is infallibly free.[13] There is no conflict between human freedom and divine concurrence properly understood.

Divine Foreknowledge and Concurrence

A consideration of God's so-called "foreknowledge" may clarify the issue. We say that God knows the future. Then, since God cannot be mistaken, what God knows of the future will certainly occur. Does it follow that we are not free in determining our own future? Certainly not. The fallacy lies in the very term "foreknowledge." This term suggests that there is a future in God just as there is a future for us and that God looks into that future and so knows what will occur for us. But God is beyond the created world of space and time. There is no time in God. In God all is present. What to us is history and what to us is the future, simply *is* to God. God knows our future not because God looks into it as if gazing into a crystal ball. Rather, God knows our future because our future is present to God. Just as God knows our present, God also knows our future. Just as God's knowing our present does not prevent us from acting freely at this very moment, so

God's knowing our future does not prevent us from acting freely when that future comes for us. If what God knows of our future will certainly come to be, that is so not because God makes things happen as God decrees they shall be but because God already knows in an eternal present what we will freely do in our future.

Now, what God knows, God also wills. If God did not will it, it would not be and it would not be there to be known. For God, to know is to will. This must be so, for "God" must be absolutely simple.

God is simple. There can be no parts, no distinctions in God (acknowledged only as Creator). If there were, something beyond God would be needed to explain the union of these distinct parts. That something would be an explanatory principle more ultimate than God. But by definition God is the ultimate explanatory principle. So there can be no distinct parts in God. By the same token, there can be no time in God. If there were, something else would be needed to explain the passage in God from past to future; something else would be needed to explain the temporal difference in God, the change from what God was not to what God will be. Then that more ultimate explanatory principle would be God, and by definition the temporal reality in question would not have been God to begin with. So there can be no time in God, conceived according to the demands of intelligent explanation, just as there can be no parts in God. God is absolutely simple.

Then God's "will" is not different from God's "mind." So what God knows, God also wills. Since God knows our future, God also wills our future. So our future as God wills it will certainly occur. Yet there is no destruction of human freedom here. If God's eternal knowledge of our future does not preclude human freedom in the determination of that future precisely because God eternally knows that future as freely determined, then God's eternal willing of our future does not preclude human freedom in the determination of that future precisely because God eternally wills that future as freely determined. There is no conflict between God's will and human freedom, just as there is no conflict between God's knowledge and human freedom. In God, knowing and willing are one and the same.

Now, divine concurrence is not *really* distinct from God's knowing or God's willing. Concurrence is but a *logically* distinct aspect of the operation of God's will, God's creative power. It is distinct only in the human mind's conception of the matter but not in the reality of God. So just as God's knowing and God's willing in no way preclude human freedom, so God's concurrence with every contingent historical act in no way precludes the freedom of that act. Divine concurrence, correctly understood, does not threaten but rather sustains human freedom.

Divine Providence and Concurrence

Consideration of two specific issues, divine Providence and human sin, will confirm this understanding. Two questions will test the present understanding. First, if God does not omnipotently manipulate human freedom, how does Providence achieve God's good will in historical process? The simple answer is this: because of the Creator's unique relationship to created agents and to the universe as a whole, God can bring about good within the free historical process that God sustains in being. All the causes in the universe, both the determinative and the free ones, are part of the divine plan for the universe. Because the overall plan, which leaves room for free agents, is God's, the end will be as God plans it, good.

A more detailed answer will recall that a number of factors account for human freedom. In any particular situation within the concrete world order, any number of courses of action are possible. Then, human understanding grasps some of these possibilities and so makes them available for human deliberation. Finally, from among the possible choices, the human agent freely opts for a particular course of action.[11] The divine plan is operative in each of these factors. For human freedom is not unlimited freedom. Human freedom operates within the universe as it in fact is. The laws that govern the universe restrict human choice: one may not choose to fly down a flight of stairs or to live without eating or to relive yesterday. Even one's internal intellectual activity unfolds according to a given pattern. Lonergan's four levels of consciousness articulate that pattern. So even if one would commit the perfect crime, one must use one's intelligence as it actually is even while misusing it. Human freedom is exercised within the order of the universe created by God.

Moreover, divine agency is operative ultimately as the divine order that guides the universe as a whole. For every contingent event depends on an infinite number of prior conditions. To human understanding these conditions can only be understood as random occurrences, amenable only to statistical method. Yet in themselves each condition could be explained if one could trace back the causal influences for each through an overwhelmingly intricate interaction of ever-prior events, each in itself also explainable by means of a repeat of the same kind of investigation. But only the very order of the universe provides an explanation for this ever branching interaction of an infinity of conditioned conditions. And only the Creator provides an explanation for the order of the universe. God guides the universe to its intended good end, ordering each contingent being according to its own operation. God does not control the course of the universe by manipulating the individual event. Rather, "God controls each event because he controls all, and he controls all because he alone can be the cause of the order of the universe on which every event depends."[12]

Providence refers to the creative activity by which God guides the universe by ordering the whole, including both determinate and free elements, toward a goal that "God" alone explains. Insofar as only God as Creator can explain and so determine the entire order of the universe—and God has determined it for good—God guides the universe and everything in it toward its good end. Part of that overall order of the universe is the good of created free agents, so the order of the universe and the unfolding of that order already take human freedom into account. So belief in Providence does not preclude acknowledgment of what to humans are mere random occurrences. Nor does belief in Providence presume routine miraculous interventions, disrupting the determinate order of the universe. Nor does belief in Providence suggest that the universe exists at the mercy of an omnipotent demiurge. Nor does belief in Providence preclude the acknowledgment of free, human acts. An adequate notion of Providence poses no conflict between God and human freedom.

Human Sin and Divine Concurrence

Human sin raises a second set of test questions for an understanding of human freedom and divine concurrence. How can sin be explained if nothing happens apart from divine concurrence? Is God responsible for sin? An adequate understanding of sin will provide an answer to these questions.[13]

Sin is a term that finds its proper context within the theist viewpoint. It refers to deliberate deviation from the divine will. Sin is a free human act that is not what God would want. In contrast, conceived within the philosophic viewpoint and then better named culpable wrongdoing, sin is deliberate deviation from what is humanly known as true and good. It is deviation from human authenticity, as defined above. Granted that the human true and good is but a participation in that fullness, divine truth and goodness, the human act that is unauthentic from one viewpoint is one and the same act that is known as sin from another viewpoint. Movement from the philosophic to the theist viewpoint adds the understanding that from a broader point of view human unauthenticity entails disorder also in relationship to God. As human authenticity is directed toward the fullness of truth and goodness that is God, so human unauthenticity implies deviation also from the full order of the universe that God knows and wills. For this reason such a human act is called sin: it regards not only the human who commits the act but also God who orders the universe. Within a theist viewpoint human wrongdoing is recognized to be sin. But the substance of sin, that which makes it what it is, is the same in either case. It is a lack. It is a deviation from what ought to be.

The sin in any particular case is not the human action—pulling the trigger of a murder weapon, speaking the words that express an untruth, taking money that belongs to someone else. These human actions merely express the sin. In themselves, they are real contingent events. As such they must be directly willed by God through divine concurrence. Otherwise they simply would not exist; they could not happen. That God concurs in the positing of these actions does not mean that God is responsible for the sin. God does not will sin. One could say, rather, as Augustine did, that God merely permits sin.

God permits sin in this sense: God concurs with actions that express sin when God sustains in being and activity creatures who posit sinful acts. For they could posit no act at all without God's concurrence. But God also permits sin in a more fundamental sense: God chose to create creatures endowed with freedom. In granting freedom, God granted the possibility of abuse of that freedom. Were God to disallow sin, human freedom itself would be disallowed. In respect for the universe God created, including creatures who act freely, God permits sin.

Note carefully again, however, that the sin that God does not will but merely permits is not the specific actions that express human sin. These God must will; otherwise they would not occur. Nor is the sin the physical evils that result from the sinful acts—the gunshot wound in the victim, the decisions based on false information, the hardship resulting from lack of funds. These, too, in one way or another are real and so are in some way effects of the creative will of God. All of these, realities in the created universe, apparently random happenings, unfortunate concatenations of conditions and of still other conditioning conditions, physical evils—all of these fit in one way or another into the overall order of the universe. Within that order God can and does deal with them.

But the sin itself is other. It is moral evil that emerges from the free agent and affects that agent and the universe as a whole. This moral evil is a disorientation, a flaw introduced into the system. It is a tear in the garment, a hole in the picture. Sin is a lack of order that ought to be there. As a lack of order, it has no intrinsic intelligibility. It is irrational, a surd, like the square root of minus one.

> We can know sin as a fact; we cannot place it in intelligible correlation with other things except *per accidens;* that is, one sin can be correlated with another, for deficient antecedents have defective consequents; but the metaphysical surd of sin cannot be related explanatorily or causally with the integers that are objective truth; for sin is really irrational, a departure at once from the ordinance of the divine mind and from the dictate of right reason. The rational and the irrational cannot mix, except in fallacious speculation. And this precept is not merely relative to man; it is absolute. The mysteries of faith are mysteries only to us because of their excess of intelligibility; but the *mysterium iniquitatis* is mysterious in itself and objectively, because of a defect of intelligibility.[14]

An adequate understanding of sin grasps that sin, like motion in Newton's first law, is nothing to be explained. Sin is irrational. It can be acknowledged as a fact but cannot be understood in itself. It can be handled like the surd in a mathematical equation is handled: one carries it along, fully aware of what it is, in the hope that eventually

120

other factors will have the surd cancel out. Perhaps somewhat in this way and at the price of much suffering, divine Providence deals with the irrationality of sin within the order of the universe.

God deals with sin. But since sin is an irrational, a "metaphysical surd," "God" in no way explains sin. Sin can have no explanation, so it needs no explanation—other than the risky freedom that humans possess. Reference to aberrant human freedom provides an adequate account of sin. That account does not implicate God, except insofar as God granted freedom. In no way is God responsible for sin. To account for sin divine concurrence need not and must not be invoked. This understanding of sin answers the second set of test questions we posed in order to clarify the meaning of divine concurrence.

Summary on God as Creator

As stated above, theism adds nothing to the psychological explanation of spiritual development except the acknowledgment that there is a Creator of that human phenomenon. To validate this statement, this chapter explicated an understanding of God as Creator, treating the technical questions of creation, conservation, and concurrence. God was not neglected. Yet throughout, the same point was made: in no way does belief in God change scientific explanation of created reality. Belief in God adds a further metaphysical dimension to such explanation, but it leaves the empirical account intact. Therefore, even granting the existence of God, the account of spiritual development and its stages given in Part I remains valid. An adequate understanding of God as Creator does not change an adequate psychological account of spiritual development. Theology merely adds a further dimension of meaning to the psychological account. The contribution is theoretical.

Notes

Chapter Five

The Theoretical Contribution of Theism

1. Helminiak, "Four Viewpoints."
2. Lonergan, *Method*, 101-124, 340-344; *Philosophy of God*.
3. Lonergan, *Method*, 338; on Vatican Council I's statement about knowledge of God by the natural light of human reason, cf. 278, 321, 338-339.
4. Kuhn, *Structure of Scientific Revolutions*.
5. Lonergan, *Insight*, 634-686.
6. Rahner and Vorgrimler, *Dictionary*, 91, 100-101, 128.
7. *Summa Theologica*, I, q. 2, a. 3.
8. Lonergan, *Grace and Freedom*.
9. *Baltimore Catechism*, 11.
10. Rahner, *Sacramentum Mundi*, vol. 2, 424-427.
11. Lonergan, *Grace and Freedom*, 93-116.
12. Lonergan, *Insight*, 664.
13. Lonergan, *Grace and Freedom*, 109-115.
14. *Ibid.*, 113.

The Practical Implications of Theism

The previous chapter argued that theism adds a further dimension of understanding to even an adequate psychological account of spiritual development. Theism treats the metaphysical issues from which the empirical sciences prescind. But a further question arises: Does theism have any practical consequences for understanding spiritual development, that is, for furthering people along the path of that development?

The summary answer is No. The reason is this: it appears that whether or not one believes in God, God is still active in one's life. One is still created and conserved in being by God and still subject to divine concurrence in every activity. Oblivion to God's existence and action does not eliminate God from the picture. Nor does it seem that human acknowledgment of God increases the influence of God's creative activity. To think otherwise is to suppose that God's relationship with the universe changes, depending on human response. But God does not change, nor is God dependent on humankind. God's relationship to creation is constant and universally benevolent. Believing or not believing in God does not change that for better or worse. Therefore, belief in God makes no practical difference for an adequate understanding of spiritual development. And all practical questions about the "what" and "why" and "how to" of spiritual development are properly answered by psychological research within the philosophic viewpoint and not by theological scholarship.

A Theoretical, Not a Pastoral Study

That statement may sound offensive to the pious and excessive even to some who are specialists in spirituality, generally conceived as a practical art. But such reactions may misrepresent the real meaning of that statement. This essay as such is not addressed to the pious; it is not intended to be an inspirational "spiritual" book. Nor is it as such intended to address the pastoral function of helping others grow in piety and religion. This essay certainly has pastoral application, but it is not a pastoral statement. Rather, it is a theoretical account of a complex spiritual topic. It is a differentiated account that sorts out and relates the realms of competence of various disciplines that bear on that topic. The specific question here regards the practical effect of theism on spiritual development. Within the present context, it becomes obvious—and must be clearly noted—that psychology, and not theology, is the discipline that properly treats the practical issues regarding spiritual development. An adequate response to this assertion is not an emotional one. It is, rather, to question whether or not this assertion is correct.

There is no intention here of minimizing the importance of theist faith in furthering human authenticity and so spiritual development, especially within the Western world. Western civilization today is extensively secular. Calling Western civilization "secular" does not mean that it is simply non-theist, for non-theism, as in Tibetan Buddhism, may be wholly dedicated to human authenticity, to lofty spiritual values. Nor does it mean simply humanist, for humanism, too, can be authentic. Here "secular" means downright positivist. In calling our society secular I mean that human authenticity is not among its fundamental values. Since this is so, religion is practically the only carrier of transcendent values in our society. Other institutions—like the public school system, the universities, the scientific community, hospitals and social service agencies, certain voluntary associations— may still foster such values in isolated cases and in strictly circumscribed form, but this can no longer be taken for granted. In a secular society religion is generally the sole carrier of transcendent values. Now, despite the amazing growth of numerous Eastern religions in the West, in Western society "religion" still generally means theism. Therefore, insofar as religion and theism tend to be identified with one another, the role of theism is paramount when spiritual development is the concern. In no way is the role of theist faith in Western civilization to be minimized.

Nonetheless, just as music and art were once religious functions but now develop autonomously, so "the care of souls" used to be a completely religious, a pastoral function but now is achieved extensively through psychotherapy and counseling. When analyzed technically, much of what constitutes theist religion now falls within the proper domain of the human sciences. So in a theoretical account many "religious" issues are to be explained not by appeal to faith and God but by scientific research. Moreover, granted a comprehensive scheme that can integrate all the pieces, such a differential analysis is not dangerous. It runs no risk of falling into reductionism, on the one hand; and on the other, it eschews all simplistic fideism, as well. It follows that the best way to further theist or any religion in the long run is accurately to treat all the diverse aspects that constitute those religions—even if this requires turning over to the competence of psychology much of what was formerly religion and even if this approach is offensive to the pious and suspect to some professional religious practitioners. The intention here is not to undermine religion in general or theism in particular but to secure them a solid theoretical foundation.

A consideration of three religious themes central to theism will confirm the contention that appeal to God adds no practical content to an adequate psychological account of spiritual development. These three "case studies" stand as evidence. The hope is that in the face of this evidence this contention will be recognized as correct.

Religion as Inspirational

First, religion has tremendous power for inspiring people to live authentically. This power is sealed with belief in God. One acts "for God's sake" or "because God requires it." One continues to hold on in life even during hardship because one "trusts in God." Belief in God and in God's action provides strong reason to do what one ought to do.

But how much of this motivation is to be attributed to belief in God and how much by the ordinary psychological functioning of—in this case, religious—sentiment and symbol? Or said otherwise, for adequate explanation in this case, how much is already accounted for within the positivist viewpoint and really how germane is the theist viewpoint? Especially in practice it may be difficult to sort out these two, but they are not the same thing, so a theoretical account must treat them differently.

In fact, much of what people profess as belief in God is simply their commitment to their own ideas and images of God. Religious literature repeatedly warns believers against personally appealing but misguided notions of God. The story of Job is the classic example in the Hebrew Bible. For many—and for all, to some extent—"God" is a convenient blank screen onto which one may project one's own deepest felt fears and fancies and then, for better or worse, feel justified in living by them. Genuine theism is a rare phenomenon. Few live for long in explicit relationship with the real God. If this is so, would not what generally passes as theism be more properly studied by the psychologist than by the theologian? Is not the operative issue in such religion more the human physical, psychic, and spiritual forces that grip a person than the actual living God of the Universe?

As explained in Chapter 5, the living God of the Universe acts in and through those other forces and not in addition to, or in conflict with, them. But the point relevant to the present study is precisely this: one will better understand religion and its functioning by focusing on the human factors through which the divine operates than by focusing on God, whom we cannot understand in any case. Insofar as God may truly be operative in any person's theism, God is operative as the ever transcendent goal that constantly calls one to purify and renew one's ever inadequate images and ideas of God. The true effective power of one's "belief in God" is in the motivating images and ideas, and these are human, not divine. So, for a real explanation of the functioning of religion, a human-scientific rather than a strictly theological study would be more productive. And further appeal to the God of the Universe would add nothing concrete to the scientific study.

The same point can be made from another approach. Much else of what people profess as belief in God is merely their commitment to values learned in association with some religious tradition or discovered during life's journey. The weight of human sentiment deposited in religious symbolism and ritual over the long years of life gives those values power to sustain one when life is bereft of meaning. The sustaining power of a religious funeral at the death of a loved one provides a ready example. But is what is operative there, just because it includes reference to God, really any different from the affective power of a civil ritual? For a soldier's family, a military funeral might be as supportive. Even a parade can tap deep sentiments, bring tears to the eyes, and inspire strong patriotic commitment. And who is to say if any of these rituals really expresses belief in the true God—or even commitment to authentic human values!—or merely unlocks the powers of the human psyche?

The shrewd—and often unscrupulous—politician is quick to invoke religious rhetoric if it will further the desired purpose. But such "religion" may not even be authentically human, let alone theist.

Or again, the pastoral counselor may well quote a Bible story to clinch a point for the client, but the skilled counselor would as willingly use some other source if it would better make the point for that particular client. Quoting the Bible or one's theist tradition, even in the name of God and religion, provides no guarantee that one is really relating to God. From the point of view of good counseling, the effectiveness of the intervention and not its form is what really matters. One would hope that the intervention does foster authentic human growth. But in whatever case, for therapist and counselee alike, the focus of the session had better be on human growth and not specifically on God. Otherwise both would be wasting their time in counseling. So "pastoral counseling" and "spiritual direction" may be nothing more than humanly adequate psychotherapy—that is, psychotherapy within the philosophic viewpoint—couched in religious symbols. And religious symbols may be used simply because they most powerfully express the worldview of the client and so are the most effective clinical tools available.

Grant, Thompson, and Clarke's *From Image to Likeness* is a superb example of how one can use elements within a religious tradition to foster psychological integration along specific lines. That book provides a chapter on each of the four Jungian functions—sensing, thinking, feeling, and intuiting—in each case highlighting numerous apposite elements in Roman Catholicism.

Of course, the importance of the pastoral counseling movement is that it offers psychotherapy in a context that recognizes transcendent values. According to the present analysis, such a context is essential to adequate psychotherapy. However, the danger in this movement looms up on two fronts. On the uncritical liberal front, it may result in reductionism as theist (and Christian) language is used to treat questions really only about human authenticity. Then the distinctive meanings of the religious symbols are watered down and lost, and the religion that pastoral counseling intends to support is unwittingly undone. On the overzealous conservative front, this movement may result in naive fideism. Such an outcome is especially evident in Fundamentalism, which refers only to the Bible to deal with all counseling issues, even those never imagined in biblical times. The outcome here is the loss both of sound psychotherapy and of responsible religion. That is to say, here not even human authenticity is served.

In every case, the inspirational power of theist religion will be traced not to belief in the one, true God but to the psychological-sociological mechanisms whereby all symbolism and ritual function. An adequate understanding of theism would make no significant contribution to an understanding of religion's functioning.

At the same time, it remains that belief in God is an effective force to move one along the path of ever self-transcending human authenticity, for God is the never attained yet ever attracting goal of that path. So true theism offers a sure safeguard against any domestication of true religion's unruly thrust toward constant self-transcendence. To provide this safeguard is precisely a primary value of theism. The prophetic tradition in Israel bears witness to this value.

Yet that very thrust toward self-transcendence that theism guarantees is none other than that which defines the philosophic viewpoint and is the driving force of spiritual development as explained apart from theist presuppositions. In other words, the deepest trans-

128

forming power within theism expresses itself through the *human* dynamism toward authentic self-transcendence. Things could not be otherwise. We live in this world, so if God wanted to attract us, God would have to meet us in this world and attract us through this-worldly means, through the human. Moreover, though we know that God is, we do not understand what God is. We understand God only analogously. And the very basis of that analogy is the same dynamism of the human spirit that is in question here. An understanding of the human spirit and its dynamism is the only appropriate guide to statements about the metaphysical. So, when one would say something practical and be true to the theist tradition, one must return to the philosophic viewpoint, from which the theist is a responsible projection. In the treatment of practical questions, the theist emphasis on the divine Creator inevitably gives way to the philosophic emphasis on human authenticity.

Theist analysis adds nothing to an adequate analysis of the human within the philosophic viewpoint except the acknowledgment that the human is created. Theism has already made its profound yet limited specific contribution when it bows before the Ultimate that metaphysically explains all. The inspirational power of theist religion is not particularly attached to belief in the true God. This inspirational power is not even necessarily a function of human authenticity. This power is rather attributable to the common psychological-sociological mechanisms operative in any profound symbolism and ritual, and the whole issue is properly studied by human sciences within the positivist viewpoint. That in theism this symbolism and ritual are structured around belief in the transcendent God of the Universe is a plus—for then it is likely to foster human authenticity—but the belief in God is not the telling issue.

The conclusion regarding spiritual development follows obviously. Religious inspiration plays an important role in furthering spiritual development. But belief in the existence and action of the Creator adds no practical content to an understanding of religion's inspirational power. Therefore, even from the point of view of personal inspiration, belief in God adds nothing practical to, and changes nothing theoretical in, an adequate psychological account of spiritual development. This statement needs no qualification insofar as the religion in question is authentic. For such religion adequately expresses the human dynamism toward the true and the good and moves its adherents along the path of authenticity. That path is fully open to the God of the Universe, the Creator, conceived as the Fullness of Truth and Goodness. As best as is humanly possible, that path represents the will of God. And unless one presumes miraculous intervention—which would still need to be subject to responsible human judgment and so still implicate human authenticity as its ultimate practical criterion—there is no other human way to know God's will. Adding to this state of affairs even firm and true belief in the God of the Universe would change nothing. All this is so whether the religion is theist or not, as long as it is humanly authentic.

So theism is not the telling issue when one would explain the inspirational power of religion. Likewise, theism is not the telling issue when one would explain religion's inspirational role in furthering spiritual development. Certainly, belief in God plays an important role in structuring religious symbolism and ritual that actually promote human authenticity. Certainly, too, the resultant inspirational power of theist religion plays an important role in the spiritual development of those who believe in God. Still, it remains true that appeal to God adds no practical content to an adequate psychological account of spiritual development.

Prayer to God and Miracles

Another important aspect of theist religion is prayer. "Prayer" is a specifically theist conception. It refers to devotional practices of one kind or another that relate the believer to God. Similar practices occur in non-theist religions. Meditation or sitting practice in Tibetan or Zen Buddhism are clear examples. But there these practices are not called prayer, and they are not thought to relate one to God.

Prayer is an appropriate topic here because in a concrete way it raises the issue of the natural unfolding of world process and the possible miraculous intervention of God. For popular piety holds that prayer to God is useful for gaining desired ends. "More is wrought by prayer than the world imagines," it has been said.[1] The implication is often taken to be that prayer influences God to grant petitions. If this is so, at least to some extent world process is controlled by God at the request of fervent believers. Then belief in God makes a significant difference to world process and, of course, to one's own spiritual development. For if one believes in God and prays fervently, one could further one's spiritual growth through the direct intervention granted by God in response to prayer. Thus, theist faith would appear to be an important practical addition to any psychological account of spiritual development. But one could argue otherwise.

It has already been noted that there is no time in God. All is eternally present. The argument was that if there were time in God, the difference between past and future would represent some change. The change would need to be accounted for by something other than God. Then that something other, which provides ultimate explanation, would by definition itself be God, and the original discussion would not have been about God at all. God does not change.

One might claim that in the case of God the change is self-explanatory; but the intelligent demand for adequate explanation balks at such tautology. To insist that precisely in the case of God this is not tautology simply because God's very essence is to change is merely to obscure the fallacy in a cloud of unthinking. Since we do not understand what God is but can speak of God only analogously, any reasonable talk of God must conform itself to the analogue, dynamic human spirit and the demands of its unfolding: attentiveness, intelligence, reasonableness, and responsibility. To ignore these canons is to disqualify the argument by excluding it from the realm of reasonable discourse. The product of such argument, like good fiction, might be inspiring, but it could not be taken as true. The argument of process theology for a developing God is fraught with self-contradiction.[2]

Since God is in fact more concerned about us than we can imagine, the desire of process theology to make God more relevant is a laudable one. But doing so by suggesting that God is so involved with us that God emotes and changes as the world does eliminates the primary contribution theism has to make—to lead people to ever further self-transcending authenticity in the face of the Ultimate Transcendent. The notion of a developing God undercuts the very thrust toward human authenticity, for in its Ultimate Principle it rejects the need for reasonable account. It provides no absolute norm against which all else must be measured. Its only absolute is variation itself. So its every possible norm, including God, varies as history does; and how can one say what is for better or worse?

131

God does not change. This does not mean that God has no concern for us or that God does not care for us. The treatment of Providence above already gave an account of the unchanging God's care for us. That God does not change means only that God's relation to created reality is unlike anything else we can name. This relation is not, for that reason, unreal;[3] it is merely beyond our full comprehension. It is too much for us to grasp. More than simply being concerned about us and precisely because of divine immanence-transcendence, God's care for our good exceeds our wildest imagination.

If God does not change, it is mistaken to think that prayer changes God's action in the world. This is not to say that prayer has no effect. As has often been noted, prayer has its effect not by changing God but by changing us, who pray. Of course, the presupposition of that insight is that one has a more or less adequate notion of God. If one's "God" is merely a projection of one's own self, prayer will only confirm one in one's present situation and will change nothing, especially not oneself. But genuine prayer changes us, not God.

As the Fullness of Truth and Goodness, God is the ultimate goal of the human spiritual thrust toward the true and the good. By opening ourselves to the transcendent God in prayer, we open ourselves to the demand for unending self-transcendence. Through prayer and because of this openness, in increasing authenticity we move beyond our narrow selves to the affirmation of all that is true and to the embrace of all that is good, as best we know it. Then we cannot but more surely be following the will of God as we are increasingly able to discern what is right and good in our daily living. The effect of prayer is to change us, to make us more authentic.

This growth in personal authenticity through prayer is not merely a personal affair. On the contrary, it is cosmic. Because through prayer we are different, the universe of which we are a part is also different. Insofar as we are better rather than worse people, we are more open to the good, which God has built into the universe as its ultimate goal. So in us the ultimate goal of the universe is more intensely at work than it would otherwise be. Moreover, our free decisions for the good, a result of our prayer, release into the universe a flood of contingent influences that really affect the universe and that are in flow with the ultimate movement of the universe as God wills it. These influences, which would not *be* apart from us, God eternally takes into account in divine governance of the universe through Providence. So it is true that, without changing God nor apart from God, our prayer influences the process of history by changing us for the better.

Note, however, that the authenticity of the human agents is the presupposition of the human influence for good in the universe. Once again, not belief in God but human authenticity is the key factor for a practical account of a spirituality question.

It follows that this account holds equally well for theists as for non-theists, provided these are authentic human beings. Whether one can be authentically human—attentive, intelligent, reasonable, and responsible—without believing in God may be debatable; but to win the argument the negative would have to discredit the goodness and the good will of the greater portion of the human race, non-theist but also not atheist nor irreligious. There is no reason to believe that theist believers are any better people, any more authentic, than their non-theist counterparts.

Moreover, even on theoretical grounds, this account must hold also for non-theists. If God exists and if God is operative, as the present account suggests, through creation, conservation, and concurrence in every human's life whether the person in question believes in God or not; then, insofar as even a non-theist is authentic, that one, unknowingly yet as best as is humanly possible, is in harmony with the will of God as it operates in the concrete universe. This is not to suggest that, despite all protestations, this person really believes in God or that this person is an "anonymous theist."[4] It is merely to insist that within the theist viewpoint, insofar as one wants to give a coherent explanation of the matter, the present conclusion must follow. Then this non-theist's spiritual practice—like meditation in Zen Buddhism—though not correctly called prayer, is nonetheless substantively identical with what theists call prayer and has the same practical effects as does the theist's prayer.[5] Belief in God is not a significant practical issue here.

It will be useful briefly to consider two other topics often related to prayer. First, it is said that prayer brings us "closer" to God. This statement is obviously a metaphor. The account just given explains what that metaphor means. Prayer makes us more authentic and so more surely directed by God's will and more freely cooperative with

God's creative power. Note well that there is no suggestion of "sharing more deeply in God's life" or of any other such notion here. Such notions are Christian, not theist. They do not belong in the present context. Theism does not envisage participation in divine life; it merely acknowledges "God" as Creator of human life.

Then there is the question of miracles. By miracles I mean direct divine interventions that change, reverse, circumvent, or in some other way disrupt the natural order of world process. Throughout, insistence has been on explaining world process without appeal to the miraculous. This is not to deny the possibility of miracles. The God who created the universe could certainly alter any or all of it. However, I do not believe that true miracles occur frequently, if at all; and I especially do not believe that one should expect miracles. God created the universe with sufficient wisdom that God can achieve the divine purpose without interference in the natural order of things; the universe is already sufficiently directed toward the good by God's ordinary Providence. Of course, to the extent that true miracles do occur and as a result of prayer, the present account needs to be supplemented. For then explicit theist faith can make a direct and practical change in world process and so in spiritual development.

This opinion about miracles is not intended to deny that extraordinary events do occur. Cases of telepathy, precognition, distant viewing, and psychokinesis, as well as the occurrence of psychic or faith healing, have all been scientifically verified.[6] Such things do occur. In fact, research suggests they probably occur more often and more easily than most people suppose.[7] But for this very reason, one should not call these occurrences true miracles. Rather, they result from the effective use of powers that many and probably all humans have, powers that in our day are generally neglected and even suppressed. This is to say, the capacity to effect such "extraordinary" occurrences is part and parcel of the universe as God created it. That these powers are not yet understood nor easily accommodated within our present scientific account of the universe does not mean that they are "supernatural." Then, if these powers are but natural, there is no need to invoke special divine intervention to explain unusual occurrences. They are not miracles in the strict sense of the term.

This understanding allows a connection between prayer and extraordinary occurrences. The link is not prayer's supposed ability to enlist divine power to effect its request. The link is rather prayer's enhancement of human authenticity. Insofar as increasing authenticity makes a person ever more fully all that he or she can be, that person would likely also be more open to accepting, and more skilled in using, the full range of human powers, including capacity to effect psi phenomena. The teaching of some religious traditions affirms this supposition.[8] Nonetheless, it is well known that some people are born with extraordinary psychic gifts and these have nothing to do with spiritual development. One must recall that in addition to "white magic" there is also "black magic." These issues are real, but they are also hardly at all understood. Accordingly, this topic can receive no further treatment here. Besides, as noted in Chapter 2, preoccupation with psi phenomena obscures the centrality of what is essential to spiritual development, human authenticity.

These considerations about prayer as another practical function of theism further illustrate the major point here. Insofar as theism's specific contribution is but to acknowledge the Creator of the universe, personal belief in God makes no practical addition to an understanding of spiritual development. Apart from possible but unlikely miraculous intervention, the God acknowledged as Creator operates through the built-in mechanisms that explain the functioning of the universe, including the free activity of human beings. So an account of these mechanisms already provides an adequate account as far as practicality is concerned. Whether or not one acknowledges God, God is operative in the universe. So explicit acknowledgment of that divine factor makes no practical difference.

The Forgiveness of Sin

A third practical religious theme specific to theism is the forgiveness of sin. Within theism people's deliberate wrongdoings are recognized to relate not only to humanity and its intrinsic demand for responsible living but also to God, the source of that humanity and the goal to which the authentic unfolding of humanity points. So what within the philosophic viewpoint is deliberate wrongdoing, unauthenticity, is named sin within the theist viewpoint. In adding the further understanding that human wrongdoing has reference also to the Creator, theism conceives a possibility not available within the philosophic viewpoint—the forgiveness of sin. By the same token, belief in God then appears to introduce an important practical advantage that the human sciences, even when conceived within the philosophic viewpoint, do not offer. But again, one could argue otherwise.

What does it mean to say that God forgives sin? Certainly the anthropomorphic metaphors generally used to speak of God's forgiveness must not be taken literally. Forgiveness does not mean that God relents in anger and now smiles again on us—simply because God has no feelings and no face. Nor does forgiveness mean that now God relates benevolently again toward us whereas before God was hostile. Such conceptions imply change in God, but God does not change.

Still, if forgiveness is real, it must make a difference. There must be a change somewhere. Since there is no change in God, the change must be in us. What is that change that forgiveness of sin entails?

Certainly, that God forgives does not mean that God undoes our sinful acts or their effects. History cannot be reversed. What has occurred has occurred and stands as fact forever. The natural consequences of our acts perdure and have their ripple effect in world process. Obliteration from history of the act of sin and its consequences is not the change that forgiveness of sin entails.

Nonetheless, forgiveness of sin does mean in part that God deals benevolently with our sin and its effects. God takes sin into account in the eternal divine plan and in Providence neutralizes the noxious effects of sin. This is not to suggest that whether we sin or not is irrelevant since good will prevail in any case. For though good will prevail, the course of history and the shape of its outcome, known and willed eternally by God, do depend on human involvement. To a significant and ever increasing degree, human agents freely determine the unfolding of world process.

Moreover, the neutralization of evil is not without a price. Those who do good in the face of evil pay that price, for sin and its effects often demand a martyr's death before they are undone. The prophetic tradition in Israel, the life of Jesus, and the case of contemporary martyrs—Mahatma Ghandi, John and Robert Kennedy, Martin Luther King, Anwar Sadat, Oscar Romero, and other unknown millions who die because of human injustice—bear witness here.

The change that forgiveness of sin entails is still to be pinpointed. That change appears to be the undoing of the unauthenticity that human wrongdoing introduces into human beings themselves. It seems to be the actual reversal of unauthenticity, which the human agents effected in themselves by their own unworthy decisions.

Recall that our decisions affect us as much and more than they affect the outside world. We make ourselves be what we will be as a function of every decision of every day. Human being is becoming. Humans are self-constituting beings.

When we act responsibly, we make ourselves responsible. We confirm and enhance the very structures of our human spirit that intrinsically call for responsibility. On the other hand, when we act irresponsibly, we ourselves become irresponsible. We dull and blunt the very urgency of our own intrinsic drive toward authenticity. Habits of irresponsibility make irresponsibility easy; responsible behavior becomes more and more difficult, more and more unlikely. With the dulling of the need to be responsible, in one way or another there follows the dulling also of our intrinsic spiritual dynamism on all its other levels. One is only selectively attentive, selectively insightful, selectively reasonable. This selectivity serves to maintain at least a pretense of the consistency that the human spirit demands. Biases are confirmed.[9] Rationalization becomes ingrained. A most remarkable phenomenon! The human being is capable of misusing the intrinsic human spiritual capacities to short-circuit these very capacities. One can, for example, use one's intelligence to rationalize effectively, but by so doing one deprives oneself precisely of the possibility of ever understanding completely—for one does not want to admit all that is really happening! Intelligence subverts intelligence. Through embraced bias and winked-at rationalization, one becomes insensitive to the full range of insistence of the transcendental precepts operative within oneself.

Granted this state of affairs, it is not to be expected that a reversal will occur. The cumulative self-mutilation of unauthenticity debilitates the very capacity needed to effect such a reversal. When one has deliberately dethroned one's delight in the good in order to honor one's pleasure in mere satisfaction, it does not seem possible that this very same agent, now oblivious to the good, would again exult the good as supreme. Having once jumped down, we cannot pull ourselves up by our bootstraps.

Nonetheless, and even more remarkably, we routinely catch ourselves at our rationalizations, admit our mistakes, and change our ways. Oftentimes the very forces of the universe seem to conspire against us to call us up short. At other times the very calm of ill-won complacency provides an opening for the prick of conscience. Howsoever it occurs, the internal phenomenon is the same: we repent and begin on a new path. This happens routinely, so one could argue that such conversion is simply part of being human. Acknowledging the facts of the case, one would have to agree that it is so. But as the present analysis demonstrates, it need not be so and perhaps it even ought not be so; it only happens to be so.

From the theist viewpoint, what happens to be so is so because God made it so. The rather routine human reversals that restore authenticity in the self-debilitated agent is the work of God. Now, what from the philosophic viewpoint is human unauthenticity is from the theist viewpoint nothing other than sin. And the reversal of human unauthenticity that appears to be part of the routine order of the universe is none other than God's forgiveness of sin. The change that forgiveness of sin entails is precisely the restoration of authenticity in the self-debilitated subject. In question here is the phenomenon treated in medieval theology under the topic of *gratia sanans*, healing or medicinal grace.[10] The Christian would insist that such healing is possible only because of Christ's redemptive work. But apart from belief in Christ and to one who believes only in the Creator-God, the possibility of this restoration appears to be built into the structure of the universe, so each occurrence of such restoration must be the work of God, the Creator. Yet, if forgiveness of sin is the work of God, an account of it requires appeal to no special intervention on the part of God and certainly to no change in God. The Creator works through natural causes. The change is in the human agent.

Why does the change occur in some cases and not in others, why here more readily and there only after long delay? A general answer to the question is contained in the treatment on Providence and human freedom given above. A specific answer in each concrete case would require an analysis of each separate case, and even then a conclusion could not be drawn. For the change in question is a free choice, and no general law can explain free choices: if free choices could be deduced, they would be necessary, not free.

The change in question is a free choice. It is the return to authenticity from former unauthenticity. It is a self-made change within the human subject him- or herself. It is a restoration through human free choice of the very structures of human authenticity, including free choice, debilitated by human free choice. In the three senses of the term—creation, conservation, and concurrence—God is the Creator of those structures, so this change is a work of God. Still, this change cannot occur apart from the human agent, for its very essence is the agent's willing cooperation with the structures of his or her own being and so, by implication if not by explicit faith, his or her willing cooperation with God, the Creator. A work of God in the ever free human agent, precisely this change is the forgiveness of sin.

It is mistaken, then, to imagine that first we repent and ask God's forgiveness and then God forgives us in return. For our very repentance is already God's forgiveness; our repentance is the very undoing of the effect of our sin in us. Theist faith allows the marvel of forgiveness to be ritualized. But the ritual of prayer for forgiveness does not induce God to forgive. Its function is more humble than that. It simply acknowledges humanity's utter dependence on God, praises God's love at work among us always, and celebrates and confirms the change of heart already effected through God's forgiveness.

On this analysis forgiveness of sin is not something available only to those who believe in God and ask for it. If it were, forgiveness would depend on human request and not on God's love. Rather, forgiveness of sin is an ever available expression of God's constant love for humankind; it is built into the design of the universe, determined by the Creator. Though only within theism can forgiveness of sin be thematized, belief in God does not make forgiveness of sin more available or more effective. Though awareness of God should make believers better people, more open to God's gracious forgiveness, there is little evidence to suggest that this is the case. Once again, the conclusion must be drawn. While belief in God allows an explanation of forgiveness of sin, an adequate understanding of forgiveness of sin suggests that belief in God makes no practical difference in obtaining this gift of God. Authenticity, not belief in God, is the key factor.

Conclusion

This chapter has discussed three themes central to theist piety: the inspirational power of religion, prayer, and the forgiveness of sin. In each case the conclusion was the same. Though theism may usefully highlight certain otherwise neglected issues, belief in God makes no practical difference in following the path of one's spiritual development, and the introduction of these religious issues requires no change in the account of spiritual development already given.

This is not to say that theism makes no contribution to an understanding of spiritual development. But that contribution is theoretical. It adds a broader dimension of understanding to the phenomenon in question by acknowledging the Creator of that phenomenon. This acknowledgment may also have a practical effect insofar as an understanding of God, the Ultimate Transcendent, clarifies the goal of the human dynamism toward authentic self-transcendence and so may foster growth toward that goal. However, an adequate understanding of theism is so little a part of most theist religion as practiced that even attainment of this possible practical effect is usually frustrated. Rather than foster growth in human authenticity, popular "belief in God" often hampers that growth by proposing a picture of God that resembles Santa Claus or the Fairy Godmother. Then faith becomes a shield from the responsibilities of life, and childish believers look for magical solutions to life's problems rather than accept them as God-given challenges that they themselves can meet.[11] Since this is the unfortunate case and since the topic here is precisely spiritual growth, in an attempt to counter false understandings, this chapter has insisted repeatedly on what theism is not.

The distinctive contribution of theism is in the realm of theory. Belief in God allows a more comprehensive explanation than is possible within the philosophic viewpoint. But the practical implications of theism make no significant addition to an adequate psychological account of spiritual development. Moreover, from whatever perspective, practical or theoretical, theism certainly changes nothing in such a psychological account.

Notes

Chapter Six

The Practical Implications of Theism

1. Alfred Tennyson, *The Idylls of the King. The Death of Arthur.*
2. Cousins, *Process Theology;* Pittenger, *Catholic Faith.*
3. Lonergan, *De Deo Trino,* 291-315.
4. Rahner, "Anonymous Christians."
5. Helminiak, "How is Meditation Prayer?"
6. Tart, *Transpersonal Psychologies,* 113-151.
7. Targ and Harary, *Mind Race.*
8. Tart, *Transpersonal Psychologies.*
9. Lonergan, *Insight,* 191-206, 218-242.
10. Fortman, *Man and Grace,* 193-194; Rondet, *Grace of Christ, passim.*
11. Bonhoeffer, *Letters and Papers.*

Growth in Holiness and Spiritual Development

Holiness is another specifically theist notion. It is a central issue in spirituality. Moreover, talk of "growth in holiness" raises the question, How does growth in holiness relate to spiritual development? Are the stages of spiritual development also stages of growth in holiness? So a treatment of holiness is essential to the present study.

The Notion of Holiness

Rudolf Otto's *The Idea of the Holy* is the classic study on holiness. In one way or another Otto's idea of the holy as the *mysterium tremendum et fascinans* colors almost every presentation on the topic.[1] Otto's work is a phenomenology of religion. It examines in detail the human experience of the numinous. Otto argues that as history progresses rational/ethical elements are integrated into the understanding of what was originally fearful and threatening; eventually the numinous is known to be God. Discernment within this process occurs because of some supposed *a priori* category of the human mind: "the mental predisposition necessary for the experience of holiness, to wit, the category of the holy,"[2] "the faculty of *divination*."[3] Otto's whole exposition rests on the *a priori* possibility for human experience of the holy as such; and the existence of the holy as a reality in itself is similarly confirmed by its being experienced. Those who experience it will know that they have. No further criteria can be given.

Otto's approach obviously differs significantly from the one followed here. Here the notion of holiness is introduced only after an extensive treatment of theism. Further, theism itself is introduced only as a possible, if reasonable, elaboration of the experience of the dynamism of the human spirit. The dynamism of the human spirit toward authentic self-transcendence and the transcendental precepts this dynamism entails—Be attentive, Be intelligent, Be reasonable, Be responsible—provide the ultimate basis and criteria for all subsequent assertions. The claim is that this principle of authentic self-transcendence is intrinsic to the human, so here, too, some *a priori* structures are in question. Yet these are open to verification in one's personal experience and are absolutely content-free. Unlike their Kantian counterparts, which Otto imitates, they do not predetermine what reality must be; rather, they are open to discover whatever reality really is.[4]

The danger in the Kantian position is extreme. By means of a historical survey Otto does come to integrate the rational into the notion of the holy. But this survey gratuitously presupposes theism and Christianity; there is nothing in the theory that demands integration of the rational. If so moved, one could claim that what had imposed itself upon oneself with "numinous" force was indeed the numinous, the holy, God. And using only Otto's explicit criteria, no one else could gainsay it. Rather than being a study of something on the side of the object, the holy, Otto's work is really a study of subjective phenomena, "religious experiences," in the broadest possible connotation of the term.[5] Otto's presentation presents the real danger of confusing the spiritual with the parapsychological—as does Assagioli's[6]—or even with the psychotic. At best, that presentation lacks precision of language and conception. One might claim, "The hush that nature brings to our turmoil, the invitation to stop pushing or analyzing and commune, is the beckoning finger of the holy."[7] But one could not cogently maintain that one had really *experienced God;* one might have experienced merely the effects of alcohol, marijuana, or some other drug.[8] Even Otto sees the need somehow to distinguish between the numinous as daemonic and as holy.[9] Indeed, limited to the theist viewpoint and apart from Christian or some such similar presuppositions, one cannot cogently claim an experience of God except as an extraordinary divine intervention, and even then one would need clear criteria to make the case. Accordingly, Otto's study of the holy is not necessarily a study about God as understood here and so is not very relevant to the present question.

Definition of Holiness

Here the term "holiness" receives a technical meaning; it is a strictly theist concept. In one way or another holiness has reference to God. Otto agrees with this most prevalent usage: "It is then to God and Deity, as 'numen' rendered absolute, that the attribute denoted by the terms *qādôsh, sanctus,* ἅγιος, holy, pertains, in the first and directest sense of the words."[10] Such usage is fully in accord with the Jewish Testament. Furthermore, according to this same Jewish usage, the rational—specifically, the ethical—is integral to the notion of holiness. If the earliest usage links holiness merely with cult and ritual purity, every major tradition of the Jewish Bible as we know it relates holiness with ethical demands.[11]

According to the Bible, holiness is properly the quality of God. Etymologically the word implies being set apart, separated. God is like no other. God alone is holy. This is so much the case that in Hebrew vocabulary "holy" could mean "divine." By association anything that pertains to God is called holy—the places where God appeared, the sanctuary where God dwells, the instruments used in worship, the priests dedicated to God's service.

Most importantly, once Israel is chosen and bound by covenant to Yahweh, Israel, too, is holy, Yahweh's holy people. "For you are a people holy to the Lord your God; the Lord your God has chosen you to be a people for his own possession, out of all the peoples that are on the face of the earth."[12] The holiness of this people brought with it the responsibility not only to worship Yahweh and Yahweh alone but also to live according to the commandments of Yahweh. In this way all would know that Israel was Yahweh's people, set apart from all the rest, holy. In the Mosaic tradition the ethical implication of being

145

God's holy people is obvious in the conferring of the Decalogue.

Beyond all others the Prophetic tradition insists on the ethical content of holiness, calling Israel to task for its neglect of social justice. Experiencing God as the "Holy, Holy, Holy," Isaiah recognized himself as guilty and sinful, part of a sinful people. Once cleansed, he himself can be called holy because "in his prophetic role he stands in direct contact with God."[13] Isaiah characterized Yahweh as "The Holy One of Israel" who would bring judgment on his people and later, according to Deutero-Isaiah, salvation. Likewise, the prophet Micah, speaking for Yahweh, rejected mere ritual purity: "He has showed you, O man, what is good; and what does the Lord require of you but to do justice, and to love kindness, and to walk humbly with your God?"[14]

Finally, the priestly tradition, which re-edited the Jewish texts, emphasizing cult and ritual, could nonetheless hardly ignore the prophetic insistence on true justice and righteousness. So the Leviticus injunction, "You shall be holy; for I the Lord your God am holy," continued the demand for personal holiness in addition to ritual purity. "These words are now applied to every facet of Israel's existence, but wherever men are involved with each other holiness means love—love to neighbor, to the resident alien, the blind, the deaf, and the slave."[15]

According to the Jewish Testament, one is holy because one is related to God, one is like God. That is to say, the holy one is the one who does God's will, who is faithful to what God desires, who "walks humbly with God." This is the meaning of holiness in this essay.

Holiness as Authenticity Before God

The two preceding chapters spelled out the implications of theism for certain issues related to spirituality. Theoretically, belief in God adds a further dimension of meaning to even an adequate psychological account of spiritual issues. Theism relates to God as Creator whatever psychology and other human sciences come to understand about the human situation. Practically, belief in God adds nothing to what an adequate human-science account can give. The substance of whatever phenomenon in question does not change when one begins to believe in God, for God is active as Creator whether acknowledged by humans or not. These insights also apply to holiness.

Within a theist viewpoint one speaks of walking with God, following God's call, doing God's will, remaining close to God. One who acts in this way would be holy. From a merely philosophic viewpoint these same activities would be named doing what is right, being committed to the good, living honestly and justly. In brief, and using the technical terminology developed above, one who acts this way would be an authentic person. The substance of human authenticity and human holiness does not differ. Holiness and all that it implies is nothing other than authenticity recognized by theist believers as having reference to God. In this sense holiness is the opposite of sin. Deliberate wrongdoing is to sin as authenticity is to holiness.

Though authenticity may be defined on the basis of structures intrinsic to the human, the theist recognizes that these very structures are God's creation. So whoever lives authentically, in accord with these structures, is living in harmony with God and in every free act is cooperating with God in achieving the goal of the universe. Within a theist context, such a one can rightly be called holy. An explanatory account suggests there is nothing more to the matter.

This conclusion presumes a differential analysis of the issue. One and the same phenomenon is analyzed and named according to different technically defined and interrelated sets of presuppositions. From the philosophic viewpoint the phenomenon in question is human *authenticity,* human integrity, lived human commitment to the true and the good. This same phenomenon conceived within the theist viewpoint is called *holiness* because concretely authenticity is God's will for humans and so orients human beings toward God.

Holiness as relationship with God is often conceived in terms of "union with God." This metaphor calls for clarification. Insofar as holiness is conceived only within the theist viewpoint, there is no suggestion of additional "union with God" over and above that between Creator and the responsive free creature. Within the theist viewpoint all must be conceived only within terms of creation. Though a spiritual factor intrinsic to humanity allows humans to relate to God in a way that other creatures cannot—namely, through free self-determination—the relationship is nonetheless merely the actualization of what is given in creation itself and what is proportionate to the human as such. The "union" is simply human cooperation with the divine plan for the universe. The relationship is merely one between Creator and creature and nothing more.

Explicit acknowledgment of this relationship in true lived theism—which is rare—adds only a higher degree of being[16] to the relationship: the relationship of creature to Creator is now not only given but also understood, known, and freely embraced for what it is. As such, the relationship with the Creator in theism can be said to be more human, for it is proper to humans not only to experience but also to correctly understand and freely to affirm what they experience. It is proper to humans not only to live life but also to correctly understand and to freely accept the life they live. Since theism entails knowledge and acceptance of humanity's relationship to the Creator, granted that the Creator really exists, in acknowledging God the theist lives life more humanly—that is, intelligently, reasonably, and responsibly—than the non-theist. This is true, of course, only from the limited point of view under consideration here.

Yet the substance of the relationship between the Creator and the human, whether acknowledged or not, is the same. Over and above living human life—and so necessarily an implicit relationship with the Creator—authentically, explicitly recognizing the relationship as holiness adds nothing to the human authenticity that is the essence of that relationship; and explicitly recognizing the relationship as holiness changes nothing in the essence of that relationship. Authenticity is the sum and substance of the proper relationship between the Creator and the created human being. Further intensification of the human authenticity *may* result from theism, but no further "union with God" is in question here.

However, within the Christian viewpoint one can speak of some further "union." This further possibility explains the need for clarifying this issue. For Christian belief insists that, over and above what is proper to humans as created intellectual beings, through the saving work of Jesus Christ and the gift of the Holy Spirit the very life of the Heavenly Father is given to humans. Then, because of the Indwelling of the Trinity, one can speak of a new basis for human union with God, and the very substance of holiness changes. What before was merely human authenticity orienting one toward the Creator-God is now seen to be some actual sharing in the very life of the Trinitarian Family. What is now at stake in some sense is participation in divinity. Now one speaks not of human holiness but of human *divinization*. A new term is needed to name this new reality and conception. This further issue will be the topic in Part III. However, it is necessary to anticipate that analysis here so that the meaning of holiness will be clear. When the theist and Christian viewpoints are not clearly distinguished, factors specific to the Christian are too easily imported into the theist. Only confusion results.

Pious Inflation: Seeking "More" in the Name of Holiness

Holiness is nothing other than human authenticity recognized as related also to God. Naming it differently and conceiving it more or less adequately does not change the reality. (Even when understood within the Christian viewpoint as divinization, the criteria of human authenticity still remain the only practical criteria available for determining and fostering this reality.) Yet, popular piety insists that there is something more to holiness than being an authentic human being. Consideration of two examples will clarify this issue.

When is the appropriate time for a person to seek spiritual direction? These are suggested criteria: "Has the person made, or does the person want to make a decision to surrender to the Lord? Not just to become a self-actualized person. Not just to serve others. Spiritual direction implies at least the desire to reach beyond merely human or ethical growth to genuine religious growth."[17] The suggestion here is that "surrender to the Lord" and "genuine religious growth" are something more than "human or ethical growth" and service to others. Theoretically the suggestion is accurate, but practically it is misleading. What more is there to surrendering to the Lord than being the best person one can be, a self-actualized person, and growing as best one can as an ethical person, concerned for others as for oneself? Granted, insofar as one might understand spiritual direction to be strictly at the service of religious—that is, at least theist—commitment, then one really should not seek spiritual direction before making "the fundamental religious act."[18] But once this commitment is made, how does such "surrender to the Lord" express itself if not through one's daily activities in life? How does one evaluate one's religious commitment if not by one's human and ethical growth? In practice any realistic concern for the spiritual must come back to the human or become obscurantist. Chapter 6 already dealt with prayer and religious inspiration, those phenomena usually singled out as specific foci of spiritual direction. In practice they, too, must be judged against the same criteria of human authenticity. To suggest that talk of God and religion introduces some practical "more" results in mystification, at best, and at worst actually distracts from the real issues of authentic spirituality.

The second example deals with discernment of spirits, the religious name for the process of making responsible decisions. Supposedly, the concern of discernment is "not simply to distinguish good from evil, or the better from the good, or even the most suitable course for me that human wisdom can select. The object is *to do God's will*."[19] If the intent of this rhetoric is merely to insist that in a theist context everything must be referred to God, all well and good. But the intent seems to be something else. The suggestion could not be that God's will may be something other than the good, for this suggestion is ludicrous. Then the suggestion must concern the human discovery of God's will. Yet even in this case the statement makes no practical sense. If God's will for humans is something other than what can be humanly determined as the good to be done in this particular case, why even talk about God's will? It is nothing accessible to human beings. Granted, one may be mistaken even in the best intentioned attempt to make a responsible decision in some particular situation. Then one's decision could not rightly be called God's will. But this theoretical clarification has no practical relevance for the person of good will, religious or not. One is still left to determine as best one can what ought to be done. When the determination is made, one can still only say that as best as one knows, one has determined God's will. Nothing more is possible, so nothing more can be expected. Unless one has access to the divine mind through means other than what is given mediately in the created order of the universe, in practice talk of God's will is merely a theist way of speaking about the authentically human. Only a case of miraculous intervention would be an exception, and it, too, would need be subject to a process of discernment in light of available human criteria. There is no "God's eye view" of things available to human beings. There is no human knowledge apart from a human agent, and the accuracy of the human agent is specified by the criterion of human authenticity.[20]

Belief in God adds nothing more to human life than a dimension of faith that situates life in a broader context. Holiness is nothing other than human authenticity before God. Expecting to find something "more" because one is concerned for holiness, and not "mere" human goodness, is to misunderstand theism and to distort one's appreciation of life in general.

Growth in Holiness and Spiritual Development

Holiness is nothing other than human authenticity viewed from the theist viewpoint. So growth in holiness can be understood as growth in authenticity.

If authenticity is defined by the transcendental precepts—Be attentive, Be intelligent, Be reasonable, Be responsible—it can grow insofar as one becomes more faithful to those precepts.

> Human authenticity is not some pure quality, some serene freedom from all oversights, all misunderstanding, all mistakes, all sins. Rather it consists in a withdrawal from unauthenticity, and the withdrawal is never a permanent achievement. It is ever precarious, ever to be achieved afresh, ever in great part a matter of uncovering still more oversights, acknowledging still further failures to understand, correcting still more mistakes, repenting more and more deeply of hidden sins.[21]

One can grow in authenticity. Yet the sum and substance of authenticity remain constant. Insofar as the four levels of consciousness[22] remain constant and the transcendental precepts, which express the dynamism of consciousness on those four levels, remain constant, so does the essence of authenticity also remain constant. Accordingly, one would not accurately speak of the development of authenticity, at least not in the same sense in which we have spoken of human development or spiritual development. Authenticity does not pass through stages; its meaning remains constant across all the stages of human development. Authenticity is an intensive quality. It corresponds to what Loevinger calls polar variables.[23]

Then holiness, too, is an intensive quality. It does not allow of

151

stages. So degrees of holiness and stages of spiritual development are not the same thing. They differ from one another both in reality and in conception. This is clear insofar as the term spiritual development, wholly within the philosophic viewpoint, has been used to refer to a set sequence of stages in the developing human being; whereas holiness, conceived within the theist viewpoint, is the authenticity of the human being in question at any stage of spiritual development.

The difference and the relationship between holiness and spiritual development, and the various possible combinations of the two, give rise to several important considerations.

First, that one passes through all the stages of spiritual development does not necessarily mean that one is intensely holy, a saint. It merely means that one is quite healthy psychologically. Holiness and psychological wholeness are not absolute correlates. Still, I have argued that the intrinsic human dynamism toward authentic self-transcendence is indispensable to explain people's movement through the upper stages of human development.[24] One would not move into the Conscientious Stage and real spiritual development apart from some response to that inner dynamism, some authenticity, some degree of holiness. Yet in every case holiness need not be profound. Though one will not develop spiritually without holiness, reaching the Cosmic Stage of spiritual development does not necessarily mean that one is a saint.

Second, the contrary is also true. One may be profoundly holy without ever achieving full spiritual development. The intensity of a person's authenticity at any stage is the gauge of holiness, and not the stage itself. Here, then, there is no suggestion that only the "beautiful people" are holy, only those completely psychologically integrated.

Third, the anomaly in those two points requires discussion. Evidently, it is possible to be a "neurotic" and still a saint. The case of Blessed Pierre de Luxembourg (1368-1387 C.E.) suggests as much.

> This descendant of the royal house of Luxembourg and relative of the King of France and the Duke of Burgundy was clearly an example of William James' "under-witted saint," a mind so narrow it could live only in a carefully isolated sphere of devotion. Because of family connections, Pierre was made Bishop of Metz at fifteen and a cardinal soon after. At first his parents opposed his propensity for extreme asceticism, but soon they grew proud of

their little "saint." In an attempt to appreciate the peculiar witness of his life, we must picture him amid the unbridled luxury
and vice of the court—a sickly, undergrown boy, dressed in rags,
horribly dirty, and covered with vermin. He is ever occupied with
his sins and carries around with him a notebook in which he is
continually recording them. In the middle of the night, he wakes
his chaplain in order to go to confession and during the last year
of his life must always have the priest by his side should he need
to be shriven. After his death at age eighteen, an entire trunk full
of sin-slips was found! The cause for his beatification was introduced at once by two kings and the University of Paris. Only
because of the current pope's negligence was the beatification
delayed for a century and a half. Many miracles, of course, followed immediately upon Pierre's death.[25]

Here is a saint who is clearly bizarre, at least by contemporary standards.

Besides, there are many who are good people, intensely committed to what they know to be right and true, holy people, but who have
not had the benefits that modern psychology can bring—new child-
rearing practices, skill in communications and interpersonal relations, emphasis on personal integrity and individuality, professional
psychotherapy, and the rest. Or they may not have had the benefits
that education can bring. They are not bizarre like Blessed Pierre de
Luxembourg, but neither are they remarkably psychologically integrated. They live in the world as they know it, narrow by others'
standards but fully adequate as far as they can detect. They live
committed to the virtues that they learned, virtues that governed a
former age, loyal to "God and Country" with self-sacrificing dedication, never really thinking to question the *status quo*, never really
capable of extensive self-transformation. These people may be intensely holy without ever moving beyond the Conscientious Conformist Stage, without ever achieving the first true stage of spiritual
development. Such a thing is possible and needs to be acknowledged
as valid in its own right. It is possible—but it is not ideal. And since it
is not ideal, it is not to be encouraged.

It appears that the age of the eccentric saint is over. One can
hardly now be called heroic for narrow-minded insistence on some
idiosyncratic ideal of human living. As further research in the human
sciences makes a reasonable degree of psychological integration pos-

sible for more and more people, holiness demands such psychological wholeness. To ignore the benefits that ongoing human achievement makes possible is irresponsible. Irresponsibility is the antithesis of authenticity and is incompatible with holiness. So today's saint will have to pursue the quest for psychological wholeness within as well as the quest for right and justice without. Contemporary developments leave no other option.

The difference between the holiness of the "neurotic" and the holiness of the self-actualized person seems to parallel that between minor and major authenticity.

> There is the minor authenticity or unauthenticity of the subject with respect to the tradition that nourishes him [or her]. There is the major authenticity that justifies or condemns the tradition itself. In the first case there is passed a human judgment on subjects. In the second case history and, ultimately, divine providence pass judgment on traditions.[26]

Minor authenticity entails fidelity to what one has been taught— religiously, culturally, societally. To the extent that one is faithful to what one has learned, one is certainly an authentic person. One might even die for one's beliefs. But every human teaching is inadequate to some extent, and some is downright distorted and false. To the extent that one's beliefs are mistaken, through no fault of one's own, one's authenticity may be genuine, but the values to which one is committed are not. There follows a profound tragedy: "in the measure a subject takes the tradition, as it exists, for his [or her] standard, in that measure he [or she] can do no more than authentically realize unauthenticity."[27] The holiness in this case is undeniable, but the contribution to society and history is questionable. Here is the case of the martyr who unfortunately died for the wrong cause or else the case of the ascetic who unfortunately followed a warped spirituality.

On the other hand, major authenticity applies where traditions themselves are judged. Those who take it upon themselves to move beyond the narrow confines of their up-bringing, to evaluate the traditions that formed them, to reject this as aberration and retain that as genuine, these participate in increasing degree in major authenticity. They are the ones who reform and purify society, who revitalize culture, who determine the public criteria that will form a new generation. They are the ones who move beyond the Conformist Stage and into the upper stages of spiritual development. And when intense holiness coincides with advanced spiritual development, there emerges the rare great saint, the outstanding spiritual model. Such a one not only achieves profound personal holiness but also contributes significantly to the wholesome advance of history. On the cutting edge of world process, such a one becomes the locus of ready human cooperation with the Creator's plan for the universe. This is holiness in the paradigmatic sense.

Fourth, while even profound holiness may occur at any stage of human development, holiness does not express itself in the same way at every stage. The unquestioning obedience of a holy child is not appropriate for a grown man or woman. Likewise, the Conscientious Stage of spiritual development entails an enthusiasm and idealism that is not a part of the later stages. The Compassionate Stage includes a willingness to strike a compromise on certain issues. Responsible attention to conflicting moral demands may allow nothing else at this stage of development. Yet lack of willingness to compromise on basic moral principles is a key characteristic of the still later Cosmic Stage.

Holiness at any stage shows itself in the intensity of those characteristics typical of that particular stage. The one who is holy lives deeply whatever it is that he or she is living. The saint is at home with whatever he or she is called to be at that time. Holiness does not require that people develop virtues inappropriate to their age and state in life. Only a spirituality oblivious to development presents one model of holiness and expects all to follow it. Developmental theory teaches that one will achieve paradigmatic holiness, great sanctity, only by living each stage of spiritual development intently until the process of human development brings on another and only by moving in succession from one stage to the next.

Finally, there is the issue of assessing holiness. If the stages of spiritual development can be defined so that movement from one to another can be determined empirically, holiness allows of no such measurable criteria. The criteria of holiness are the criteria of authenticity—Be attentive, Be intelligent, Be reasonable, Be responsible. But these are heuristic notions. They give no concrete indication of what they entail in any particular situation. Besides, they define qualities of subjectivity, and the subject *qua* subject is not available to public observation. Who can say if someone else is being attentive or not? Even we ourselves cannot always honestly attest to the purity of our own attentiveness. Moreover, empirical indications of internal acts are difficult to assess. What might appear as outstanding achievement might really be only the half-hearted attempt of a highly gifted person, and what might appear as a niggardly attempt might really be the heroic effort of some impoverished soul. So the spiritual traditions insist that one cannot judge another's sin, that one must refrain from criticism until one has walked in another's shoes. Likewise, one cannot judge another's holiness.

Nonetheless, on the other hand, there are objective criteria of holiness—the very criteria of authenticity. And there are commonly accepted assessments of objective right and wrong. So when all evidence points to authenticity, and the effects of behavior are good, it is possible to conclude that a person is holy, especially in extraordinary cases. In less striking cases, one could perhaps more safely presume that a person is holy than presume that a person is not. Yet in the end and in all cases, only God can judge with accuracy, for only God knows the human heart. So one does not prove that someone is holy; one believes someone is holy. Like God, holiness is also an object of faith.

Summary of Part II

That a discussion of holiness conclude with God and faith is as it should be, for holiness is a theist conception. The theist believer recognizes that all things are created, so he or she sees in human authenticity reference also to God, the Creator. Insofar as one is being what one ought to be, one is not only more genuinely human but is also more surely oriented toward God, the ultimate source of one's being. One is holy.

Beyond what even the most adequate science can do, theism allows a broader understanding of reality since it places all in a metaphysical context. Theism recognizes that there must be an explanation for existence itself and names that explanation "God." God is the ultimate source of all things: creation. God maintains all things in being: conservation. And God operates in all things so that they may attain their proper ends: concurrence. Created dependence on God does not destroy human freedom but rather confirms freedom in existence.

Recognizing the marvel of God's Providence in the universe, believers extol God in religious ritual, turn to God in prayer, and thank God for the forgiveness of sin. They recognize that human goodness points toward God and is free cooperation with God, so they name human goodness "holiness." They find a sense of well-being in recognizing this deeper meaning that permeates the whole of the universe—just as others somehow also find peace in their own religious beliefs.

Belief in God makes no practical difference in the living of life as it came from the Creator. Whether one believes in God or not, God is there. Whether one prays to God or not, God is active in one's life. So to understand and deal with the practicalities of life, one turns not to theology but to the human sciences. The stages of human development that psychological research discovers are none other than the stages of spiritual development when viewed from a particular perspective. Theist believers recognize that these stages are the creation of God. God uses these very processes of human life to achieve the divine purpose for humanity and for the universe. Belief in God places these stages in a broader context of meaning, but that belief neither changes nor adds to the adequate psychological account. Within the theist viewpoint, spiritual development and its stages is nothing other than what a psychological study showed it to be.

Notes

Chapter Seven

Growth in Holiness and Spiritual Development

1. Bauer, *Encyclopedia*, 372-375; Leon-Dufour, *Dictionary*, 207-210; Richardson and Bowden, *Dictionary*, 261-262; Wakefield, *Dictionary*, 194-195.

2. Otto, *The Holy*, 160.

3. *Ibid.*, 144.

4. Sala, "A Priori in Knowledge."

5. Helminiak, "Neurology."

6. See Chapter 2.

7. Carmody and Carmody, *Religion*, 154.

8. Panke, "Drugs and Mysticism."

9. Otto, *The Holy*, 152-154.

10. *Ibid.*, 110.

11. Bauer, *Encyclopedia*, 207-210; Buttrick, *Interpreter's Dictionary*, vol. 2, 616-625; Kittel, *Theological Dictionary*, vol. 1, 88-110; Leon-Dufour, *Dictionary*, 207-210.

12. Dt. 7:6.

13. Kittel, *Theological Dictionary*, vol. 1, 93.

14. Mic. 6:8. Cf. Wakefield, *Dictionary*, 194.

15. Lev. 19:2. Cf. Buttrick, *Interpreter's Dictionary*, vol. 2, 622.

16. Lonergan, *De Constitutione Christi*, 98, 102-104, 127; Helminiak, "One in Christ," 345-346, 451-457.

17. McCarty, "Entering Spiritual Direction," 110.

18. *Ibid.*

19. Smith, "Discernment of Spirits," 441.

20. Lonergan, *Method*, 37, 292, 338.

21. *Ibid.*, 252.

22. Lonergan, *Method*, 9.

23. See Chapter 3.
24. See Chapter 4.
25. Gannon and Traub, *Desert and City,* 113.
26. Lonergan, *Method,* 80.
27. *Ibid.*

PART III

The Contribution of Christian Belief

The Possibility of Human Divinization

CHAPTER EIGHT

Human Divinization in Christ

Part I of this essay considered spiritual development as a study in psychology. Assuming the philosophic viewpoint and so presuming a spiritual component as intrinsic to the human, that part defined spiritual development as a human phenomenon and suggested its stages. Part II treated questions that arise when one presumes the existence of God. The conclusion there was that theism adds a broader understanding to the psychological account by acknowledging that the structures, mechanisms, processes, and stages of spiritual development are created by God. So when we live authentically, allowing those human processes to unfold as they ought, we are cooperating with God's purpose for the universe and are orienting ourselves and our growth toward God. Nonetheless, since the reality of God's creative activity is not dependent on human acknowledgment of it, theism makes no changes in, and no practical additions to, an adequate psychological understanding of spiritual development.

Now a further question arises: Granted the philosophic and theist contributions, what theoretical and practical differences does Christian belief make to an understanding of spiritual development?

This question presupposes that there is a cumulative movement from the philosophic to the theist and finally to the Christian understanding of things. As a religion dedicated to human authenticity, Christianity embodies whatever rightly falls within the philosophic viewpoint—like all ethical concerns and all social and ritual supports for wholesome living. As a religion that believes in "one God, the Creator of heaven and earth,"[1] Christianity also embodies whatever was said above about theism. This new question asks about any different and additional contribution that Christianity offers. This question is about the specifically Christian, the distinctively Christian. At stake here is a methodological concern. The very manner in which this further question is introduced presumes that whatever Christianity has in common with authentic humanism and with theism is already properly treated in those other theoretical contexts. At stake is a matter of having the appropriate disciplines treat their respective distinctive issues.

This question also presupposes that one asks about *authentic* Christianity. Just as any culture might inculcate values that, though structuring that society, are hardly authentically human; and just as a religion might profess belief in God but foster some form of superstition and hardly support true theist dedication to the Creator of the Universe; so many positions might go by the name Christian but hardly adhere to the heart of the matter.[2] This question presumes authentic Christianity, even as it presumes that authentic Christianity already embodies authentic humanism and authentic theism.

The query will inevitably arise, How can one maintain that the version of Christianity presented here is any more authentic than any other version? One can only respond that "authentic" is a heuristic notion. It points to what will be known when the essence of Christianity is correctly understood. Then, one could urge that there is a difference between the authentic and the unauthentic, that at least in principle the authentic can be known, and, accordingly, that the collaborative, good-willed effort to know the authentic is to be encouraged. Finally, certain conclusions are submitted here so that they may be available for criticism and so foster discussion that moves toward eventual and generally accepted correct understanding.

The Christian Viewpoint

The Christian understanding of things differs from the theist on two scores—on the reality of things and so, naturally, also on the theoretical account of things. Because Christianity believes God and the human to be somehow different from what theism proposes, Christianity offers a further understanding, an understanding not available in theism.

Notice a contrast with the contribution that theism makes. Like Christianity, theism also adds a further theoretical understanding to whatever explanation the human sciences might give. Theism notes that humankind is not only here to be understood; it is here precisely because, like all things, it is created by God. In a parallel way Christianity notes that humankind is not only here and not only created by God; in Christ in some way humankind enjoys a growing participation in divinity. So both theism and Christianity contribute a further understanding about the human reality. From a theoretical point of view, there is a similarity.

But unlike Christianity, the contribution that theism makes is only theoretical; it is a further explanation of what is already there. Theism does not presume that its acknowledgment of God as Creator implies in the human anything more than what adequate human sciences could discover. Theism adds the awareness of a new relationship in the human, the relationship of the human to the Creator; but this relationship, which only theism discloses, implies no difference in the human, no change, in comparison to what the human sciences could disclose. On the other hand, Christian belief discloses something in the human that neither the human sciences nor theism knows. Christianity discloses a further aspect of the human reality itself. This further aspect is not only a new relationship to God but also a real participation in divinity. According to Christian belief, the human reality that the human sciences and theism know is not merely human; in some way the human participates in divinity itself, and it is destined to share fully in divinity, insofar as that is possible to humanity.

So the contribution that Christianity makes is twofold. Christian belief discloses a further human reality, and so it also offers a further explanation of the human. Granted that Christian belief is correct, a comprehensive explanation of the human requires the Christian contribution in addition to the contributions of theism and the human sciences. Only within the Christian viewpoint is there a comprehensive and fully adequate account of the human. Moreover, it appears that there can be no viewpoint beyond the Christian, for fulfillment beyond divinization, which Christianity already conceives, is impossible. So analysis within the Christian viewpoint completes any study of the human. Accordingly, this section on Christianity is the final part of this book on spiritual development.

Belief in human divinization is at the core of Christianity. This belief is inextricably linked with belief in Jesus Christ as the Eternally Begotten of God who became human and in his humanity attained divine glory through his resurrection and so introduced into history a new goal for human fulfillment. Thus, in his resurrection Jesus becomes the paradigm of human divinization. Others' attainment of divinization in Christ depends on the gift of the Holy Spirit. These beliefs entail, in turn, a plurality of subjects in God—the Trinity. The advancement of the trinitarian work of human divinization further entails a community aware of, and dedicated to, this work—the Church. Thus, these four issues are inextricably united: human divinization or the doctrine of "Grace," the mystery of Christ, God as Trinity, and the Church. These distinctively Christian beliefs constitute the essence of Christianity. They determine the Christian viewpoint. The first three, different facets of one and the same phenomenon, represent Christianity's unique contribution to a complete understanding of spiritual development.

The Practical Contribution of Christianity

To say that Christianity discloses a further dimension of human reality, the process of divinization, is not to suggest that Christian belief actualizes that further dimension. That is, one need not be Christian to participate in the divine fulfillment effected by God in Christ. That is why the fourth of the core Christian mysteries, Church, is peripheral to the concerns of this book. That is also why the meaning of Church is a prime topic of contemporary theological discussion.[3] Until recently, Church was too easily conceived as the realm of the baptized graced in contradistinction to the realm of the non-baptized damned. Most mainline Christian Churches have abandoned this former understanding, and a quest for a new theology of Church is underway.

1 Timothy 2:3-5 offers some biblical support for the new under-

standing: "God our Savior. . . desires all humans to be saved. . . . For there is one God, and there is one mediator between God and human-kind, the human Christ Jesus, who gave himself as a ransom for all."[4]

The Roman Catholic teaching from the Second Vatican Council offers a clear statement from a major Christian Church:

> All this [conformity to the image of the Son through reception of the Holy Spirit and the experience of death and resurrection in Christ] holds true not for Christians only but also for all men [and women] of good will in whose hearts grace is active invisibly. For since Christ died for all, and since all men [and women] are in fact called to one and the same destiny, which is divine, we must hold that the Holy Spirit offers to all the possibility of being made partners, in a way known to God, in the paschal mystery.[5]

This statement gives a rationale for the new understanding. A further consideration could be added. Christ's redemptive work was not simply to be a teacher about God nor simply to reveal something that apart from himself was always part of the human situation. His work was, rather, to effect something new in human history. The redemption was a cognitive achievement only because it was first an ontological one. Then, what Christ effected in some way touches every person born into the human family, whether each is aware of Christ or not.[6] Because of the solidarity of the human race,[7] the redemptive work of Christ affects all humankind. All are graced, all receive the Holy Spirit, in one way or another all are called to share Christ's glorified life in heaven.

Note this in the Vatican II statement: all *people of good will* share in the paschal mystery of Christ. The line between those who are in Christ and those who are not coincides with the line that divides the good from the wicked. The parable of the sheep and the goats says as much.[8] Christian belief and baptism are not the telling issue. Human authenticity is.

The situation is similar to that in theism. Just as belief in God does not establish the Creator-creature relationship with God, so belief in Christ does not establish the redemptive participation in the mysteries of Christ. In both cases human authenticity is the telling factor. Granted that a person is authentic, seeking honestly to know and do what is right and good, holiness as relationship with God and divinization as participation in Christ both follow automatically. God,

One and Three, has built these further issues into the structure of human life. In the living, no human can avoid them.

Then, as within the theist viewpoint, so within the Christian viewpoint, no further practical considerations need be added to an adequate psychological account of spiritual development. Although Christian belief does disclose a dimension of human reality that the human sciences cannot know, that dimension, even if unknown, is real and is universally operative. So the conclusions of the human sciences within the philosophic viewpoint already but unknowingly take into account the effects of the Christian mysteries on humankind. Insofar as the Christian mysteries make a discernible effect in *human* experience, they are already available as objects of study for the authentic human sciences. Insofar as these mysteries are mysteries of *God*, they are available only to Christian faith and can be explicated only within the Christian viewpoint. Therefore, 1) Christian faith discloses a dimension of human reality unknowable apart from Christian faith. Accordingly, 2) Christian faith adds a further dimension of explanation to any account of the human; Christianity makes a theoretical contribution. But 3) since that dimension is real and effective whether known or not, like theism, Christian faith makes no practical contribution to an understanding of the human.

In principle this issue is no different from what was said above about theism, so it merits no extensive treatment here. Often what passes for Christianity is not authentic Christianity at all; so the question about the contribution of Christianity in such cases is moot. Much of the sad history of Christianity—its wars and inquisitions and persecutions—obviously not even authentically human, bears witness here. Where Christianity is authentic, as with theism, it helps the believer to live authentically. The Christian dedication to truth and love within the unity of diversified community and the Christian lesson that it is worth even dying for what one knows to be true and good, even as Jesus did, are examples here. As do other religions, Christianity has ways of communicating these important truths that pertain to human authenticity. Moreover, since the Christian believer not only lives a life in Christ but also knows and willingly embraces that life in Christ, he or she may attain a "higher degree of being" of that life in Christ.[9] Yet that life is substantively no different from the life any other authentic but unbelieving person lives. All are in Christ.

So the specifically Christian contribution makes no difference as far as the practicalities of living in Christ are concerned.

One is to live a good life. One is to do as best one knows how. Nothing more is possible. Nothing more can be expected. The issue fully patent of human investigation and elaboration is how to live authentically. And all authentic people will come to the same conclusions on this issue—Christians, theists, and humanists.[10] There is no specifically theist ethics, and there is no specifically Christian ethics.

The other issues, like the work of creation and salvation in Christ, are proper to God. Humans may know of them, but humans do not understand them. Besides, human knowledge of them and meditation on them does nothing to enhance or lessen their reality. These things can be left to God; the others are the necessary concern of humans.

So Christian religion may help one to discover and follow the authentically human course, but Christianity adds nothing practical to, and changes nothing practical in, that course. As for spiritual development in particular, questions about the practical "what's" and "why's" and "how to's" are appropriately answered by the human sciences within the philosophic viewpoint. All this was said above about theism, and it applies again *mutatis mutandis* to Christianity.

Therefore, this section will not be concerned about the practical. The concern will rather be to highlight the theoretical contribution Christianity makes to an understanding of spiritual development. This concern will entail an extended and technical treatment of the central mysteries of Christianity, particularly the Trinity, the mission of the Holy Spirit, and the divinization of the human being. Although this presentation will result in no further practical conclusions about spiritual development, this presentation will show that Christianity does make a significant and a unique contribution to a comprehensive explanation of spiritual development. This presentation will also serve to remind Christians of issues that are the heart of the Christian tradition but that often receive little or no serious attention.

If these comments seem in some way to minimize the importance of Christianity, the intent is only to highlight Christianity's true importance. There is a grave danger in the contemporary situation. On the one hand, few who call themselves Christian really appreciate the essence of Christianity. Few understand what is unique in their Christian belief. How many Christian schools and seminaries require or even offer courses on the Trinity today? On the other hand, unless the already unchristian ideology of Fundamentalism and Dogmatism prevails, it will soon become common knowledge that what is generally thought to be Christian is really found in one way or another in all the great world religions. Then "Christianity" will appear irrelevant. The grave danger is that Christianity will be lost. Even worse, it will be lost and never missed. The intent here is to highlight the essence of Christianity so that it may be known and appreciated simply for what it is and that its contribution may be preserved.

Relationship with God in Christ

In theism the fundamental relationship between God and the human is creation. Creaturehood implies an inviolable distinction. Creature and Creator are defined in opposition to one another. Although the Bible notes that woman and man were created in the image and likeness of God,[11] there is no suggestion that they are in any way divine. "Image and likeness" means that in some way they are similar to God. They are to name the animals, till the soil, and be responsible for the world. The world is subject to their dominion. In this they are like God, who shaped the world and is its Lord. They are like God, but nothing more. If the Jewish mind allowed that people could be holy by being specially related to God, it could never think of any created being as divine. Theism allows no such thing.

Christianity goes beyond theism. Its fundamental contribution is to conceive and coherently explain a bridge between the Creator and the creature. Christianity envisages the union of God and human beings. It allows for human divinization.

The Christian vision of human divinization arises from the original Christian experience of Jesus and his impact on the early Christian community, as recorded in the Christian Testament. The basic belief was that because of Jesus all believers—and ultimately all humankind—could share in a saving fulfillment that Jesus himself had attained. Jesus Christ is the paradigmatic instance of human divinization. A complete account of this matter would constitute a comprehensive christology. I have provided such an account elsewhere, elaborating not only the spiritual implication of Christian be-

lief but also tracing the historical development of this belief and legiti-
mating it on the basis of the available historical data.[12] Here a
summary of the redemptive work of Christ must suffice.

Human divinization is the central issue here. Divinization means
a human participation in certain qualities that are proper to God
alone. To be divinized implies that in some sense a human becomes
divine.

According to this understanding, Jesus' divinization occurred at
his resurrection. Then, even as human, he came to share in divine
qualities that were properly his, as divine, from all eternity. There is
no suggestion here that at the resurrection Jesus became God. There
is no attempt here to explain the Nicene definition—that Jesus Christ
is "God from God, Light from Light, true God from true God, Begotten not created, one in being (homoousios) with the Father"[13]—on the
basis of the resurrection. The notion of anything ever *becoming* God is
self-contradictory; it is absurd. Rather, the suggestion is this: precisely
because Jesus was Eternal-Son, it was proper that even in his *human*
state he share in divine qualities, insofar as such sharing is possible
for any human.

Note that the human state is a created one. It is an instance in
reality of that inviolable distinction between Creator and creature. So
no human can become God. Even when Eternal-Son becomes human,
he subsists in a created reality, and even the created reality of Eternal-
Son cannot at some point become uncreated. What is created could
never become uncreated; what has a temporal beginning could never
become eternal. So no human, as human, could become divine in the
sense of becoming uncreated and eternal. Yet it might be possible that
a human share in certain divine qualities, but only certain ones. And
the qualification is important: insofar as such sharing is possible for
any human.

Especially in the case of a human who actually is God, it is
eminently proper—nay, it appears to be required—that that one share
in divine qualities. So an earlier christology held that from the first
moment of his human existence Jesus knew all things and had access
to divine power. Contemporary biblical scholarship shows that, in
fact, that was not the case. Despite what human wisdom would expect, God chose that Eternal-Son surrender all divine prerogatives
and live during his earthly days as every other human being, like us in

all things but sin. According to divine wisdom, only after a life of perfect fidelity and even at the cost of misunderstanding, anguish, abandonment, and bloody death on a cross, would Jesus as human share in the divine qualities that could have, should have, been his from the beginning of his human life. So God raised Jesus from the dead, raised him in glory, raised him divinized. Jesus' humanity was transformed, raised to its highest possible perfection.

Human Divinization

What does human divinization mean? As a mystery of participation in the divine nature, like God, divinization cannot be understood. Still, in faith it can be affirmed, and some analogous account of it can be given.

Certain human capacities point toward the divine, especially the spiritual capacities to know and to love. In fact, this very dynamism of knowing and loving, the dynamism of the human spirit, intrinsic to the human, is a basis for understanding human development as spiritual development. In a theist account of the matter, self-transcending human authenticity, which entails living in accord with the exigencies of that dynamism, finds its ultimate term in God. Insofar as one is following the exigencies of the human spirit, one is living in accord with God's will for humanity and for the universe, and so one is oriented toward God. One is not only authentic, one is also holy. But although the philosophic viewpoint allows that the object of the human desire to understand correctly is limitless and although theism allows that to understand everything about everything and so to be able to explain all things is to be God, apart from Christianity there is no suggestion that a human could ever attain the limitless goal of the human intellect and so share the divine quality of understanding everything about everything. That the human mind attain this fullness proper only to God would be an instance of human divinization. Likewise, although the philosophic viewpoint allows that the human desire to love is boundless, and although theism allows that to love everything insofar as everything is lovable is to be God, apart from Christianity there is no suggestion that a human could ever love boundlessly and so share that divine quality. That the human capacity for love attain a fullness proper to God alone would be another instance of human divinization.

The suggestion is that to share in the divine mind and in the divine love would, in this limited sense, be to share in divinity. This would be divinization.

Belief in a human participation in divinity lies at the heart of the Christian tradition. The Christian Testament refers to this mystery often. The Second Letter of Peter says that we are called to God's own "glory and excellence" and that we are to "become partakers of the divine nature."[14] 1 John 3:2 says that, indeed, "we are God's children now; it does not yet appear what we shall be, but we know that when he appears we shall be like him." In 1 Corinthians 13:12 Paul writes, "Now we see in a mirror dimly, but then face to face. Now I know in part; then I shall understand fully." And Paul repeatedly refers to our participation in divine life in Christ under the metaphor of adopted childhood: "God sent his Son so we might receive adoption as sons [and daughters]."[15] Moreover, the early Fathers of the Church preached at length about this mystery.[16] Their teaching is summed up in a prayer still used in the Roman Catholic Mass at the mixing of the water and wine: "By the mystery of this water and wine, may we come to share in the divinity of Christ, who humbled himself to share in our humanity."

It is clear that such sharing is a participation in divinity and not merely a human perfection—even though the self-transcending dynamism of the human spirit itself ever points toward such a fulfillment. In fact, humans do not understand everything about everything. Human knowing is cumulative, it proceeds bit by bit. It entails a process of passage from potency to actuation. But understanding everything about everything transcends this very process and suggests a state of pure actualization, beyond all further potency. Though we might project such an achievement, imagining the build-up of bit upon bit until the whole is attained, what the result would be is fully beyond us. If we are able to speak of such an achievement, we cannot properly conceive it. We merely project into an ideal state our ordinary experience of knowing. On the basis of the dynamism of the human spirit we may heuristically conceive that state. That is, we may know it analogously. Still, we have no experience of such a thing and no proper understanding of it. If the human longs for such an achievement, the achievement is nonetheless beyond the human. On the other hand, because of that very longing, an expression of the relentless dynamism of the human spirit toward authentic self-transcendence, the achievement does not seem to be impossible for the human. Yet attaining it must entail some transformation of the human spirit, some perfection that moves one beyond what is properly human and into what is properly divine.[17]

And something similar could be said about love.

Here, then, is an understanding of human divinization. The suggestion is that this is precisely what happened to Jesus in his resurrection. Jesus Christ became the first instance of human divinization.

The Saving Work of Christ and the Holy Spirit

Jesus introduced a new reality into history, a divinized human being. Taking human achievement to a new high, he provided a new and now real terminus for human becoming. He changed the meaning of human life. According to God's unfathomable wisdom and at the personal cost of suffering and death, God the Eternal Son reversed the course of human history from within. Formerly deviating from God and God's will for the universe, in Christ human history was now again moving toward God. Reconciliation between God and humankind, effected from the human side where alone it was lacking, had been accomplished. Now, because of the solidarity of the human race, all humankind is involved in a history that moves toward God and whose epitome is divinization. That is to say, Jesus redeemed the human race.

The contribution of Jesus Christ Eternal Son to human salvation is the redemptive work just described. Jesus offered a new possibility for humankind. What has never happened may be possible; then again, it may not. One can speculate. But what has happened is certainly possible. When Jesus was raised from the dead to divine glory, the possibility of human divinization moved from the realm of mere speculation and into reality. Opening this new possibility to humankind was Jesus' significant yet limited contribution.

However, human salvation is not achieved until this possibility is actualized in other human beings. According to Christian understanding rooted in the Christian Testament experience and clarified by subsequent doctrinal definition, actualization of this new possibility in humankind results from the gift of the Holy Spirit. As Paul writes, "God's love has been poured into our hearts through the Holy Spirit which has been given to us,"[18] and again, "God has sent the Spirit of his Son into our hearts, crying, 'Abba! Father!' So through God you are no longer a slave but a son [or daughter]."[19] Completion of the work of human salvation requires a second intervention of God in human history. Human salvation requires the sanctifying mission of the Holy Spirit in addition to the redemptive mission of the Son. The mission of the Holy Spirit, the resultant Indwelling of the Trinity in human hearts, and the consequences for an account of spiritual development will be the topic of the following chapter.

The Divine Side of the Christian Vision

Christianity envisages a new human reality, divinization. The intervention of the Eternal Son into human history and the parallel intervention of the Holy Spirit makes human divinization possible. According to the Christian understanding, two divine missions condition human divinization. So Christianity's new disclosure of reality on the human side entails a new disclosure of reality also on the divine side. The missions of two divine ones from God into human history imply a plurality in God. The Christian experience reveals God as Trinity.

The Christian affirmation of a Trinity in God is inextricably linked with the Christian affirmation of the divinity of Jesus Christ. Both stand or fall together. Belief in Jesus Christ as Savior and Lord, God Incarnate, is the hallmark of the Christian tradition. This belief was clarified beyond dispute at the Council of Nicea, which itself can be shown to be in full continuity with the teaching of the Christian Testament and so with the early disciples' experience of Jesus.[20] So Christian belief in the divinity of Jesus rests on a remarkable historical experience at the beginning of the Common Era. Granted that this belief is correct and Jesus Christ is God, there arises already an unavoidable duality in God. Jesus addressed himself to God as to another individual; he prayed to God as Father. If Jesus is God and if the Father is God, there are two in God. Deny the divinity of Jesus Christ

175

and the duality in God is eliminated—but so is the Christian tradition eliminated. Affirm the divinity of Jesus Christ and there must be a duality in God. A similar analysis can be made regarding the Holy Spirit, whose divinity was clarified definitively in 381 C.E. at the First Council of Constantinople. So the Christian affirms a Trinity in God.

The logic moves from Christian experience in this world to the reality of the Divinity itself in eternity. The economic Trinity, the divine Three as experienced in the present order—or economy—of salvation, reveals and is identical with the immanent Trinity, the divine Three as they are eternally in God. This must be so. If the Father sent the Son, there is a relationship between the Father and the Son. If this relationship is real in the Son—that is, if the Son was really sent by the Father—then this relationship must also be real in the Father. If it is real in the Father, it must be eternal in the Father. Likewise, if it is eternal in the Father, it must also be eternal in the Son. There must be an eternal relation of derivation between the Son and the Father. The contingent mission of the Son from the Father in history implies an eternal procession of the Son from the Father in God. And a similar argument can be made regarding the procession of the Holy Spirit from the Father and the Son.

So Christian belief professes three divine Subjects in one God. (The term "Subject" is more accurate today than the traditional term "Person," whose technical theological meaning is in no way retained in contemporary usage, whether popular or philosophical.)[21] In 1442 C.E. the ecumenical Council of Florence summarized Christian belief about the Trinity as follows: the Church

> believes, professes and teaches one true God, omnipotent, unchangeable, and eternal, Father, Son and Holy Spirit, one in essence, threefold in persons. The Father not begotten, the Son begotten of the Father, the Holy Spirit proceeding from the Father and the Son . . . These three Persons are one God, and not three gods. For the three have one substance, one essence, one nature, one godhead, one immensity, one eternity, and all things are one (*in them*) except where there is the opposition (*confrontation*) of relationship. 'On account of this unity the Father is wholly in the Son, and wholly in the Holy Spirit; the Son wholly in the Father and wholly in the Holy Spirit; the Holy Spirit wholly in the Father and wholly in the Son. None precedes the other in eternity, none exceeds in greatness, nor excels in power. For it is from eternity

176

and without beginning that the Son took his origin from the Father, and from eternity and without beginning that the Holy Spirit proceeds from the Father and the Son' (*Fulgentius*). What the Father is or has, he has not from another but from himself; he is the origin without origin. What the Son is or has, he has from the Father; he is origin from origin. What the Holy Spirit is or has, he has at the same time from the Father and the Son. But the Father and Son are not two origins, but one origin. As the Father and the Son and the Holy Ghost are not three origins of creation but one origin. . . .[22]

Theological speculation on the Trinity resolved the apparent contradictions in the doctrine through the refinement of important philosophical concepts—person, nature, essence, substance, and others noted in the above creedal statement. This is not the place to rehearse that historical process or justify its conclusions.[23] Here the Christian belief must be accepted as such. The task at hand is to apply the doctrine and so to show its relevance to an understanding of spiritual development.

Christianity discloses new reality in God, a trinity of Divine Subjects, correlative to a new reality in humanity, divinization. According to this Christian understanding, over and above the Creator-creature relationship that theism allows, humans have also relationships with the three divine Subjects. Precisely these new relationships account for the new human reality, divinization.

The Disproportionate Nature of Human Divinization

Human divinization is a fulfillment disproportionate to the human as such. More than human, it is a participation in divinity. As such, it cannot be explained merely by appeal to God as Creator. Although it is a created reality, for it is a *human* participation in divinity, it is not adequately understood as a part of creation within the theist viewpoint. Human divinization implies more than the theist order of creation.

The difference is not a question of chronology or statistics but of intrinsic intelligibility.[24] Whether or not human divinization as known in Christianity was a possibility available to all humankind from the beginning of creation is not the issue. Even if it was—and contemporary theology suggests that in view of the future redemption such salvation was available from the beginning—it is still a fulfillment disproportionate to the human. The universality of the phenomenon among humankind does not of itself make the phenomenon human, for the nature of a reality is not determined by its statistical incidence but by its intrinsic intelligibility. And human divinization requires more than humanity to explain it. In addition to humanity, one must also posit the missions of the Son and of the Holy Spirit in order to account for human divinization. These latter two factors are not human, they are divine. Moreover, they are not necessary, they are contingent. This latter point is obvious in the case of the redemption.[25] To deny the contingency of the redemption is to deny freedom and all virtue in the human Jesus, and to deny saving virtue in the human Jesus is to vitiate the incarnation of all but symbolic significance. So certainly the redemptive mission of the Son entails contingencies. Then factors other than what is intrinsic to the human condition human divinization. Unable to be explained on the basis of humanity alone, dependent on divine factors, human divinization is obviously disproportionate to the human. It represents an intervention of God that in its intrinsic intelligibility transcends creation as understood in theism. To make this very point, the Christian Testament speaks of a *new* creation when it refers to salvation offered in Christ.[26]

Of course, by appealing to the additional factor of the missions of the Son and of the Holy Spirit in order to make its point, this argument presupposes the Christian understanding of the issue. But how else can the issue be structured? The notion of divinization does not occur elsewhere. Hinduism may have something akin to it, but on closer inspection the Hindu problematic appears to be significantly different from the Christian and, indeed, from the Jewish and Muslim.[27] Like Neo-platonism and like gnostic speculation[28] and hopelessly obscured in a preference for multivalent metaphors over precise concepts, Hinduism does not seem to posit a real distinction between God and the human: Atman is Brahman. So no real question of divinization can even arise. At its depths, the human is not really human at all. The human is really a diffuse and dull form of the divine. Then, to suggest that the human shares in divinity is nothing startling. If the human is really divine, then obviously the human already is divine! It may even be God, as well. In Hinduism bridging humanity and divinity is no issue at all.

However, granted the distinction between the necessary and the contingent, between the Creator and the creature, a coherent account of divinization does not come easily. Such an account requires factors beyond the merely human, for divinization is no merely human reality. Christianity provides those factors by insistence on the divinity of Jesus Christ, his resurrection unto divine glory, and the sanctifying work of the Holy Spirit. If this approach appears complex and even parochial, it does at least address the issue, and it does provide a coherent explanation. Then, although divinization may actually be a universal human possibility, it is nonetheless a fulfillment disproportionate to humanity as such. On this understanding, the Christian viewpoint is really distinct from the theist viewpoint and represents a real advance over the theist viewpoint. A comprehensive explanatory account of spiritual development that envisages human divinization requires the treatment that only the Christian viewpoint provides.

Notes

Chapter Eight

Human Divinization in Christ

1. *The Roman Missal*, 413; Neuner and Roos, *Teaching of Catholic Church*, 423-438.

2. Lonergan, *Method*, 80, 162, 291, 199.

3. Dulles, *Church to Believe in, Models of Church, Resilient Church*; Küng, *The Church*; McBrien, *Church, Do We Need the Church?, Remaking the Church*; Minear, *Images of Church*; Rahner, *Church after Council, Shape of Church to Come*; Schnackenburg, *Church in New Testament*.

4. Cf. also Rom 5:15-19, 8:32; 2 Cor. 5:14-15, 19; 1 Tim. 4:10; Jn. 1:9.

5. *Gaudium et Spes*, art. 22, in Flanery, *Vatican Council II*, 924; cf. also *Nostra Aetate*, art. 1, *Ibid.*, 738, and *Lumen Gentium*, art. 13-16, *Ibid.*, 364-368.

6. Hick and Hebblethwaite, *Christianity and Other Religions*.

7. Helminiak, "One in Christ."

8. Mt. 25:31-46.

9. Chapter 7, n. 16, above.

10. Lonergan, *Method*, 235-266; Swain, "Conflict and Resolution."

11. Gen. 1:26-27.

12. Helminiak, *The Same Jesus*.

13. Neuner and Roos, 424.

14. 2 Peter 1:3-4.

15. Gal. 4:4-5; cf. also Eph. 1:3-5; Rom. 8:15, 23, 9:4.

16. Helminiak, "One in Christ," 33-111.

17. Lonergan, *Collection*, 84-95.

18. Rom. 5:5.

19. Gal. 4:6-7.

20. Helminiak, *The Same Jesus*.

21. Lonergan, *Collection*, 164-197; *Second Collection*, 69-86, 239-261; *De Constitutione Christi*; *De Deo Trino*; Rahner, *The Trinity*.

22. Neuner and Roos, *Teaching of Catholic Church*, 100-101.

23. DeMarjorie, *The Christian Trinity*; Hill, *Three-Personed God*; Kasper, *The God of Jesus*; Lonergan, *De Deo Trino*; Rahner, *The Trinity*.

24. Lonergan, *Grace and Freedom*, 13-19.

25. Helminiak, *The Same Jesus*, Chapter Eight, n. 40, Chapter Ten, n. 30.

26. 2 Cor. 5:17; Gal. 6:15.

27. Panikkar, *Unknown Christ*.

28. Louth, *Origins of Christian Mysticism*; Williams, *Christian Spirituality*.

The Holy Spirit and Human Divinization

In addition to the contributions that adequate human sciences and theism can make to an understanding of spiritual development, Christianity makes a further contribution: all human growth is in fact a growing participation in divinity. The redemptive work of Jesus Christ introduced divinization as a real possibility into human history. Granted this possibility, an understanding of human growth as growth in divine life consists primarily in an understanding of the sanctifying work of the Holy Spirit. Traditionally, this issue is the theology of grace. The key to the matter is an understanding of the Holy Spirit as God's own Love. Because the Holy Spirit is given to us, God transforms the human spirit, making it receptive to God's Love, the Holy Spirit. Then, possessing God's own Love and so loving with divine Love, the human advances in authenticity and so in holiness. But since within the Christian viewpoint these advances are not mere human progress but increasing participation in divinity, one is actually growing in divinization as one grows in holiness. Moreover, since the goal of life in Christ is not mere holiness but actual participation in the glory of the resurrected Christ, one also looks forward to the perfection of one's spiritual development "when the perishable puts on the imperishable, and the mortal puts on immortality."[1] This chapter presents an account of this further understanding, proper to Christianity.

The Personal Properties of the Three Divine Subjects

Christian belief in the missions of the Son and of the Holy Spirit necessitates that there are three distinct Subjects in God: Father, Son, and Holy Spirit. These three are the one God, Creator of heaven and earth. Except for the distinct identity proper to each, all that they have and are is common to all.

God is absolutely simple; there is no composition in God. If there were, God would be changeable; and something else would be needed to account for the union of the distinct factors in God. Then this supposed "God" would not be God. This point was already made above. Apart from the distinctions that determine the three Subjects, there are no distinctions in God.

Because of the limitations of human understanding and conception, we speak of distinct aspects of God—the divine mind, the divine will, the divine power, the divine essence, the divine existence. But these are not really distinct; they are distinct only in our minds. This point was also made above in the treatment of Providence. It was noted that for God to "foreknow" is for God to "forewill." In God knowledge and will are one and the same thing: what God knows to exist does exist. Everything in God is one, except for distinctions of the three Subjects who are God.

The Three are one Divinity. It follows, using the human categories, that the Three share one mind, one will, one power, one essence, one existence. Take existence, for example. Each of us has our own separate act of created existence. My existence makes me be and be what I am, myself and not someone else. Each of us is constituted as a separate reality by our own individual existence. But in God there is only one existence which accounts for the reality of the Three divine Subjects. If each of the Three had His/Her own existence, there would be three Gods, not one—and the very meaning of "God" would have been changed. Then we would be dealing with polytheism where there are many gods and where each differs from the other in function

184

and power and so on. But if each differs, each must lack that which is proper to the others. If they lack, they are not God in the sense defined in Chapter 5. They are not the Creator-God of the theist viewpoint. So within the presuppositions of this essay, they are not really God at all. There is only one God and so only one divine existence. The Three in God must exist by the one and the same divine existence. A similar argument can be made about the divine mind and will and power and essence.

Note how different this is from the human situation. Each of us has his or her own mind, his or her own feelings, his or her own imagination, his or her own free self-determination, his or her own capabilities. We speak of all these qualities as "personal," and a "person" is determined by that one's unique understanding, knowledge, feelings, freedom, power, and so on. In contemporary usage, the words "person" and "personal" are used to refer to such a reality. But the situation is not the same in God. The Three divine Subjects have in common one mind, one will, one power. According to the contemporary meaning of the word, Each is not a person, having His/Her own mind, will, dignity, and so on. The meaning of the theological term "person" is not the same as the meaning of the contemporary term. So a different term must be used to indicate a different meaning. There are three Subjects in God. There are Three who are God, Three who share only one mind and will and power. These Three are *distinct* Subjects: the one is not the other. Yet these three Subjects, who really are and who are really distinct from one another, have all in common.

If the Three have all in common, what determines them as distinct Subjects? What constitutes their distinct identities? Certainly, there must be something proper to each of the Three. Otherwise they would not be distinct.

The difference among the Three in God does not lie in what they have or what they are. The difference lies in how they are and how they have what they have. The Son is God as proceeding from the Father. As Son of the Father, all that the Father has, the Son also has. The Son exists by the very existence that is also the Father's: they are one God. As God, they are identical in all things. But the Father does not proceed. The Son does. This very quality—procession from the

Father—is precisely what determines the Son as Son. One might say that the very identity of the Son is "bornness" or "proceeding-from-the-Father-ness." It is that which is distinctive of the Son.

If the Son proceeds from the Father, clearly the Son is distinct from the Father. The Father is *that from which* the Son proceeds, and the Son is *that which* proceeds from the Father. This mutual relationship of opposition introduces a distinction in God and determines the identity of the two Subjects, Father and Son.

Moreover, nothing other than the Son's proceeding from the Father distinguishes the Son from the Father. Apart from their distinction as Subjects in mutually constitutive relationship with one another, they share all in common. So the only thing one can say about the Son as God that is not true also of the Father is that the Son proceeds from the Father. Likewise, the only thing that one can say about the Father that is not true also of the Son as God is that the Father generates the Son. All else is common to the two.

Notice that the property that constitutes the Son in relation to the Father in the immanent Trinity is the very same one that is revealed about the Father and the Son in salvation history: the Father sent the Son; the Son was sent by the Father. As indicated in Chapter 8, Christianity derives its understanding of the inner life of the Trinity from what is known of the divine Subjects in history.

Now, a similar presentation can be made regarding the Holy Spirit. The Spirit, too, has a distinctive property that distinguishes the Spirit from the Father and from the Son. In salvation history it is known that the Father and the Son sent the Holy Spirit; the Holy Spirit was sent by the Father and the Son. So, in the Trinity itself it is known that the Holy Spirit proceeds from the Father and the Son; the Father and the Son spirate the Holy Spirit. This relationship of being spirated sets up another relation of opposition between the One who is spirated and the Father and Son who spirate and so constitutes a third distinct Subject in God.

Thus, all Three in God are distinct from one another while all Three are all equally God. The Father is God without source who generates the Son and, with the Son, spirates the Holy Spirit. The Son is God proceeding from the Father and, with the Father, spirates the Holy Spirit. The Holy Spirit is God proceeding from the Father and the Son. (According to the equally valid Eastern Christian formula, the Holy Spirit proceeds from the Father *through* the Son.[2]) These are the properties, these alone, that distinguish the three divine Subjects among themselves. In God nothing else can be said properly about any of the Three.

Appropriation and the *ad extra* Rule

Evidently, very little can be said accurately and properly about the Father or the Son or the Holy Spirit. Only that which constitutes them as distinct from one another is proper to each, and that is summarized in one brief paragraph above. Yet the Christian tradition says much about these Three, attributing to Them qualities and activities that are not actually proper but that nonetheless seem appropriate in each case. This way of speaking is called appropriation.

For example, the Father is said to be Creator of the world, the Son the Savior, and the Holy Spirit the Sanctifier. Clearly, however, creation is not a property of the Father. Creation is an act of all Three in God, an act of God precisely as Trinity, as the One Creator-God. Likewise, though the Son saved humankind by his redemptive work on earth, the Father sent the Son to redeem us, and the Holy Spirit continues the same saving work of the Son among humankind. In one way or another all Three are Savior of the world. Moreover, insofar as salvation actually occurs in any human being, it is a created effect and so is not proper to any of the Three alone but is common to all as the one Creator-God. Accordingly, the supposed work of the Holy Spirit, sanctification, is the work of God as One.

Nonetheless, there is some appropriateness in speaking of the Father as Creator, the Son as Savior, and the Holy Spirit as Sanctifier. Since the Eternal Parent is the unsourced source of the inner-trinitarian life, it may be appropriate to think of the Father also as the ultimate source of all reality and so as Creator. Likewise, as the one sent among us to reconcile humankind with God, Jesus Christ, the Only-begotten of the Parent, may appropriately be called Savior of the world. And as the one whose mission to humankind is a key factor in their sanctification, the Holy Spirit may appropriately be called Sanctifier.

Appropriation is the most common way of speaking about the Three in God. Little is ever said properly about the Three in God.

Almost everything that is said or written about the Father, Son, or Holy Spirit is said by way of appropriation. This is especially so in the case of spiritual writings about the Holy Spirit. Such practice is acceptable insofar as it is useful, insofar as it aids people in loving God and in living wholesomely. It is acceptable as long as one recognizes that only appropriation is at work[3]—which today means almost never!

There is a usage becoming more common today, one that may not be acceptable. In a laudable attempt to avoid the pro-male sexist bias built into the Christian symbols inherited from the Christian Testament, some now make the sign of the cross "In the name of the Creator and of the Redeemer and of the Sanctifier, Amen." For the reasons just noted, this usage is not an accurate substitute for "Father, Son, and Holy Spirit." As a replacement for naming the Three in God, if taken literally, it actually dissolves the trinitarian doctrine. Other substitutes need to be found.[4] The Father could correctly be called the Parent, as above. When softened with appropriate adjectives, like Loving or Eternal, this term could even become an acceptable liturgical usage. The Father could also be called the Mother, even as the Council of Toledo in 675 used the undeniably feminine image to speak of the generation of the Son: "not generated or born from nothing or from some other substance but *from the womb* of the Father."[5] Mother-Father would also be an excellent alternative, excellent precisely because the notion is mind-boggling and serves to remind us that God is not like us and that we do not understand what God is. Only Begotten or Eternally Begotten or even Eternal Offspring would be theologically correct alternatives for Son. Daughter or Daughter-Son would also be an adequate substitute here insofar as only trinitarian life is concerned, but because the Eternally Begotten incarnated as a male, such usage might blur the identity of this Divine One with Jesus Christ. In any case, two things are beyond doubt. First, though human language usually represents them as one or the other, the Subjects in God are neither male nor female, so both female and male symbols and pronouns may correctly be used to refer to the three Subjects in the Trinity. Second, whatever symbols are employed, the usage must preserve the notion of generation or procession of one Subject from the Other or Others; otherwise the Trinity is lost.

However, speaking of Jesus Christ the Eternal Offspring as *Redeemer* may be completely accurate. Insofar as "redemption" is taken to refer specifically to the saving work of Jesus Christ—this usage, if not standard, is common in Christian theology[6]—the Eternally Begotten and the Eternally Begotten alone is the Redeemer. The position of the Eternally Begotten is peculiar in comparison with that of the Parent and the Holy Spirit. Among the Three, the Only Begotten alone is able to effect things apart from the other two—because only the Eternal Offspring became incarnate. Taking on a human nature, the Only Begotten acquired a second principle of operation. In addition to the divinity, through which the Parent, Offspring, and Holy Spirit all act and act as One, the Eternal Offspring also has his humanity. As human, the Eternal Offspring can do things that are his own proper acts and that are not acts proper to the Eternal Parent and the Holy Spirit. Only the Eternally Begotten became incarnate. Only the Eternally Begotten thought with a human mind, spoke with a human voice, walked with human legs, and worked with human hands. Only the Eternally Begotten was born in time, and only the Eternally Begotten died on the cross. Insofar as these acts of the Only Begotten effected the redemption of the world and the reconciliation of humankind with God, the Only Begotten alone is the Redeemer. The Eternally Begotten could act alone as the sole and proper agent of his acts, apart from the Mother-Father and the Holy Spirit, because he became human.

Of course, this is not to say that the human Jesus acted apart from divine concurrence, which pertains to every created activity, whether Jesus' or anyone else's. Divine concurrence is not to be denied here, but neither is it to be confused with the specifically trinitarian issue under discussion here. Furthermore, this is not to suggest that the incarnate Only-Begotten was alone when he acted. Because of their shared Divinity and because of the mutual relationships that constitute the Divine Ones as Themselves, None is ever alone, without the other Two. This aspect of the trinitarian mystery is called the circuminsession or perichoresis or mutual indwelling or inexistence of the Divine Three.[7] Jesus' Eternal Parent and the Holy Spirit were always with Jesus. Yet as human Jesus Christ, Eternal Son, was the sole subject, the sole agent, of his historical actions.

In contrast, whenever the Father or the Son as God or the Holy Spirit acts outside the Trinity, each must act by using the divine power. There is no other possibility. Yet the divine power is common to all

Three; it is not one of the properties of any of the Three. Of course, each of the Three has the divine power in His/Her own way, just as each has the divinity in a peculiar way—as unsourced source, as begotten, or as spirated.[8] But this consideration must not obscure the point being made here: the creative power of God is common to all Three in God. So when One acts through the divine power, the Others act as well. As God, using the divine power to effect anything outside of God, none of the divine Three ever acts alone. Therefore, God's creative work is always and necessarily the work of the Three as Trinity, as the One Creator-God.

Theology speaks of this axiom as the *ad extra* rule. The Latin *"ad extra"* means "toward the outside"; it refers to any divine act apart from the inner-trinitarian processions and their correlative missions. Within God, the Parent alone generates the Begotten One, the Begotten One alone proceeds from the Father, only the Parent and the Begotten One spirate the Holy Spirit, and the Holy Spirit alone is spirated by the Parent and the Begotten One. Since these acts of generation, procession, and spiration are determined precisely by the relationships of opposition that they entail—the One comes from the Other(s)—these acts constitute the divine Subjects as distinct from one another and define the properties of each One. Likewise, when the Mother-Father sends Her/His Eternally Begotten, only the Mother-Father sends the Eternally Begotten, and only the Eternally Begotten is sent. And when the Mother-Father and the Eternal Offspring send the Holy Spirit, only those Two send the Holy Spirit, and only the Holy Spirit is sent. As parallels to the processions in God, the missions and the relations they entail are proper to the Divine Subjects involved in each case. However, when God effects anything outside of the Trinity, the creative act of the divine power is common to all Three. The formal formulation of this axiom occurs in the creed of the Council of Florence, quoted in Chapter 8: "all things are one (in them) except where there is the opposition (confrontation) of relationship."

The Role of the Holy Spirit

In the present study the *ad extra* rule comes to bear with particular importance in the case of the mission of the Holy Spirit. It is too simple—it is erroneous!—to say simply that the Holy Spirit sanctifies us. Insofar as human sanctification is a created effect in us, it is the work of the Trinity, the One Creator-God. This point cannot be made strongly enough. Christian piety speaks all too easily about the Holy Spirit as the source of spiritual experiences. Whenever we receive some inspiration, supposedly the Spirit inspires us. When we are inclined to do some good, supposedly the Spirit moves us. When we feel some religious sentiment, supposedly it is the action of the Holy Spirit that we feel. Likewise, supposedly the Holy Spirit enlightens us, gives us strength, brings us tears of repentance, gives us rest in labor, refreshes us in life's heat, and consoles us in life's sorrow. In fact, these things are not said properly of the Holy Spirit; they are all said by way of appropriation. Since human inspiration, enlightenment, consolation, and all the rest are created effects, they cannot but be the work of God as One. It is simply not true literally that the Holy Spirit is *the* One who effects these spiritual phenomena in us.

At the same time, it must be recognized that the Holy Spirit is God. Then, insofar as it is God that effects these things in us, the Holy Spirit does effect them in us.[9] So we can appropriately pray to the Holy Spirit and thank the Holy Spirit for such things. Still, the point here is this: in effecting such things, as God the Holy Spirit acts in common with the Father and the Son. The Holy Spirit does not act alone in effecting such things. In fact, like the Eternal Parent but unlike the Begotten One who became human, the Holy Spirit alone cannot effect anything in us. Moreover, when effecting such things along with the Parent and the Begotten One, the Spirit is not doing His/Her "own thing," so to speak. For these works are not proper to the Holy Spirit. Only to proceed from the Father-Mother and the Begotten One is proper to the Holy Spirit. These works are only appropriated to the Holy Spirit.

Still, the Christian tradition—even the best of the Christian tradition—is insistent on linking such activities with the Holy Spirit. For example, the above paragraph listing all the things that are *supposedly* the very works of the Holy Spirit, echoes not only the contemporary charismatic renewal movement but also the classic hymns from the Pentecost Sunday liturgy by Thomas Aquinas, *Veni Creator Spiritus* and *Veni Sancte Spiritus*. There must be some valid link between these spiritual experiences of the human soul and the Holy Spirit Him/Herself. Besides, if no such connection can be named, it makes no sense even to speak of the Holy Spirit as distinct from the other Two in God. Appeal to the Holy Spirit would have no real consequences. Talk of the Holy Spirit would simply be part of some Christian fairy tale, inspirational perhaps, but still mere fantasy. Yet Christian belief claims to disclose another dimension of *reality*, human reality as well as divine reality. So, granted the validity of the Christian insight, the Holy Spirit must be real, and some connection between the Holy Spirit and human spiritual experiences must be discernible. What is that connection?

That question has plagued Christian thinkers for centuries.[10] Various solutions have been suggested. M.J. Sheeben suggested that the indwelling of the Holy Spirit made the Church be "a kind of incarnation of the Holy Spirit."[11] Supposedly the Holy Spirit could take possession of each of our human natures in a way proper to the Holy Spirit, just as the Only Begotten took on a human nature in a way proper to the Only Begotten. But this notion is vague, and it confuses the presence of the Holy Spirit with the incarnation of the Only Begotten, suggesting a modern adoptionist heresy.[12] Again, since the *ad extra* rule disqualifies any possibility of explaining the proper work of the Holy Spirit on the basis of efficient causality, some have tried to explain that work as "quasi-formal causality." Supposedly, by dwelling in us the Holy Spirit impresses His/Her own proper quality, to be "of the Father and the Son," on us, just as a seal makes its mark, but in reverse, on wax.[13] But this approach is metaphorical rather than systematic. And when technical explanation is given, the theory dies the death of over-qualification, for the very essence of form and then the very essence of causality are both interpreted away.[14] Another approach would try to attribute a particular role in the creation of sanctifying grace to each of the Three in God and so account for a work proper to the Holy Spirit.[15] But what was said above about efficient causality already highlights the inadequacy of this approach.

In fact, there can be no answer to a question that asks about the proper sanctifying work of the Holy Spirit. Every such "work" is a created effect. As such, it is common to the Trinity. In no way can it be predicated properly of the Holy Spirit. But there is a connection between the Holy Spirit and the sanctification of humankind. That connection is found not in what is done *by the Holy Spirit* but in what is done by God *because* the Holy Spirit is sent by the Mother-Father and the Begotten One. "By the Holy Spirit" would entail efficient causality, disqualified by the *ad extra* rule. "Because of the Holy Spirit" suggests final causality. The mission of the Holy Spirit is that *because of which* God effects a transformation in the human. Because the Holy Spirit is sent to dwell in us, God creates in us the capacity to receive and respond to the Holy Spirit.[16] This appeal to final causality provides a real and valid link between the sanctification of humankind and the Holy Spirit as distinct from the Father and Son. At the same time this approach respects the *ad extra* rule about God's creative activity.

Uncreated and Created Grace

These considerations suggest that grace, the divine gift that sanctifies, is double. The primary gift of God is none other than the Holy Spirit, Who comes to us from the Mother-Father and the Eternal Offspring. The Holy Spirit is God's uncreated gift, Uncreated Grace. Note that when the issue is conceived in this way, reference is properly to the Holy Spirit as distinct from the other Two, for the Holy Spirit is sent *from* the Father-Mother and the Begotten One. The Holy Spirit Him/Herself and no one or nothing else is God's gift to us.

At stake here is a divine mission, an intervention into human history as real as the mission of the Only Begotten. Both the mission of the Only Begotten and the mission of the Holy Spirit result in a created effect in history. If there were no such created effect, it would not be true to say that Either of Them had been sent. When contingencies are predicated of the Divinity, which is Itself necessary and in which there is no change, the predication can be true only if there is some created, contingent effect.[17] In the case of the Only Begotten, the humanity of Jesus is the created effect correlative to the divine mission. In this case the effect is visible. In the case of the Holy Spirit, the created effect correlative to the divine mission is the transformation of the human spirit that allows the human to receive and respond to the Holy Spirit, Who is given. In this case the effect is invisible, but it is no less real. This is to say, the Uncreated Gift of God entails in the human also a created gift, a transformation in the human.

To Uncreated Grace there corresponds a created grace. This created grace, the transformation of the human spirit that correlates with the uncreated gift of the Holy Spirit, is called sanctifying grace. Sanctifying grace is the second aspect of grace. Chronologically simultaneous, it is logically secondary to the primary gift, the Holy Spirit. Because the Eternal Parent and the Eternally Begotten send the Holy Spirit to dwell in our hearts, God transforms us to receive that Divine Gift. It is this transformation that makes human divinization possible.

The Trinitarian Order of Human Salvation

Created grace correlates with Uncreated Grace. So any understanding of the nature of the transformation that opens the human to divinization must be based on an understanding of the Holy Spirit. Unfortunately, there is very little to be said properly about the Holy Spirit. The Holy Spirit has this only one property: the Spirit proceeds from the Eternal Parent and the Eternally Begotten.

Starting with this doctrinal fact, theology could suggest that the Holy Spirit must then somehow be a link between the Father and the Son. In some way the Spirit is the bond between the Two of Them. Then, created grace, somehow corresponding to this property constitutive of the Holy Spirit, Uncreated Grace, must also be said to unite us with the Eternal Parent and the Only Begotten. In view of our knowledge of the particular work of the Only Begotten, Jesus Christ, that leads us to the Loving Parent, we might conclude that the trinitarian order of human divinization is this: because of the Holy Spirit, Who is given to us, we are somehow united with the death and resurrection of Jesus and so come to share in the life of the Eternal Parent; we are divinized. Our union with Jesus in the Holy Spirit could be further explicated as follows: because the Holy Spirit is given to us, God transforms our spirits. Then we are able to recognize Jesus as the Only Child of the Mother-Father, and we make him our model. Living our lives as he did his, faithful to the divine principle in us just as he was faithful to his divine self, we will pass through death to glorified life and share the Eternal Parent's life as divinized, adopted sons and daughters in Christ.

This account already gives some understanding of the trinitarian order of salvation. Yet the account remains sketchy. The redemptive work of the Only Begotten was a space/time, this-worldly reality, accessible to historical investigation. So the saving work of the Only Begotten can be explicated in some detail.[18] However, the invisible saving mission of the Holy Spirit to human hearts transcends the categories of space and time and so is not easily investigated. So our understanding of the Holy Spirit's specific role in human salvation remains vague. Metaphors, not systematic formulation, fill in the gaps in understanding: bond, union, transformation. In order to understand the role of the Holy Spirit better, some richer understanding of the Holy Spirit Him/Herself and of the Holy Trinity is needed.

The Psychological Analogy

The Christian tradition has attempted various ways of gaining deeper understanding about the Trinity. One of the most fruitful, especially in the context of this essay, is the so-called "psychological analogy."[19]

Since we have no immediate knowledge of God while in this world, we must attempt to understand the revealed mysteries of God on the basis of other things that we do know. We must use analogies. In Chapter 5, an understanding of the Creator-God, projected as the ideal fulfillment of the dynamism of the human spirit, was one such analogy. But what in our experience might the Trinity be like? The sun, its ray, and the light; the spring, the stream, and the river; or the three-leafed clover—these popular images of the Trinity may be suggestive, but as physical metaphors they are obviously too gross to allow accurate understanding of the Trinity. What other analogy might we use?

Augustine pondered that question, and taking a lead from Genesis 1:26: "Let us make man in our image, after our likeness," Augustine concluded that the image of the Trinity would be in the highest part of the human. So Augustine reflected on the human mind or soul or spirit and searched there for a triadic pattern, the image of God, that might reveal the divine Trinity. In his *De Trinitate* (*The Trinity*) Augustine related several such patterns. The most important is the *mind* that *knows* and *loves* itself: *mens, notitia,* and *amor.* Thomas Aquinas refined this analogy, especially by analyzing the production of a mental word in the mind[20] and the resultant love as an act of the will.[21] Bernard Lonergan further elaborated the psychological analogy on the basis of his analysis of intentional consciousness.[22] Obviously, the term "psychological" analogy does not refer to contemporary empirical psychology. Rather, it refers to a former "rational psychology," whose concern was "the elaboration of mental faculties, powers, or functions."[23]

When one understands something, the mind expresses that understanding in a "word."[24] Word here does not refer to the external spoken word nor even to the internal concept which external words can express in multiple ways. For example, the words *"Ha fallecido," "Sie ist gestorben,"* "She died," "She passed away," all express the same concepts in different ways. Rather, the inner word is the understanding itself that the concepts express. The inner word is the immediate product of an act of understanding. The inner word underlies the concepts that express it, and these, in turn, underlie the spoken or written words. The process of the production of an inner word[25] is wholly within the realm of intentional consciousness.

Insofar as one has understood correctly, this inner word is an expression of that which was understood. It is, as it were, a replica of the understood in the one who understands. So by an act of understanding, the understood is somehow in the understander.

But the human intellectual process does not stop here. The very nature of the human spirit urges one on to some evaluative response to what has been understood.[26] Recall that, according to Lonergan's four-level analysis of consciousness, once one has determined that this or that is so, one is spontaneously faced with the further question, What am I going to do about it? The further issue is one of value and choice. In medieval faculty psychology that further issue would be a question of the will. At stake is the movement of the human spirit toward the goodness of something understood or known. To use a general term, at stake is the movement of love.

Now, when that which was understood is the goodness of some reality, the human spirit follows up that act of understanding with an act of love. So there can be distinguished here two movements within human consciousness or mind: the production of a word expressing the goodness of that which was understood as good, and the loving of that goodness as understood and expressed.

Notice that the word proceeds from the mind through an act of understanding. The loving, on the other hand, proceeds from the mind as well as from the word, which expresses the goodness of that which is loved. The presupposition in this particular case[27] is that love follows knowledge, that the spontaneous response to something known as good is love of that thing. But the movement of love depends on the prior expression of the goodness in a word. So, while the word proceeds from only one source, love proceeds from two.

Notice another difference between the act of understanding and the act of love. The act of understanding results in some expression of the understanding, a word. So there is a process that moves from 1) the mind through 2) an act of understanding to the production of 3) a word. This process terminates in the word, which is the expression of the understanding and so some replica of that which was understood. On the other hand, the loving does not produce some replica of the beloved. Rather, loving terminates in the beloved itself. The essence of loving is positive regard for the beloved. The object of loving is not some replica or expression of the beloved but the beloved itself. So in loving there is a process that moves from 1) the mind and its word to 2) an act of love, the loving.

This difference is important.[28] Insofar as one loves, not some replica or mental expression of the beloved but the beloved itself is the term of the loving. That toward which the love is directed—and so that which actualizes the love—is the beloved. This means that by love the beloved is in the lover. ". . . the presence of the beloved in the lover is exactly the same entity as the act of love in the lover. . . ."[29] The very meaning of loving is the presence of the beloved in the lover. It is this presence of the beloved in the lover that explains the loving of the beloved, for the beloved is that *because of which* the lover loves. And that because of which one loves must be in the lover him- or herself. If not, then the "lover" is not really the one loving the "beloved"; there is no act of love occurring on the part of the "lover." Rather, as one might imagine it, the "lover" would be pushed or pulled toward the beloved. But imagination is not at issue here; spiritual acts are. Now, in fact, the lover loves the beloved, and insofar as the beloved is that because of which *the lover* loves *the beloved*, the beloved is in the lover precisely as a motive force of the loving in question. Insofar as there is loving, the beloved is present in the lover as being loved. And on the side of the lover, that "being loved" of the beloved is nothing other than the loving of the lover. The loving is the presence of the beloved in the lover. In technical terms, the beloved is the final cause of the loving.[30] But a final cause is in the agent acting; it is precisely that because of which the agent acts. So, as final cause of the loving, the beloved is in the lover.

This same point might be made another way. The beloved is not really the beloved unless it is actually loved. Only when the lover loves the beloved is it beloved. But the appreciation of the goodness of the beloved that makes the beloved be beloved is in the lover. So it is in the loving that the beloved is the beloved. Then, the beloved is in the lover, where the loving occurs. Moreover, the beloved is really in the lover. If it is really the beloved that is loved—and not some fantasy—then the beloved itself and nothing else, precisely as loved, is in the lover.

There is a parallel here with what occurs in the act of understanding.[31] According to the Scholastic axiom, *intellectus in actu fit intellectum in actu*: in the moment of actual understanding, the intellect becomes that which is understood. The sense here is deliberately double: the intellect becomes something else, and it is itself that the intellect understands. So in the moment of understanding there occurs an identity between the understanding intellect and that which is understood. Then, in being present to itself, the intellect is also present to that which it understands; and in understanding itself, the intellect also understands what is not itself but what has in the moment of understanding become identical with it. The spiritual act of understanding entails a presence of understander to understood that is an identity between the understander and the understood.

In a similar way, the spiritual act of love entails a presence of the beloved to the lover. Loving is that presence. In the loving the beloved actually becomes the beloved—but only in the *lover's* loving. So the beloved is in the lover who is actually loving the beloved. Otherwise, it is not really the beloved that is being loved, and the lover is not really doing the loving.

The presence of the beloved in the lover is real; it is the essence of love. But its reality must be correctly understood.[32] This is not the spatial presence of two physical objects to one another; in fact, such presence attributed to inanimate objects is just an analogue of the primary human presence that is under discussion here. Likewise, this is not the presence of an image of the beloved in the imagination of the lover; here again this imaginative presence, a form of spatial presence, is but an analogous form of personal presence, which is the primary meaning of human presence. Still, though the presence in question is the primary meaning of human presence from which the others derive, people are generally more able to understand those other more physical kinds of presence than the spiritual presence in question here. Spiritual presence—the presence of the known in the knower through a word and of the beloved in the lover through loving—is more subtle, more difficult to grasp. It is so close to us that we miss it. Like the air we breathe and take for granted, we overlook personal presence. More to the point, like our minds that we do not notice, we are usually oblivious to spiritual presence—like our very minds, of which we are seldom clearly aware but without which we can be aware of nothing. Of course, when one is in love, one is well aware of the abiding presence of the beloved within oneself. Perhaps we are oblivious to such spiritual presence because we actually understand and love so seldom. After all, all that is said here is true only of understanding and of loving that is real, that is actual. And we may seldom really be engaged in acts of understanding and love.

Application to the Trinity

This analysis of human consciousness and its acts provides a basis for achieving some understanding of the inner-trinitarian life of God. The presupposition of this theological enterprise is that God is intelligent and loving. Granted this, one may posit an act of understanding and an act of love in God. Since God is infinite and these acts are therefore perfect, the result of them would be nothing other than a procession of God from God—in two different ways, by understanding and by love.[33]

Assuming that God understands, there is in God an act of understanding. This act is perfect and infinite. The object of this act is no other than God, the Divinity itself. In understanding God, God understands completely and expresses that understanding in a Word. This Word is the perfect expression of all that God understood. As perfect, it is identical in every way with that which was understood.

199

Moreover, since there is no real distinction in God between the divine intellect and the Divinity itself, the Word that is the perfect expression of the divine intellect is the perfect expression also of the Divinity. As identical with the Divinity, the Word is God. As the Word which proceeds from God, however, the Word is also distinct from God from which the Word proceeds. So there are relations of opposition in God on the basis of what appears to be in God a procession of God from God. Granted Christian revelation, there is reason to understand that the Word in God is the Son and the Divinity from which the Word proceeds is the Father. Thus, the psychological analogy suggests some understanding of the procession of God from God and gives reason for understanding this procession as the generation of the Eternally Begotten from the Eternal Mother-Father.

Similarly, assuming that God loves, there is in God an act of love. Since love arises via some expression of goodness grasped as good, the divine act is a loving response to the divine Goodness precisely as expressed in the Word. Thus, the movement of divine love proceeds from God who loves and from the Word. But the divine love that proceeds from God via the Word is love for nothing other than God. The Beloved is God. So, since in loving the beloved is present in the lover, God who is loved is present in God on the basis of divine loving. Since this loving in God is not really distinct from divine being, this loving, which is the presence of God to God as loved, is also God. This divine loving itself is God present in God, on the basis of God's love and the Word. Again the psychological analogy suggests some basis for a second procession of God from God. This procession sets up mutual relations of opposition in God and so founds another set of distinctions in God. These distinctions are different from the others because these depend on loving rather than on understanding. As dependent on loving, this second procession results from two principles, the divine being itself as loving and the intellectual expression of that divine being in a word. Granted Christian revelation about the mission of the Holy Spirit from the Father and the Son, there is reason to see in this second procession an analogous account of the spiration of the Holy Spirit. Thus, the psychological analogy suggests some understanding of the eternal spiration of the Holy Spirit from the Eternal Parent and the Eternal Word.

The Holy Spirit as God's Loving

According to this understanding, the Holy Spirit is precisely God's divine Loving itself. The Holy Spirit is not the result of God's Loving; the Holy Spirit is that Loving. Use of the present participle, "loving," rather than a mere noun, "love," helps make it clear that actual, active love is in question here. In question is not the divine capacity to love or the divine will, if we can use these human concepts. In question is the act of a dynamic consciousness, the actual act of loving. In question is the actuation of that will or that capacity to love. As already noted, the psychological analogy highlights two acts of dynamic consciousness, the act of understanding and the act of loving. The act of understanding terminates in a word and so, when applied to God, allows us to speak of a generation in God, the procession of a Divine Word from the Divinity, the procession of the Son from the Father. But the act of loving does not produce any word or replica of the beloved. The loving terminates with that act itself just as the loving terminates in the beloved, making the beloved present in the lover. The presence of the beloved in the lover and the loving in the lover are one and the same entity. So the loving in God that makes God present to God as the beloved in the lover, that loving that is nothing other than the divine being itself, is God. God's active loving itself is God the Holy Spirit. The Holy Spirit is God's love, God's active loving.

It follows that the Holy Spirit is the mutual love of the Father and the Son. The love-capacity of God, the divine essence, is the capacity/essence common to the Parent and the Offspring. So the Holy Spirit, the divine Loving, is the Loving both of the Parent and of the Eternal Offspring. In this context, to say that the Holy Spirit proceeds from the Eternal Parent *and* the Eternally Begotten is another way of making this same point. Furthermore, the object of the divine loving is also the divine essence itself, with which both the Parent and the Offspring are identical. So the divine loving for the goodness of the divine essence is also the love of the Parent for the Offspring and of the Offspring for the Parent. What from one perspective is the divine loving as an act of the Divinity is from another perspective the mutual love of the Mother-Father and the Son-Daughter. The Holy Spirit, who is the active love of God, is also the love of the Parent and Child for one another. Metaphorically we say that the Holy Spirit is the bond or the union between the Father and the Son. Here is a technical explanation of what those metaphors might mean.

Since the Holy Spirit is God's Love itself, it also follows that when God loves us, God loves us with the Holy Spirit: "God's love has been poured into our hearts through the Holy Spirit which has been given to us."[34] Then God loves us with the very same love with which the Eternal Parent and the Eternally Begotten One love one another. Through the gift of the Holy Spirit, we are introduced into the trinitarian life. We share in the love that passes between the Eternal Parent and the Eternally Begotten of God. Obviously, this participation in the inner-trinitarian life is a gift that is completely disproportionate to the human as such. It is an inchoate participation in divinity.

Human Transformation Because of the Holy Spirit

The above analyses now allow some technical explanation also of the transformation that human divinization entails. The key to this explanation is, again, an understanding of loving.

Because the Father-Mother and the Eternal Offspring give the Holy Spirit to me, God also enables me to receive the Holy Spirit. There is a created grace in me that corresponds to the Uncreated Grace given to me. This created grace in me is precisely the capacity to love the Holy Spirit. This describes one side of the issue. The other side is this: because I love the Holy Spirit, the Holy Spirit is in me as the Beloved in the lover. Notice how the two sides of the issue correspond to one another. Because God's gift, the Holy Spirit, is present in me, God enables me to love the Holy Spirit. Because I love the Holy Spirit, the Holy Spirit is present in me. These two factors co-condition one another. Created Grace and uncreated grace are the presuppositions of one another. Of course, God's free gift of the Holy Spirit holds the logical priority. But the point here is this: at the heart of the Christian mystery of grace is love. Human love and divine love meet in love, and, according to the nature of love, the lovers are present in one another, so the human participates in the divine.

God's own infinite Love is in the human precisely by means of the human's disproportionate act of love for It. But if a human loves

202

God's Love and God's Love is in him or her, then that one can love with God's own love. The human love has been transformed by participation in divine Love. Insofar as this is so, the human love comes to its highest perfection as the furthest possible reach of dynamic human consciousness is attained.

However, it is obvious that what is described here is not an earthly occurrence. It is only what is to be expected when the process in question reaches its fulfillment. Though the transformation in question results from a double act of God—Uncreated Grace and created grace—it is still understandable that the effect is not instantaneous. For the effect occurs also as a result of human love, and although this human love is disproportionately perfected, it remains nonetheless human love. So the perfection of the human, even within the Christian viewpoint, still depends on human freedom. For this reason it is necessary to distinguish within created grace two aspects, the human and the divine. The latter refers to the disproportionate capacity to love that God creates in the human because the Holy Spirit is given. This dimension constitutes what Rahner calls the "supernatural existential."[35] It means that by God's good design all humans are born into a situation that opens them to divine life, to supernatural—that is, disproportionate—fulfillment. The former is the human response, the human free actuation of this capacity in actual acts of love for the Holy Spirit. But since this human response, like every created act, cannot occur apart from divine concurrence, in every actual occurrence even this response is a gift from God, a disproportionate gift, a divinizing grace—even as Paul writes: "God is at work in you, both to will and to work for his good pleasure."[36] In brief, within sanctifying grace, the created gift, one must distinguish operative and cooperative grace, operative in the initiative of God and cooperative in the response of humans.[37] An understanding of the mutual interaction of these two, God's irresistible grace and human freedom, entails all the same issues already treated in Chapter 5 under the topic of divine concurrence and divine providence. This discussion need not be rehearsed here. The relevant point here is this: an understanding of human divinization on the basis of disproportionate grace within the Christian viewpoint loses nothing of what has already been said within the theist and philosophic viewpoints. Rather, it presupposes that. The effective transformation of the human spirit because of the gift of the Holy Spirit still partially depends on and results from human cooperation with God and is but the fulfillment—disproportionate, though it be—of human self-determination in self-transcending authenticity.

The Trinitarian Order of Human Salvation Revisited

Because the Holy Spirit is in me, God's own Love is mine. So when I love, I love not only with a human love but also with God's own Love that is one with mine, present in me as the beloved in the lover. As a result, I move toward ultimate self-transcendence, wholly oriented in my love toward the Absolute Fullness itself. As a result, I respond lovingly to all that is good and to all insofar as they are good. My growth in human authenticity is fueled with divine Love. More about this below. Here the specifically Christian contribution, divinizing participation in Trinitarian life, needs to be highlighted.

The presence of Divine Love within me, transforming my human spirit, affects my every act. Most importantly, loving with Divine Love, I am able to love the Divine One who dwelt among us. In the human Jesus I recognize the Eternally Begotten. I give myself to Him and follow Him as my Lord: "no one can say 'Jesus is Lord' except by the Holy Spirit."[38] In Jesus I recognize a visible historicization of that to which I feel drawn invisibly because of God's work within me through the gift of the Holy Spirit.[39] As a true child of God, adopted into divine life, I cry out, "Abba, Father."[40] Loving Jesus, my brother in the flesh and in the divine life, and so conforming myself to the Eternally Begotten of God, and ever faithful to the Divine Spirit within me, I am willing to give of myself for all that is right and true and good, even to the point of death, if need be. Then, like the Incarnate Son in death as well as in life, I can hope to share also in His resurrection. In Christ through the Holy Spirit, I attain to the divine life that comes from the Eternal Parent. Divinized, I share the life of the Eternal Parent in the Eternally Begotten One through the Holy Spirit.

Thus, Christian belief provides a coherent account of the process of human growth as actually a process of growth in divine life. Presupposing Jewish belief, Christian belief acknowledges the logically necessary and inviolable distinction between God and the human. But inspired by the disclosure of divine mysteries in the experience of Jesus Christ, Christian belief accounts for a bridge over the gap between the human and the divine. Without concluding that humans ever could become God, Christianity allows that because of two divine missions from God humans can attain a created participation in divine life. The Christian viewpoint envisages and coherently accounts for the possibility of human divinization.

Experience of God's Saving Work Within Oneself

The creative work of God that accompanies the mission of the Holy Spirit results in a real change in the human being. As already noted, if there were no such created effect correlative to this divine mission, it would not be true that the Holy Spirit had really been sent. The created effect correlative to the mission of the Eternally Begotten is the human life of Jesus Christ. The created effect correlative to the mission of the Holy Spirit is created grace in human hearts. Since, like the former, this latter created effect is real, since it is within humans themselves, and since it is a dynamic reality, it ought to be subject to human experience. So the question arises, what aspects of human experience result from sanctifying grace in us? What does the experience of grace feel like?

In his later treatment of religious experience and conversion, Bernard Lonergan suggests the experience that can be conceptualized as sanctifying grace:[41] "the dynamic state of being in love with God." "Being in love with God, as experienced, is being in love in an unrestricted fashion. All love is self-surrender, but being in love with God is being in love without limits or qualifications or conditions or reservations."[42] This state is not one that is chosen; rather, it comes upon us to "dismantle and abolish the horizon in which our knowing and choosing went on."[43] "It can come as a thunderclap as when, in the prophet Ezekiel's words, God plucks out man's heart of stone and replaces it with a heart of flesh. But more commonly it comes so quietly and gently that it is conscious indeed but not adverted to, not inquired into, not understood, not identified and named, not verified and affirmed."[44] Although this state is conscious, it may not be known. "It remains within subjectivity as a vector, an undertow, a fateful call to a dreaded holiness."[45] ". . . the gift of God's love is an experience of the holy, of Rudolf Otto's *mysterium fascinans et tremendum*. It is what Paul Tillich named a being grasped by ultimate concern. It corresponds to St. Ignatius Loyola's consolation that has no cause, as expounded by Karl Rahner."[46] This dynamic state of being in love "manifests itself in acts of kindness, goodness, fidelity, gentleness, and self-control (Gal. 5:22)."[47] ". . . the dynamic state of itself is operative grace, but the same state as principle of acts of love, hope, faith, repentance, and so on, is grace as co-operative."[48]

Lonergan speaks of the experience of grace primarily in theist terms: being in love with God. Behind this expression of the matter is also the Christian conceptualization of it, for that which is experienced can be called sanctifying grace, with its operative and cooperative dimensions, the result of "God's love flooding our hearts through the Holy Spirit given to us."[49] Yet, the primary notion, unrestricted falling in love, could also be interpreted in terms of self-surrender to the dynamism of human consciousness that moves one toward authentic self-transcendence. Indeed, "Just as unrestricted questioning is our capacity for self-transcendence, so being in love in an unrestricted fashion is the proper fulfillment of that capacity."[50] The ideas of conversion, gentle or abrupt, and of subsequent acts of genuine virtue would be appropriate to such an understanding also within the philosophic viewpoint.

Evidently, then, at stake here is a set of experiential data that are open to various interpretations. Fundamentally, the data are human, the experienced movement of the heart or soul, the inner longing for the "more" in life, the urge to commit oneself to what is right and good, true and worthwhile, lasting and positive. These very notions describe the dynamism of the human spirit, the intrinsic principle of authentic self-transcendence, introduced into this discussion in Chapter 1 and in one way or another uncovered in the developmental theories of Part I. Within that context, within the philosophic viewpoint, what is experienced is no more than human. The presuppositions of that viewpoint allow no other conclusion. But within the theist viewpoint these very same data are validly interpreted as falling in love with God, though within mere theism there would be no notion of actually attaining the object of that love and of sharing in divinity. Within the Christian viewpoint these very same data are validly interpreted as the result of God's disproportionate creative act, transforming the human capacity to love because God's own Love, the Holy Spirit, is given. Then, what is experienced as the movement of the human heart toward all that is true and good is recognized to be none other than the process of divinization at work among humankind.

That is the point. God's divinizing work in the human heart is available to human experience, but what is experienced would not be recognized as that divinizing work apart from Christian revelation and faith. Who would have suspected that the urging of conscience and the desire for the transcendent is actually in part the result of God's own Love, the Holy Spirit, being poured into the human heart? Who would have suspected that growth in human virtue is actually also growth in divine life? Who would have suspected that noble commitment to the responsibilities of human living, involvement in this world, is actually the path to life in God? Apart from the Christian viewpoint, these interpretations would simply not follow. But granted the Christian viewpoint, they become the obvious part of a coherent understanding of human life.

Rightly, then, Christians can speak—but only by appropriation—of the promptings of the Holy Spirit within them. Absolutely accurately they can speak of experiencing the saving work of God within them and can know that this work results because the Holy Spirit has been given to them. Accurately, again, then, they can speak of loving the Holy Spirit in Him/Herself, of relating specifically to the Eternally Begotten, and of addressing the Eternal Parent as Father-Mother. For, if the mission of the Holy Spirit does not result in any specific *ad extra* work attributable individually to the Holy Spirit, that mission does establish distinct relations with the Holy Spirit and so also with the Begotten One and the Mother-Father, as well. In fact, the very goal of the divine missions is to establish new relations with God and specifically with the Three in God;[51] the created effects that accompany those missions are but the necessary means to that primary end. The primary goal, the establishment of these new relations between the human and the Three in God is none other than the introduction of the human into the divine life. If the divine life itself is not yet the immediate object of human experience, the divine life given to humankind promises to become that when humankind reaches divine perfection. Besides, humankind already experiences the divine life mediately, via those spiritual impulses that Christians recognize to be none other than the divinizing work of God in them. "For now I see in a mirror dimly, but then face to face. Now I know in part; then I shall understand fully, even as I have been fully understood."[52]

These legitimate conclusions follow on the basis of both experience *and* Christian belief. On the basis only of one or the other, no such conclusions can be drawn. Experience alone cannot lead to a legitimate conclusion about a disproportionate divine work in the human heart; no merely human evidence could justify such a conclusion. On the other hand, belief apart from some data of experience cannot arrive at a reasonable conclusion about anything; ungrounded belief is mere opinion.[53] The available data can be interpreted variously. One reasonable interpretation is that which constitutes the Christian viewpoint. This viewpoint allows that the process of human development is actually a growth in divine as well as human life and that in some way this growth in divinization can be experienced.

Christian Holiness and Spiritual Development

Through the gift of the Holy Spirit and the human love of that Spirit, God's own Love is present in the human as Beloved in the lover. Present through love, God's Love is present through spiritual actuation proper to the fourth level of human consciousness.

> It is the type of consciousness that deliberates, makes judgments of value, decides, acts responsibly and freely. But it is this consciousness as brought to a fulfillment, as having undergone a conversion, as possessing a basis that may be broadened and deepened and heightened and enriched but not superseded, as ready to deliberate and judge and decide and act with the easy freedom of those that do all good because they are in love. So the gift of God's love occupies the ground and root of the fourth and the highest level of man's [and woman's] intentional consciousness. It takes over the peak of the soul, the *apex animae*.[54]

By what might be styled a "trickle down" effect, the divine Love that occupies and perfects the fourth level of human consciousness, the level of love, affects the other levels, as well. Because one loves fully and responsibly, one is also more capable of judging more reasonably, understanding more intelligently, and experiencing more attentively. That is to say, divinizing grace perfects the human spirit, the intrinsic principle of authentic self-transcendence. This very principle is an essential factor in human spiritual development. Under the influence of grace and because of the gift of the Holy Spirit, the process of spiritual development that is proportionate to the human is intensified and enhanced. The presence in the human spirit of that which is the ideal goal of that spirit, Divine Love, draws the human toward that ideal goal in increasing authenticity, holiness, divinization.

Note that divinizing grace enhances the dynamism of the human spirit and fosters the appropriate unfolding of the human organism. There is no suppression, cancellation, invalidation of the spontaneous human dynamism. There is only the enhancement of all that is truly human. Therefore, all that is accurately said about the human and its development within the philosophic and theist viewpoints remains valid also within the Christian viewpoint. The processes and stages of spiritual development that adequate human sciences can discern are the processes and stages also of Christian spiritual development. Those processes and stages are the ones outlines in Part I. Christian insight changes nothing of this.

The theist notion of holiness also remains valid within the Christian viewpoint, though its meaning is enhanced. Within theism "holiness" names the orientation toward God and within God's universe that is proper to the human. Within Christianity this human attitude is known to be not only an orientation toward God but an actual share in divine life itself, destined to reach fulfillment when God will be all in all.[55] Because within the Christian viewpoint this fulfillment is assured, the inchoate reality in this life is known also to be a new reality, not just holiness but actual divinization in process. So, far from disqualifying the theist notion of holiness, the Christian viewpoint adds a deeper understanding here, as well. What is known within the philosophic viewpoint as human authenticity, and within the theist viewpoint as human holiness, is known within the Christian viewpoint as human divinization.

Furthermore, the Christian viewpoint makes a further contribution to understanding the whole process of spiritual development. Within the theist viewpoint holiness is an intensive quality. It may pertain to anyone at any stage of spiritual development, and it does not necessitate that anyone reach the final stages of that development. One may be holy without being fully spiritually developed. The situation is somewhat different within the Christian viewpoint. Insofar as Christianity envisages divinization of the human, its goal in God is the ideal perfection of the human being. This perfection includes resurrection of the body as well as any merely spiritual perfection. That is to say, Christian belief envisages the perfection of the whole human being. Now, to be human is to develop. So in envisaging the perfection of the human, Christian belief also envisages the perfection of the stages of human development. This perfection would entail the ultimate transformation of the psychological structures of the human and the attainment of that ideal final stage projected in Chapter 4: "the integration of the drive toward authenticity with the structure of the personality." In fact, such an understanding seems to be a valid interpretation of Paul's conception of the resurrection in 1 Corinthians 15: 44—"a spiritual body." To the Hebrew mind this seemingly self-contradictory juxtaposition of words suggests that "The risen body will be *pneumatikon* [spiritual], the perfect instrument of man's [and woman's] *pneuma* [spirit], which in the life of glory will be completely possessed by and perfectly docile to the divine Spirit."[56] Accordingly, within the Christian viewpoint, not only is holiness more radically than in theism conceived as divinization, but the divinization process also insures that each one will in God also attain the highest stage of spiritual development.

Conclusion

Thus, Christian belief offers further insight into and further promise about the process of human spiritual development. "Divinization" summarizes the Christian contribution insofar as it bears on the human. An adequate account of the divinization process requires systematic treatment of the Christian mystery of the Trinity, for the mission of the Holy Spirit is at the core of this process. Granted an adequate understanding of this Christian mystery, it is clear that the Christian viewpoint discerns a dimension of meaning in human development that is unavailable elsewhere. To reveal this further insight is precisely the Christian contribution on this matter. On the other hand, the Christian viewpoint neither alters nor invalidates anything of what adequate human sciences and theism make known about this same matter. Even at the end of this study, the stages of spiritual development and the processes inherent in them remain valid as presented in Part I. Spiritual development, whether understood within the philosophic, the theist, or the Christian viewpoint, is nothing other than human development conceived according to a particular set of concerns.

Notes

Chapter Nine

The Holy Spirit and Human Divinization

1. 1 Cor. 15:54.
2. DeMarjorie, *The Christian Trinity*, 160-178.
3. *Ibid.*, 193-198.
4. Helminiak, "How to Talk about God."
5. Neuner and Roos, *Teaching of Catholic Church*, 93, emphasis added.
6. Richardson and Bowden, *Dictionary*, 487; Cross, *Oxford Dictionary*, 1144.
7. DeMarjorie, *The Christian Trinity*, 178-186.
8. Aquinas, *Summa Theologica*, I, q. 45, a. 6.
9. Lonergan, *De Deo Trino*, 203-204.
10. Rondet, *Grace of Christ*, 365-377.
11. Congar, *I Believe*, 88.
12. Rondet, *Grace of Christ*, 373-374.
13. Tromp, *Corpus Christi*, 124-138; Rahner, "Some Implications."
14. Helminiak, "One in Christ," 172-173.
15. *Ibid.*, 416-419.
16. Lonergan, *De Deo Trino*, 226-238, 249-260.
17. *Ibid.*, 217-219, 232-235.
18. Helminiak, *The Same Jesus*.
19. DeMarjorie, *The Christian Trinity*, 297-321.
20. Lonergan, *Verbum; De Deo Trino*.
21. *Ibid.* Crowe, "Complacency and Concern."
22. Lonergan, *Insight, De Deo Trino*.
23. Reese, *Dictionary of Philosophy*, 467.
24. Lonergan, *Verbum; Insight; De Deo Trino*.

25. Lonergan, *Insight.*

26. Aquinas, *Summa Contra Gentiles,* IV, 19, par. 2.

27. Lonergan, *Verbum,* 204-205.

28. Lonergan, *De Deo Trino,* 109-114.

29. Lonergan, *Verbum,* 203.

30. *Ibid.,* 202-203.

31. Helminiak, "Consciousness," 224-225.

32. Lonergan, *De Deo Trino,* 249-256.

33. Lonergan, *Verbum,* 206-215.

34. Rom. 5:5.

35. Rahner, "Experience of Grace," "Nature and Grace," "Relationship between Nature and Grace."

36. Phil. 2:13.

37. Lonergan, *Grace and Freedom.*

38. 1 Cor. 12:3.

39. Crowe, "Son and Spirit"; Dunne, "Trinity and History."

40. Gal. 4:6.

41. Lonergan, *Method,* 105-107, 240-241; Price, "Conversion," "Lonergan and the Foundations."

42. Lonergan, *Method,* 105-106.

43. *Ibid.,* 106.

44. Lonergan, *Second Collection,* 245.

45. Lonergan, *Method,* 113.

46. *Ibid.,* 106.

47. *Ibid.*

48. *Ibid.,* 107.

49. *Ibid.,* 241.

50. *Ibid.,* 106.

51. Lonergan, *De Deo Trino,* 249-259.

52. 1 Cor. 13:12.

53. Helminiak, *The Same Jesus,* Chapter Two.

54. Lonergan, *Method,* 107.

55. 1 Cor. 15:28.

56. Kugelman, *First Corinthians,* 51:86.

Bibliography

Assagioli, Roberto. *Psychosynthesis: A Manual of Principles and Techniques.* New York: Penguin Books, 1976. (Originally published in 1965.)

Augustine. *The Trinity,* trans. Stephen McKenna. Washington, D.C.: Catholic University of America Press, 1963.

Aumann, Jordan. *Spiritual Theology.* Huntington, Indiana: Our Sunday Visitor Press, 1980.

Baltimore Catechism No. 2. New York: W. H. Sadlier, Inc., 1945, 1965.

Bauer, Johannes B., ed. *Encyclopedia of Biblical Theology: The Complete Sacramentum Verbi.* New York: Crossroad, 1981.

Beard, Ruth M. *An Anthology of Piaget's Developmental Psychology for Students and Teachers.* New York: The New American Library, Inc., 1972. (Originally published in 1969.)

Bickhard, Mark. "A Model of Developmental and Psychological Processes." *Genetic Psychology Monographs,* 102(1980): 61-116.

_____ . "The Nature of Developmental Stages." *Human Development,* 21(1978): 217-233.

Bonhoeffer, Dietrich. *Letters and Papers from Prison.* New York: Macmillan Publishing Co., Inc., 1972.

Bourke, Vernon J. "Augustine of Hippo: The Approach of the Soul to

God." In E. Rozanne Elder, ed., *The Spirituality of Western Christendom*. Kalamazoo, Michigan: Cistercian Publications, Inc., 1976.

Bouyer, Louis. *Introduction to Spirituality*. Collegeville, Minnesota: Liturgical Press, 1961.

Breger, Louis. *From Instinct to Identity: The Development of Personality*. Englewood Cliffs, New Jersey: Prentice-Hall, Inc., 1974.

Brewi, Janice and Brennan, Anne. *Mid-Life: Psychological and Spiritual Perspectives*. New York: Crossroad, 1982.

Buttrick, George Arthur, ed. *The Interpreter's Dictionary of the Bible*, 5 vols. Nashville: Abingdon Press, 1962.

Campbell, Robert L. and Bickhard, Mark H. *Knowing Levels and Developmental Stages, Contributions to Human Development*, vol. 16, ed. John A. Meacham. Basel: Karger, 1986.

Carmody, Denise Larder and Carmody, John. *Religion: The Great Questions*. New York: The Seabury Press, 1983.

Case, Robbie. *Intellectual Development: Birth to Adulthood*. London: Academic Press, Inc./Ltd., 1985.

Chávez-García, Sylvia and Helminiak, Daniel A. "Sexuality and Spirituality: Friends Not Foes," *The Journal of Pastoral Care*, 39(1985):151-163.

CHD Report: A Report on Phase One of the Ministry to Priests Program in the Diocese of Pittsburgh. University of Notre Dame, The Center for Human Development: September, 1979.

Commons, Michael L., Richards, Francis A. and Armon, Cheryl, eds. *Beyond Formal Operations: Late Adolescent and Adult Cognitive Development*. New York: Praeger Publishers, 1984.

Congar, Yves. *I Believe in the Holy Spirit*, vol. II: *Lord and Giver of Life*. New York: The Seabury Press, 1983.

Conn, Walter E. "Moral Development As Self-Transcendence." *Horizons*, 4(1977):189-205.

Cousins, Ewert H., ed. *Process Theology: Basic Writings*. New York: Paulist Press, 1971.

Cross, F.L., ed. *The Oxford Dictionary of the Christian Church*. London: Oxford University Press, 1971.

Crowe, Frederick E. "Complacency and Concern in the Thought of

Saint Thomas." *Theological Studies,* 20(1959):1-39, 198-230, 343-395.

―――――. "Son and Spirit: Tension in the Divine Missions." *Science et Esprit,* 35(1983):153-169.

DeMargerie, Bertrand. *The Christian Trinity in History.* Trans. by Edmund J. Fortman. Still River, Massachusetts: St. Bede's Publications, 1982.

Dember, W.N. "The New Look in Motivation." *American Scientist,* 53(1965):409-427.

Doran, Robert J. "Jungian Psychology and Christian Spirituality." *Review for Religious,* 38(1979):497-510, 742-752, 857-866.

―――――. *Psychic Conversion and Theological Foundations: Toward a Reorientation of the Human Sciences.* Chico, California: Scholars Press, 1981.

―――――. *Subject and Psyche: Ricoeur, Jung, and the Search for Foundations.* Washington, D.C.: University Press of America, 1977.

Dulles, Avery. *A Church to Believe In: Discipleship and the Dynamics of Faith.* New York: Crossroad, 1982.

―――――. *Models of the Church.* Garden City, New York: Doubleday & Co., Inc., 1974.

―――――. *The Resilient Church: The Necessity and Limits of Adaptation.* Garden City, New York: Doubleday & Co., Inc., 1977.

Dunn, Patricia J. and Helminiak, Daniel A. "Spiritual Practices for the Elderly." *Spirituality Today,* 33(1981):122-136.

Dunne, Tad. "Trinity and History." *Theological Studies,* 45(1984):139-152.

Edwards, Tilden H., Jr.; Mead, Loren B.; Palmer, Parker J., and Simmons, James P. *Spiritual Growth: An Empirical Exploration of its Meaning, Sources, and Implications.* Washington, D.C.: Metropolitan Ecumenical Training Center, Inc., 1974.

Erikson, Erik. "Eight Ages of Man." In *Childhood and Society.* New York: W.W. Norton and Co., Inc., 1963. (Originally published in 1950.)

Flannery, Austin, ed. *Vatican Council II: The Conciliar and Post Conciliar Documents.* Northport, New York: Costello Publishing, 1975.

Flugel, J.C. *Man, Morals and Society.* New York: International Universities Press, 1945.

Fortman, Edmund J. *The Theology of Man and Grace: Commentary: Readings in the Theology of Grace.* Milwaukee: The Bruce Publishing Co., 1966.

Fowler, James W. *Becoming Adult, Becoming Christian: Adult Development and Christian Faith.* San Francisco: Harper & Row, 1984.

————. "Faith Development Theory and the Aims of Religious Socialization." In Gloria Durka and Joan-Marie Smith, eds., *Emerging Issues in Religious Education.* New York: Paulist Press, 1976.

————. *Stages of Faith: The Psychology of Human Development and the Quest for Meaning.* San Francisco: Harper & Row, 1981.

————. "Stages of Faith: The Structural-Developmental Approach." In Thomas Hennessy, ed., *Values and Moral Education.* New York: Paulist Press, 1976.

————. *To See the Kingdom: The Theological Vision of H. Richard Niebuhr.* Nashville: Abingdon Press, 1974.

————. "Toward a Developmental Perspective on Faith." *Religious Education,* 69(March-April, 1974):207-219.

Fowler, James W. and Keen, Sam. *Life Maps: Conversations on the Journey of Faith.* Oak Grove, Minneapolis: Winston Press, 1978.

Gannon, Thomas M. and Traub, George W. *The Desert and the City: An Interpretation of the History of Christian Spirituality.* New York: Macmillan, 1969, and Chicago: Loyola University Press, 2nd printing.

Gelpi, Donald L. *Experiencing God: A Theology of Human Experience.* New York: Paulist Press, 1978.

Gilligan, Carol. *In a Different Voice: Psychological Theory and Women's Development.* Cambridge, Massachusetts: Harvard University Press, 1982.

Goldbrunner, Josef. *Holiness is Wholeness.* New York: Pantheon, 1955.

Goleman, Daniel. "Meditation as Meta-Therapy: Hypotheses toward a Proposed Fifth State of Consciousness." *The Journal of Transpersonal Psychology,* 3(1971):1-25.

Grant, Harold W.; Thompson, Magdala, and Clarke, Thomas E. *From Image to Likeness: A Jungian Path in the Gospel Journey.* New York: Paulist Press, 1983.

Groeschel, Benedict J. *Spiritual Passages: The Psychology of Spiritual Development*. New York: Crossroad, 1983.

Gwaltney, James A. "Spiritual Development through Designed Exercises in a Small Group Setting." *Perkins Journal*, 28, #4(1974-75):1-24.

Helminiak, Daniel A. "Consciousness as a Subject Matter." *The Journal for the Theory of Social Behavior*, 14(1984):211-230.

_____ . "Four Viewpoints on the Human: A Conceptual Schema for Interdisciplinary Studies." *The Heythrop Journal* (in press).

_____ . "How Is Meditation Prayer?" *Review for Religious*, 41(1982): 774-782.

_____ . "Lonergan and Systematic Spiritual Theology." *New Blackfriars*, 67(1986):78-92.

_____ . "Meditation—Psychologically and Theologically Considered." *Pastoral Psychology*, 30(1981):6-20.

_____ . "Neurology, Psychology, and Extraordinary Religious Experiences." *The Journal of Religion and Health*, 23(1984):33-46.

_____ . "One in Christ: An Exercise in Systematic Theology." Unpublished doctoral dissertation, Boston College and Andover Newton Theological School, 1979.

_____ . Review of James W. Fowler, *Becoming Adult, Becoming Christian*. In *The Journal of Pastoral Care*, 39(1985):280-282.

_____ . *The Same Jesus: A Contemporary Christology*. Chicago: Loyola University Press, 1986.

_____ . "Modern Science on Pain and Suffering: A Christian Perspective." *Spirituality Today*, 38(1986):136-148.

_____ . "Where Do We Stand as Christians? The Challenge of Western Science and Oriental Religions." *Spiritual Life*, 28(1982):195-209.

Henry, Paul James. "Relationship between Personality Integration and Clergy Effectiveness." Unpublished doctoral dissertation, University of Massachusetts, 1977.

Hick, John and Hebblethwaite, Brian. *Christianity and Other Religions: Selected Readings*. Philadelphia: Fortress Press, 1980.

Hill, William J. *The Three-Personed God: The Trinity as a Mystery of Salvation*. Washington, D.C.: The Catholic University of America Press, 1982.

219

Holmes, Urban T. *A History of Christian Spirituality: An Analytical Introduction*. New York: The Seabury Press, 1980.

Howe, Leroy T. "A Developmental Perspective on Conversion." *Perkins School of Theology Journal*, 33(1979):20-35.

Johnston, William. *The Inner Eye of Love: Mysticism and Religion*. San Francisco: Harper & Row, 1978.

———. *Silent Music: The Science of Meditation*. New York: Harper & Row, Perennial Library, 1976. (Originally published in 1974.)

Jung, Carl G. "The Stages of Life." *Modern Man in Search of a Soul*. New York: Harvest, 1933. (Originally published in 1930.)

Kasper, Walter. *The God of Jesus Christ*, trans. Matthew J. O'Connell. New York: Crossroad, 1984.

Kegan, Robert. *The Evolving Person: Problems and Process in Human Development*. Cambridge, Massachusetts: Harvard University Press, 1982.

Kittel, Gerhard, ed. *Theological Dictionary of the New Testament*. Grand Rapids, Michigan: Wm. B. Eerdmans Pub. Co., 1964.

Koch, Sigmund. "The Nature and Limits of Psychological Knowledge: Lessons of a Century qua 'Science.'" *American Psychologist*, 36(1981):257-269.

———. "Reflections on the State of Psychology." *Social Research*, 38(1971):669-709.

Kohlberg, Lawrence. "The Child as Moral Philosopher." *Psychology Today*, Sept., 1968:25-30.

———. "The Implications of Moral Stages for Adult Education." *Religious Education*, 72(1977):183-201.

———. "Stages and Sequence: The Cognitive-Developmental Approach to Socialization." In D.A. Goslin, ed., *Handbook of Socialization Theory and Research*. Chicago: Rand McNally, 1969.

Kohlberg, Lawrence and Armon, Cheryl. "Three Types of Stage Models Used in the Study of Adult Cognitive Behavior. In Michael L. Commons, Francis A. Richards, Cheryl Armon, eds., *Beyond Formal Operations: Late Adolescent and Adult Cognitive Behavior*. New York: Praeger Publishers, 1984, 338-394.

Kohlberg, Lawrence and Gilligan, Carol. "The Adolescent as Philosopher." *Daedalus*, 100(1971):1051-1086.

Kohlberg, Lawrence and Power, Clark. "Moral Development, Religious Thinking, and the Question of a Seventh Stage." In Lawrence Kohlberg, *The Philosophy of Moral Development: Moral Stages and the Idea of Justice, Essays on Moral Development*, Vol. I. San Francisco: Harper & Row, 1981, 311-372.

Koplowitz, Herb. "A Projection Beyond Piaget's Formal-Operational Stage: A General System Stage and a Unitary Stage." In Michael L. Commons, Francis A. Richards, Cheryl Armon, eds., *Beyond Formal Operations: Late Adolescent and Adult Cognitive Behavior*. New York: Praeger Publishers, 1984.

Kugelman, Richard. "The First Letter to the Corinthians." In Raymond E. Brown, Joseph A. Fitzmyer, and Roland E. Murphy, eds., *The Jerome Biblical Commentary*. Englewood Cliffs, New Jersey: Prentice Hall, Inc., 1968, art. 51, vol. II, 254-290.

Kuhn, Deanna. "Cognitive Development." In Marc H. Bornstein and Michael E. Lamb, eds., *Developmental Psychology: An Advanced Textbook*. Hillsdale, New Jersey: Lawrence Erlbaum Associates, Publishers, 1984, 133-180.

Kuhn, Thomas S. *The Structure of Scientific Revolutions*, 2nd ed. Chicago: The University of Chicago Press, 1970.

Küng, Hans. *The Church*. New York: Sheed and Ward, 1967.

Laskey, Harry M. and Moore, James F. "Current Studies of Adult Development: Implications for Education." Unpublished paper, written for the National Institute of Community Development, National Institute of Education, contract #400-76-0026.

Leon-Dufour, Xavier, ed. *Dictionary of Biblical Theology*. London: Geoffrey Chapman, 1967.

Levinson, Daniel. *The Seasons of a Man's Life*. New York: Knopf, 1978.

Loevinger, Jane. *Ego Development*. San Francisco: Jossey-Bass Publishers, 1977.

Lonergan, Bernard J.F. *Collection: Papers by Bernard Lonergan, S.J.* Montreal: Palm Publishers, 1967.

_____. *De Constitutione Christi Ontologica et Psychologica*. Rome: Gregorian University Press, 1958.

_____. *De Deo Trino: II. Pars Systematica*. Rome: Gregorian University Press, 1964.

_____. *Grace and Freedom: Operative Grace in the Thought of St. Thomas*

221

Aquinas. Ed. J. Patout Burns. New York: Herder and Herder, 1971.

————. *Insight: A Study of Human Understanding.* New York: Philosophical Library, 1957.

————. *Method in Theology.* New York: Herder and Herder, 1972.

————. *Philosophy of God and Theology.* Philadelphia: The Westminster Press, 1973.

————. *A Second Collection.* Philadelphia: The Westminster Press, 1974.

Louth, Andrew. *The Origins of the Christian Mystical Tradition: From Plato to Denys.* Oxford: Clarendon Press, 1981.

MacLeod, Robert B. "Newtonian and Darwinian Conceptions of Man; and Some Alternatives." *Journal of the History of the Behavioral Sciences,* 6(1970):207-218.

————. "The Phenomenological Approach to Social Psychology." *Psychological Review,* 54(1944):193-210.

Maddi, Salvatore R. *Personality Theories: A Comparative Analysis,* 4th edition. Homewood, Illinois: The Dorsey Press, 1980.

Maslow, Abraham H. "Critique of Self-Actualization." *Journal of Individual Psychology,* 15(1959):24-32.

Matson, Katinka, with Horton, Lyn. *The Psychology Today Omnibook of Personal Development.* New York: William Morrow and Co., Inc., 1977.

McBrien, Richard P. *Church: The Continuing Quest.* New York: Newman Press, 1970.

————. *Do We Need the Church?* New York: Harper & Row, 1969.

————. *The Remaking of the Church: An Agenda for Reform.* New York: Harper & Row, 1973.

McCarty, Shaun. "On Entering Spiritual Direction." *Review for Religious,* 35(1976):854-867. Reprinted in Kevin G. Culligan, ed., *Spiritual Direction: Contemporary Readings.* Locust Valley, New York: Living Flame Press, 1983, pp. 99-115.

Mead, George Herbert. *Mind, Self and Society.* Chicago: University of Chicago Press, 1974. (Originally published in 1934.)

Minear, Paul S. *Images of the Church in the New Testament.* Philadelphia: The Westminster Press, 1960.

Misiak, Henry and Sexton, Virginia Staudy. *Phenomenological, Existen-*

tial, and Humanistic Psychologies: A Historical Survey. New York: Grune and Stratton, 1973.

Murray, John Courtney. *The Problem of God: Yesterday and Today.* New Haven, Connecticut: Yale University Press, 1964.

Neuner, Josef and Roos, Heinrich. *The Teaching of the Catholic Church,* trans. Geoffrey Stevens. Staten Island, New York: Abba House, 1967.

Otto, Rudolf. *The Idea of the Holy,* trans. John W. Harvey. Oxford: Oxford University Press, 1958. (Originally published in 1923.)

Panikkar, Raimundo. *The Unknown Christ of Hinduism: Towards an Ecumenical Christophany.* Maryknoll, New York: Orbis Books, 1981.

Panke, W.N. "Drugs and Mysticism." *International Journal of Parapsychology,* 8(1966). Also in John White, ed., *The Highest State of Consciousness.* Garden City, New York: Doubleday & Co., 1972, pp. 257-277.

Perry, W.G., Jr. *Forms of Intellectual and Ethical Development in the College Years.* New York: Holt, Rineholt and Winston, 1970.

Philibert, Paul J. "Conscience: Developmental Perspectives from Rogers and Kohlberg." *Horizons,* 6(1979):1-25.

Piaget, Jean. "Equilibration Processes in the Psychobiological Development of the Child." In H.E. Gruber and J.J. Voneche, eds., *The Essential Piaget.* New York: Basic Books, 1977. (Originally published in 1958.)

_____. *The Moral Judgment of the Child.* New York: The Free Press, 1965. (Originally published in 1929.)

_____. *The Origins of Intelligence in Children.* New York: Norton Library, 1963. (Originally published in 1936.)

_____. *Structuralism.* New York: Basic Books, 1970. (Originally published in 1968.)

Pittenger, Norman. *Catholic Faith in Process Perspective.* Maryknoll, New York: Orbis Books, 1981.

Powell, Philip. "Stage 4A: Category Operations and Interactive Empathy." In Michael L. Commons, Francis A. Richards, Cheryl Armon, eds., *Beyond Formal Operations: Late Adolescent and Adult Cognitive Behavior.* New York: Praeger Publishers, 1984.

Price, James Robertson. "Conversion and the Doctrine of Grace in

Bernard Lonergan and John Climacus." *Anglican Theological Review*, 62(1980):338-362.

———. "Lonergan and the Foundations of a Contemporary Mystical Theology." In Fred Lawrence, ed., *Lonergan Workshop*, IV. Chico, California: Scholars Press, 1985, pp. 163-195.

Progoff, Ira. *The Symbolic and the Real*. New York: Dialogue House Library, 1975.

Rahner, Karl. "Anonymous Christians." *Theological Investigations*, vol. VI, trans. Karl-H. and Boniface Kruger. New York: The Seabury Press, 1974, pp. 390-398.

———. *The Church after the Council*. New York: Herder and Herder, 1966.

———. "Concerning the Relationship between Nature and Grace." In *Theological Investigations*, vol. I, trans. Cornelius Ernst. Baltimore: Helicon Press, 1961, pp. 297-317.

———. "Nature and Grace." In *Theological Investigations*, vol. IV, trans. Kevin Smith. Baltimore: Helicon Press, 1966, pp. 165-188.

———. "Reflections on the Experience of Grace." In *Theological Investigations*, vol. III, trans. Karl-H. and Boniface Kruger. Baltimore: Helicon Press, 1967, pp. 86-90.

———, ed. *Sacramentum Mundi: An Encyclopedia of Theology*, 5 vols. New York: Herder and Herder, 1968.

———. *The Shape of the Church to Come*, trans. Edward Quinn. New York: The Seabury Press, 1974.

———. "Some Implications of the Scholastic Concept of Uncreated Grace." In *Theological Investigations*, vol. I, trans. Cornelius Ernst. Baltimore: Helicon Press, 1961, pp. 316-346.

———. *The Trinity*, trans. Joseph Donceel. New York: Herder and Herder, 1970.

Rahner, Karl and Vorgrimler, Herbert. *Dictionary of Theology*, 2nd edition. New York: Crossroad, 1981.

Ravindra, R. "Self-surrender: The Core of the Spiritual Life." *Studies in Religion/Sciences Réligieuses*, 3(1973-74):357-363.

Reese, William L. *Dictionary of Philosophy and Religion: Eastern and Western Thought*. Atlantic Highlands, New Jersey: Humanities Press, 1980.

Richardson, Alan and Bowden, John, eds. *The Westminster Dictionary of Christian Theology.* Philadelphia: The Westminster Press, 1983.

Ricoeur, Paul. *The Symbolism of Evil.* Boston: Beacon Press, 1969.

Rogers, Carl R. *On Becoming a Person: A Therapist's View of Psychotherapy.* Boston: Houghton Mifflin Co., 1961.

Rondet, Henri. *The Grace of Christ: A Brief History of the Theology of Grace.* New York: Newman Press, 1967.

Sala, Giovanni. "The A Priori in Human Knowledge: Kant's *Critique of Pure Reason* and Lonergan's *Insight.*" *The Thomist,* 40(1976):179-221.

Santrok, John W. *Life-Span Development.* Dubuque, Iowa: Wm. C. Brown Co. Publishers, 1983.

Schachtel, E.G. *Metamorphosis.* New York: Basic Books, 1959.

Scheler, Max. *The Nature of Sympathy.* Hamden, Connecticut: Archon Books, 1973. (Originally published in 1912.)

Schnackenburg, Rudolf. *The Church in the New Testament.* New York: Herder and Herder, 1965.

Sheehy, Gail. *Passages: Predictable Crises in Adult Life.* New York: Bantam Books, 1976.

Simmons, Henry C. "Human Development: Some Conditions for Adult Faith at Age Thirty." *Religious Education,* 71(1976):563-572.

_____. "Quiet Journey: Psychological Development and Religious Growth from Ages Thirty to Sixty." *Religious Education,* 71(1976): 132-142.

Smith, Herbert F. "Discernment of Spirits." *Review for Religious,* 35(1976):432-454.

Squire, Aelred. *Asking the Fathers: The Art of Meditation and Prayer.* New York: Paulist Press, 1973.

Studzinski, Raymond. *Spiritual Direction and Midlife Development.* Chicago: Loyola University Press, 1985.

Swain, Bernard F. "Conflict and Resolution: The Development of the Notion 'Dialectic' in the Work of Bernard Lonergan." Unpublished doctoral dissertation, The University of Chicago, 1980.

Tanquerey, Adolphe. *The Spiritual Life: A Treatise on Ascetical and Mystical Theology.* Tournai, Belgium: Desclee and Co., 1930.

Targ, Russell and Harary, Keith. *The Mind Race: Understanding and Using Psychic Abilities.* New York: Villard Books, 1984.

Tart, Charles T. *Transpersonal Psychologies.* New York: Harper & Row, 1975.

Thomas Aquinas. *Summa Contra Gentiles,* trans. Anton C. Pegis. Notre Dame, Indiana: Notre Dame University Press, 1975.

————. *Summa Theologica.* Madrid: Biblioteca de Autores Cristianos, 1961.

Thompson, Helen. *Journey Toward Wholeness: A Jungian Model of Adult Spiritual Growth.* New York: Paulist Press, 1982.

Tromp, Sebastian. *Corpus Christi Quod est Ecclesia,* vol. III, *De Spiritu Christi Anima.* Rome: Gregorian University Press, 1960.

Truhlar, Carolus Vladimirus. *Structura Theologica Vitae Spiritualis.* Rome: Gregorian University Press, 1966.

Trungpa, Chogyam. *Cutting Through Spiritual Materialism.* Berkeley: Shambhala, 1973.

————. *The Myth of Freedom and the Way of Meditation.* Berkeley: Shambhala, 1976.

VanKaam, Adrian. *In Search of Spiritual Identity.* Denville, New Jersey: Dimension Books, 1975.

Wakefield, Gordon S., ed. *The Westminster Dictionary of Christian Spirituality.* Philadelphia: The Westminster Press, 1983.

White, John, ed. *The Highest State of Consciousness.* Garden City, New York: Doubleday & Co., Inc., Anchor Books, 1972.

William, Rowan. *Christian Spirituality: A Theological History from the New Testament to Luther and John of the Cross.* Atlanta: John Knox Press, 1980.

Woolfolk, Robert L. and Richardson, Frank C. "Behavior Therapy and the Ideology of Modernity." *American Psychologist,* 39(1984):777-786.

Index